Narrative Inquiry and Psycho

Rer

Narrative Inquiry and Psychotherapy

Jane Speedy

palgrave
macmillan

First published 2008 by
PALGRAVE MACMILLAN
Houndmills, Basingstoke, Hampshire RG21 6XS and
175 Fifth Avenue, New York, N.Y. 10010
Companies and representatives throughout the world

PALGRAVE MACMILLAN is the global academic imprint of the Palgrave Macmillan division of St. Martin's Press, LLC and of Palgrave Macmillan Ltd. Macmillan® is a registered trademark in the United States, United Kingdom and other countries. Palgrave is a registered trademark in the European Union and other countries.

ISBN-13: 978–0–230–57340–6 hardback
ISBN-10: 0–230–57340–1   hardback
ISBN-13: 978–0–333–99026–1 paperback
ISBN-10: 0–333–99026–9   paperback

This book is printed on paper suitable for recycling and made from fully managed and sustained forest sources. Logging, pulping and manufacturing processes are expected to conform to the environmental regulations of the country of origin.

A catalogue record for this book is available from the British Library.

A catalog record for this book is available from the Library of Congress.

10   9   8   7   6   5   4   3   2   1
17 16 15 14 13 12 11 10 09 08

Printed in China

For Audrey Speedy, 1927–1996

Contents

Acknowledgements

Foucault (1977a) suggests that we sign our writing with our own names and the names of people whose conversations shaped that writing. Immediately I find myself scuppered. If I were to take up Foucault's suggestion the list of authors would be impossibly long. This is a multi-voiced text. This book is an account of some of my forays into narrative research and practice. It is not the story of a lone inquirer, but rather, of a woman sustained by many conversations.

The co-researchers in this study, the people who have generously contributed stories from their lives, would be regarded as co-authors in another time and space dimension. They are acknowledged as such in the text, but for the most part, appear under pseudonyms and with aspects of their lives altered in order to preserve anonymity. I am grateful to the sixteen colleagues from the University of Bristol who took part in my doctoral research and particularly indebted to the (mostly different) sixteen people who appear in this book as Donald, Clare, Morag, Marie, Gina Thompson and others, Hyatt Braithwaite, the Jones family, Gregory Stanton and the 'unassuming geeks'. Their ongoing commitment to conversations about this work has been extraordinary.

Another group of co-researchers have been the staff in the University of Bristol Education Library. I am not very good at using libraries. I am very bad at getting books back on time and occasionally leave them on trains. I am also keen to get obscure articles from all over the place as quickly as possible. The Sues (Chubb and Chadwick), Jill Smallbone, Julia Jefferies and Jenny Jones have gone to enormous trouble to support this project and have treated me with patience and humour (and they have needed a lot of both).

I have been very glad of conversations with Master's and doctoral programme participants at the University of Bristol. Heather Gibbs, Ginny Bates, Dione Mifsud, Jonathan Wyatt, Ken Gale, Chris Scarlet, Bernadette Cibulskas, Francine Bradshaw, Clifford Allen, Jenny Knibb, Yin Ling Hung and Jim Lucas, in particular, have all influenced the way that I write. The group of colleagues within the Centre for Narratives and Transformative Learning will find traces of our discussions set down here, especially Dave Bainton, Tim Bond, Prue Bramwell Davies,

Laurinda Brown, Wendy Brown, Nell Bridges, Joyce Ferguson, Viv Martin, Kim Etherington, Artemi Sakellariadis, Sue Wilson, Susan Williams and Sheila Trahar.

I'm indebted to David Denborough and Cheryl White from Dulwich Centre Publications. In the end I did not come up with the book that they envisaged, but I have come up with this one and several others instead. Johnella Bird, David Epston and Michael White have been at the forefront of the narrative therapy practitioners to whom I have been apprenticed. Their company has been inspiring, in relation not only to therapeutic practice, but also to thinking outside the box.

Much of this text was written at the kitchen table and discussed with friends and family on the sofas in our front room. As my daughter Esther once observed, 'If Jane's writing a book, we are all writing a book.' Esther Speedy and Sarah Hall have been living with this book for several years as has my good friend Jeanette Murphy over many 'damned fine cups' of coffee in various cafes and at various kitchen tables. Clare Ralfs, Kate Nobbs and Hazel Johns have never met each other, living as they do, at different corners of the planet, but their ongoing companionship, has sustained me during this project. We have rarely discussed this book, but we have chopped a lot of vegetables together and come up with some wild ideas. I am very grateful for their company in my life. To my friends, family and dogs, this book owes a great deal, both for distracting me away from and sustaining me towards its production.

The 'Oz-2000' narrative online group, Artemi Sakellariadis, Wendy Drewery, Laurinda Brown, Sue Webb, Sam Chromy, Kim Etherington, Kate Nobbs, Mandy Pentecost, Clare Ralfs, Cathy Riessman, Cathy Birkett, Sarah Hall, Tim Bond, Saville Kushner, Malcolm Reed and John McLeod have all read and commented on previous drafts of different sections. None of these people is responsible for the completed book, but it has been improved considerably through all these conversations and, not least, by virtue of the (much-tested) patience and expertise of Catherine Gray and her team at Palgrave Macmillan.

Some of this book has been based on a doctoral thesis, 'Singing Over the Bones: A Narrative Inquiry into the Construction of Research and Practice Cultures and Professional Identities by Counsellor Educators' (Speedy, 2001a), and I am grateful to the Graduate School of Education of the University of Bristol for granting periods of study leave towards completing that thesis and commencing this book. Earlier versions of Chapter 5 were presented at the Dulwich Centre Summer School, Adelaide, 2003, the International Narrative Therapy and Community

Work Conference, Oaxaca, Mexico, 2004, and were also published in the *British Journal of Guidance and Counselling*, 2005. A version of Chapter 6 appeared in the *International Journal of Narrative Therapy and Community Work*, 2004, and was presented at the European Society for Research in the Education of Adults (ESREA) conference, Canterbury, 2003. Jamie Lee and Iain Henderson assisted in a 'reader's theatre' style presentation of Chapter 7 at the Festive Narrative Conference, Adelaide, 2006, which also appeared in the *Journal of Psychotherapy Integration*, December 2005. Versions of Chapters 8 and 9 were presented at the British Association of Supervision Practice and Research (BASPR) Conference 2004 and the British Association of Counselling and Psychotherapy (BACP) Research Conference, London, 2004. A version of Chapter 8 also appeared in *Counselling and Psychotherapy Research*, 2005. Chapter 10 was constructed out of earlier versions from the BACP Research Conference, Nottingham, 2005, and the International Arts-based Educational Research Conference, Belfast, 2005. I would like to thank the participants in these conference sessions as well as the editors and referees of the journals and publications listed above, for their comments on this work in progress. What I have come up with in this book is not their fault but they have all added flavour and food for thought. I consider this text a 'body of work in progress' and have been able to think of it as a fluid, unfinished endeavour rather than 'the final version' because I have been sustained by so many conversations and reflections.

Every effort has been made to contact all the copyright-holders, but if any have been inadvertently omitted the publishers will be pleased to make the necessary arrangements at the earliest opportunity.

Lastly, this book is written in both the memory and the company of Audrey Speedy (1927–96), Chris Speedy (1953–89) and Rosie Jeffries (1955–2001).

Preface

I am sitting at the kitchen table constructing myself as a writer, an identity claim that is not entirely privileged in this context. The kitchen windows are casting a pool of light into the fern-fringed darkness of the garden beyond. There is a large dog at my feet, and in the next room, door ajar, my twelve-year-old daughter is watching *Bend It Like Beckham* on a flickering television screen in the half-light of the living room. It is nearly supper-time. Under the pretext of spending time 'in the kitchen' I am beginning to write this book. A multitude of alternative identity claims (dog walker, parent, partner and meal-provider to name but a few) are tugging away at the edges of my mind's eye and disrupting my focus and sense of purpose. This space will be short lived. As Winterson (2004: 134) has so firmly asserted:

> You don't need to know everything. There is no everything. The stories themselves make the meaning. The continuous narrative of existence is a lie. There is no continuous narrative, there are lit-up moments and the rest is dark.

This 'lit-up' moment will soon retreat back into the darkness. This opening paragraph is being fitted in 'in-between' and will soon unravel between my fingers as other threads of my life encroach and tighten their grip. I have been staring out of the window into the night for quite a while now, occasionally picking up a thin pink felt pen and adding extra squiggles and scribbles to an already overfull spider diagram eked out on the pad beside me. I open my new slim silver writing machine, gently dust off the brightly lit screen and begin.

This is one of the ways that I may begin to write this book. I may well come up with others and, indeed, as we speak, there are at least seven perfectly acceptable alternatives, absent but implicit in the current text, scrunched up on the floor. Not to mention the myriad versions becoming apparent to you, the readers, as you re-tell these stories to yourselves within the conversational space that is opening up between us.

If the story I have just told you was represented by a thin line travelling across a slice of my 'mind's eye', there might be clear signs of agency, of my making choices about the stories that I prefer from those that are culturally and personally available to me. I was, for example, drinking a glass of Chianti as I was writing, but I did not mention that, lest it demonstrate a lack of gravitas on my part.

A great deal of open space is also evident in this quick mind's eye excavation – space that perhaps sustains many possible ways of linking the traces and fragments and aspects of stories that have not yet been told, may never be told, or are unsayable and unavailable for the telling.

Thus, I hope, by way of introduction, to have described some of the key ideas that sustain narrative research, specifically the notion that human identity is a social achievement, contingent on time, context, audience, culture, history, memory and personal agency and that the stories we tell ourselves and each other in our day-to-day exchanges both constitute and are constitutive of our lives.

Narrative Inquiry

This book is a distillation of my own excavations into narrative practice and research in psychotherapy over the last decade. My hope is that each section of the book reads like an invitation into a conversation. Each of these conversations contains one or more illustrative stories.

This book, a body of work in progress, constitutes what Marcus (1994) would describe as a 'messy text'. The text comprises a series of incomplete stories that collectively trace and configure my excavations into narrative and arts-based research, narrative therapy practice and the relations between them.

'Narrative' is suddenly everywhere. National narratives, global narratives and organisational narratives abound within the daily media. Politicians are 'seamlessly constructing a *New Labour narrative*' (Rawnsley, 2002), or so they would have us believe, as well as getting together after a recent election to re-construct *an overall narrative* (Kennedy, 2005). *Jazz narratives* are currently being composed and performed (Marsalis, 2004); *narrative landscapes* are being explored (Wojecki, 2004); and *narrative medicine* is being taught (Charon, 2004). I take no issue with the narrative turn within any of these fields. This book, however, is concerned with 'Narrative Inquiry and Psychotherapy' in order to specifically locate it as a space in which people, including myself, tell and re-tell the stories of their lives and, in so doing, shape the lives that they live. In this sense my work is about 'small' stories, the stories of people's everyday lives, rather than of epic or global events, although perhaps the one version of narrative sheds light upon the other.

For readers who like a map of the territory in order to find their bearings: **Chapter 1** outlines the ideas that have been informed by the versions of narrative inquiry that I have been engaged in. **Chapters 2 and 3** navigate their way through the thorny and complex issue of what rigorous, ethical research projects that traverse the landscape between arts and social sciences might look like, and **Chapter 4** illustrates the ways in which narrative therapy and narrative inquiry might usefully inform each other. This is not a book about research for narrative therapists or a book about narrative therapy for social science researchers. It is a book situated between those two worlds and hopes to encourage inhabitants of all domains to peer over the edges towards each other. **The rest of the book** is compiled of short exemplars, intended as illustrations of different genres of narrative inquiry rather than templates for others to follow.

A Layered Text

This is neither an overview of narrative research, nor a handbook of methods, nor a monograph detailing a specific, completed narrative inquiry. Indeed, excellent versions of all these genres already exist (see: Angus and McLeod, 2004a, Clandinin and Connolly, 2000; Etherington, 2000; Langellier and Peterson, 2004; Lieblich et al., 1998; Luttrell 2003; Riessman, 1993). This book is presented as a series of fragments and traces and as a conscious effort at writing against the grain of overviews, manuals and handbooks. The text begins somewhere and there are no concluding chapters. If anything this book just fizzles out.

In between these points are a divergent series of small-scale studies or fragments of research into people's lives. The first part of the book focuses on the fit between a more arts-based, literary style of narrative inquiry and poststructuralist and feminist ideas and on the blurring of boundaries between narrative approaches to therapy and research. As I suggested earlier, this book is not designed exclusively for narrative therapy practitioners wishing to research their work, although I hope it will interest them. I hope it will be of interest to a range of practitioner researchers within what McLeod (2000, 2004b, 2006) has described as the 'post-psychological age'. I suspect that many of the ideas, positions and metaphors taken up by narrative therapy practitioners and post-colonial, poststructural and feminist researchers alike (such as the uses of ethical curiosity, archaeological excavation, ethnographic imagination and social/relational worldviews) will be of interest to a range of people critically reflecting on their practice.

The rest of this book concentrates on different contexts for the telling and re-telling of stories, and the representational possibilities for those stories, and ends with imaginary futures.

The text moves transparently in and out of layers of personal narrative, more formal academic prose, fairy story, fable, fictionalised accounts, poetic documents, life stories and discussion of the blurring and layering of these genres. I hope that by experimenting with and moving between literary, scholarly, investigative, imaginary and personal styles of inquiry I will gently scrape away at the discourses of research.

The Discourses of Psychotherapy

The terms 'counselling' and 'psychotherapy' will be used interchangeably throughout the text, since, by this author's lights at least, they are identical, not competing, identity claims. The discourses of counselling extend well beyond individual relationships between therapists and the people who consult them. They include the professional regimes of truth whereby particular identity claims (such as 'integrative psychotherapist' or 'counsellor educator') are constructed. The immense growth of 'individual' counselling and psychotherapy practices along-side the decline of the welfare state in Britain during the late twentieth-century monetarist years when there was 'no such thing as society, only individuals and their families' (Thatcher, 1987) is surely no coincidence? Therapeutic encounters, albeit confidential exchanges about apparently 'private' troubles, are only available to us in our contemporary everyday lives as a result of shifts in public and social discourses. Indeed, ideas about public and private spaces are constantly shifting in the wake of the television confessional, chat show, and 'reality' TV.

There are occasions in this text when stories of therapeutic encounters with individuals are the research focus. Gregory's story (Chapter 4), the conversations with Hyatt (Chapter 6) and my explorations along-side Margie Jones (Chapter 8) are all examples of this. These encounters have, however, rarely stayed as de-contextualised 'therapy' sessions. Conversations with Gregory were soon to include the group of 'unassuming geeks' (see Chapter 7), those with Margie included not only both living and dead members of her family but also living, dead and imaginary members of my own family, and those with Hyatt moved out of the therapy room and into a poetic email exchange. Equally the 'gargoyles' stories in Chapter 10 are based on counselling supervision sessions, and Donald and Morag's stories (Chapters 4 and 7) describe counselling educators' experiences.

Throughout the book, pseudonyms have been used to describe participants, and a range of potentially identifying features of their lives have been disguised. This has not been, and never is, a simple process. In the case of the 'geeks' for example (see Chapter 7), intense debates about anonymity versus ownership and authorship went on, and continue to go on. For the Jones family (Chapter 8) and Gina et al. (Chapter 6) the choosing of pseudonyms and other elements of disguise became part of the performance of selves and the source of much ribaldry and hilarity. The outcome, inevitably, privileges my position as sole author – an uneasy space for a co-researcher to occupy, but one that we have all settled for, for the moment.

1

Introduction: Poststructuralist Ideas and Narrative Inquiry

I have struggled with writing this chapter more than any of the others. There have been many versions, most of them in different styles of academic prose/social science report writing. My tussles have been with the pros and cons of starting with an 'ideas' chapter. It seems important to 'set the scene' by embedding my work within its histories, cultures and contexts. The practice of research is akin to a series of conversations and it seems useful to locate this entry in relation to the ongoing dialogue. Nonetheless my experience of both therapy and research 'in process' is not that ideas and histories inform practices or vice versa, but rather that they sustain each other in a constant, fluid exchange as the work progresses. In many research texts where there is an 'ideas' section at the beginning, readers are invited to skip the first part and come back to it later, the implication being (or so it seems to me) that ideas are abstract and harder to absorb than the stories of 'what happened next' and also, perhaps, that if the text reflects some sense of chronological time then the ideas came first. So, there's the conundrum. How might I write a beginning chapter that destabilises certainties and clearly positions my work without preserving it in aspic? And how can I also write in engaging ways and in the spirit of my stated intention of moving without apology between different narrative genres and discourses such as fiction, auto-ethnographic narrative, re-presented conversations, and academic prose?

I routinely teach courses exploring these issues and my approach is likely to be similar to that advocated by White (1997a) in relation to supervision or consultation practices within psychotherapy, wherein he invites people to interview him and he then interviews them back. In teaching contexts I have often invited people to interview me, then each other, and then pool together our body of knowledge-in-context. In positioning ourselves, in these conversations, as curious 'ethnographers' I find that we become intrigued with the possibilities before us and tend to find ourselves excavating knowledge that we did not know

1

we had, or speaking in quite unexpected ways. I have often found myself re-interrogating my ideas rather than settling for the reproduction of that which has become familiar. This becomes a process of 'exoticising the domestic' (Bourdieu, 1988).

I thought of inviting someone to interview me, having very much enjoyed the sense of movement, and of entering into a dialogue as a reader, presented in Strong and Paré's (2004) series of unfinished conversations about discursive therapy. I also had quite a strong sense of the particular cross-section of territories that I currently inhabited and wanted to convey. Perhaps I could interview myself? I spent some time metaphorically interviewing the possible 'selves' who might apply for this job. They all seemed a bit too close to the bone, but then I remembered Mr Gingey. Mr Gingey was an 'imaginary friend' who had shared my life until I was about seven years old. Now long since forgotten, he had been invented by my brother Chris and had been a useful, but somewhat unpredictable, childhood ally and co-conspirator. In our time, we had been up to all sorts together. Perhaps we could rekindle our relationship and get up to some more?

Mr Gingey had clearly inhabited the same territories that I had for the last 50 years, whilst at the same time remaining a somewhat shadowy figure. The appeal of Mr Gingey's unexpected arrival as co-researcher in this chapter, for me at least, has been the highlighting of relationships between truths, make-believe, 'legitimate' research and the impact of the stories we tell ourselves about our lives. In inviting Mr Gingey into this text as my co-researcher (he appears again briefly in Chapter 8), I found myself 'writing against the grain' of the sorts of chapters that begin research texts.

The introduction of Mr Gingey as a character so early on in this book troubles the edges of research and practice and perhaps merges the territories mapped out as 'adult' and 'childhood' domains. To write about imaginary characters and have conversations with them is well within the conventions of therapy practice stories (especially play therapy, see Betterton and Epston, 1998; Freeman et al., 1997). It is the stuff of novels, wherein walls can dissolve, revealing different time zones (Lessing, 1974), where we are propelled into future worlds (Atwood, 1985), worlds inhabited by the occasional winged woman or bizarrely telepathic twins (Carter, 1984, 1992) or vividly portrayed ancestral spirits (Allende, 1986). In novels people float mysteriously from one part of the world to another, write and speak to each other after death and gradually talk and sing themselves into different futures (Shange, 1995; Walker, 1989, 1992).

In research texts, it is unusual for imaginary, fictional or winged characters to dwell alongside the author, whose role is more routinely to describe such characters and other people's relationships with them from a discreet distance. Exceptions from the world of counselling and counselling research are Michael White's (1997b) Mouse Stories, Miller Mair's poetics of experience (1989) and John McLeod's (1997) narrative case history of the fictional character 'Tubby' from David Lodge's (1995) novel *Therapy*.

Mr Gingey's arrival in this chapter presents me with some dangers as well as permissions as an author. Readers may mistake playfulness for lack of substance. They may also elide a stand against certainties and forms that authorise with a lack of rigour. This seems a risk worth taking, however, for Mr Gingey not only provides a useful foil who can present commonly asked questions about poststructuralism, feminism, queer studies and their relationships with the 'narrative turn', he also neatly introduces 'magical realism', itself a 'transgressive and subversive' fictional genre (Bowers, 2004: 67), very early on into this research text. The ideas presented in this section are complex and, I think, worth grappling with, but it is hard to present anything like a 'textbook' style account of them in ways that stay tentative, contingent and in the moment. Things explained in textbook style become very definite and suddenly we find 'postmodernism/poststructuralism' has become a fixed entity, rather than

the code name for the crisis of confidence in western conceptual systems.   (Lather, 1991: 159)

A conversation with Mr Gingey supports the lightness that I feel these ideas should be worn with. These ideas, and the practices that they sustain, are of their domains and of their moments in history. I have found them a useful companion in excavating people's practices of living in late twentieth-/early twenty-first-century Europe (indeed, this is where they come from), but I have no expectations of their continued endurance or universality.

No doubt from the vantage point of the future (or indeed the non-western/westernised present), 'narrative' formulations of therapy and research will look as arbitrary and lacking in complexity as most nineteenth-century treatments and theories do to me today. I am already aware that narrative configurations are anthropomorphic and privilege human understandings and constructions. I aspire to a more ecologically and globally connected way of constructing knowledge (more of which, in the last chapter; see also Byrne, 1998), a new 'code name for the crisis of confidence in anthropomorphic conceptual systems', and hope this may prevail in the future.

The advent of Mr Gingey also seemed to scatter and muddle the pages and when I came to put them back together they were not of the same size or font. There were gaps and cracks and fragments of stories that seemed not entirely to fit, traces that may not even be part of this time–space dimension. They appear to have fallen through a grating from one world, or time, to another. This is the space that Mr Gingey seemed to be inviting us all to step into. It is a space that is very familiar within a more 'literary genre', as Pullman (2003: i) eloquently demonstrates in 'Lyra's story':

> This . . . contains a story and several other things. The other things might be connected with the story, or they might not; they might be connected to stories that haven't appeared yet. It's not easy to tell. It's easy to imagine how they might have turned up though. The world is full of things like that: old post cards, theatre programmes, leaflets about bomb-proofing your cellar . . . All these tattered old bits and pieces have a history and a meaning. A group of them together can seem like traces . . .

Literatures of the Imagination

This book is not a novel, but to pretend towards such imaginary texts as the novels of Philip Pullman, Doris Lessing and Margaret Atwood immediately contextualises my relationship with narrative theory and practice. The text became a layered account (Ronai, 1992) that included multifarious 'tattered old bits and pieces' that had histories and, when put together, seemed to construct a meaning.

My own interest in multi-storied texts originates in my passionate and continuing relationship with fiction and poetry. My thirst for multi-storied, overlapping, layered accounts was not inculcated by the (much later) rich narrative research texts emerging within other disciplines such as sociology (Langellier, 2001), anthropology (Behar, 1993) or psychology (Mishler, 2000), nor by the works of the new poststructuralist ethnographers like Ronai (1992, 1999), Davies (2000a, 2000b) and Lather (1991), and Lather and Smithies (1997) (of all of whom, more later). It was inspired by the multi-voiced plays and poems of Ntozake Shange, the conversations between spirit, present and future worlds that are scattered throughout the works of Angela Carter and Isabel Allende, and the ambiguities that remain in the works of Milan Kundera and David Malouf. These are the narratives that I have lived alongside for the past thirty-plus years and through which I have made some sense of my life. My later interest in storied research was already resonant with these possibilities.

Traditionally, although there may be frequent traces of intertextuality with popular and other cultural markers, psychotherapy research and practice texts tend to cite each other and the literatures of mainstream psychological research and 'social science'. Intertextuality (the allusions and traces from one cultural reference point contained in another) within this genre is indicated via rigorously upheld traditions of academic referencing. There is considerable value in locating texts within bodies of knowledge, but this also gives a thin description of the antecedents of much therapeutic development and creativity. Despite evidence of the anthropological, theological, historical, political, literary- and arts-based backgrounds of many counsellors and psychotherapists within the UK at least (McLeod, 2001b, 2001c; Speedy, 2001), the literatures of the imagination are rarely cited. Perhaps counselling psychologists at work *really are* thinking about what stage within the framework or model they have reached and what level of intervention it would be useful to make. For myself, I am mostly listening out for 'talk that sings' (Bird, 2000: 1–47), and the literature that most commonly comes to mind as I work either as a therapist or a researcher tends to be poetry.

*   *   *

'Hello m' dear', I said. 'Haven't seen you for ages, what exactly are you up to these days?'

'Well, at the moment I'm just putting the finishing touches to my book,' she replied proudly.

'Are you indeed', I grinned, trying to look impressed, 'and what's it about, might I be so bold as to enquire?'

'You might,' she said, bowing graciously, 'It's about narrative inquiry and psychotherapy and it's all but finished.'

It was quite dark in the room. The sun was just coming up and the curtains were still half drawn. I had awoken early, my head full of memories and, armed with a mug of earl grey tea and a packet of 'ginger nut' biscuits, I had crept onto the end of the bed and begun writing down the ideas that seemed to have taken shape whilst I was asleep. I did not notice Jane at first. We reached for the ginger nuts at the same time and I looked up, startled, to find her sitting up, silently watching me. She looked much older than I remembered although she seemed to be dressed in the same crumpled pair of pyjamas that she had worn forty years ago. I felt a bit overdressed in my green Harris tweed suit and red bow tie. Then I remembered her great love of sweet biscuits and realised that I was going to have to keep my wits about me if I was to get my hands on any of these ginger nuts. And so our conversations began . . .

* * *

Mr Gingey: Is narrative just a trendy word for story or something more?

Jane: Well, 'narrative' is a rather overarching term for the stories we tell ourselves, but it's not the same as 'story' or 'life story'. There are multifarious versions of what narrative means to people, ranging from the broad Aristotelian concept of a plot, taking place over time, including a beginning, a middle and an end; to Labov's (1982; Labov and Waletzky, 1967) very specific, linguistic structuralist understanding of stories within conversation, providing an abstract, orientating the listener, describing complicating action, evaluating the meaning, resolving the action and ending with a coda; and to Sarbin's (1986: 9) claim that narrative is 'the organising principle for human action'.

Narrative researchers position themselves differently across a huge range of understandings of what it means to be human as well as across versions of 'narrative'. Some writers, such as McAdams (1993), construct their research against a range of possible archetypal stories or plots (see Booker, 2004). Others, such as Riessman (1993), Riessman and Speedy (2006) and McLeod (1997) have a looser, broader definition of narrative in conversation as significant episodes of 'sequence and consequence' and 'plot-over-time'.

In positioning myself within a narrative frame, I find myself invited into particular ways of seeing and knowing. Narrative describes forms of discourse that offer a coherence over time, within space and context, so that: 'narrators make sense of themselves, social situations, and history' (Bamberg and McCabe, 1998: iii; see also Clandinin and Connolly, 2000).

This book is not about *whole* life histories, but about the moments and turning points in people's lives that they struggle to make sense of

– the episodes that bring them into contact with therapy and counselling, or indeed, the moments that turn them into therapists and counsellors. It is about the ways these moments are storied or made sense of in different contexts, over time. It is also about different kinds of time and the ways that autobiographical time, mythical time and narrative time, for instance, would all support different tellings of the same story (see Freeman, 1998).

Mr Gingey: Aren't you prying? Why would I want to know about the stories that people tell you in therapy, isn't that their business?

Jane: Well this book isn't about the things people want to keep to themselves, but you've put your finger on one of the main reasons that I wanted to write it. This stark private/public divide comes, I think, from modern developments in western culture around what it means to be an 'individual' person. It frequently disguises the social and historical roots of what are considered to be 'personal' concerns. I have often criticised the 'personal problems industry' for making community and political issues into individual concerns (see Speedy, 2000a, 2001c). Riessman (2005) speaks of the 'social' causes of private troubles, and this book is about personal everyday accounts but also about their social and historical connotations and connections. Bird (2004b) speaks of a 'relational' practice of conversation and I have found that placing people's life stories in relation to others and in relation to situations and discourses allows people to gain a better grasp of what might be their individual 'business', as you call it, and what might lie beyond the realms of individual agency.

Mr Gingey: Okay hang on, can we just back up here? Why couldn't you have just called this book 'life stories'?

Jane: Well yes, I could have I suppose, but I also want to explore the conversations that take place at the crossroads where narrative therapy and narrative research meet. I'm interested in 'troubling the edges' between therapy and research practices. There are those that see narrative therapy as a branch of family therapy (Polkinghorne, 2004) and certainly many of its advocates come from that field. There are those who consider that narrative therapy has quite a lot to offer the whole domain of counselling and psychotherapy (Monk et al., 1997; Payne, 2006), but I also think that narrative therapy has much to offer the world of narrative inquiry and vice versa. Perhaps both these fields might gain from veering towards more arts-based 'ways of seeing'. The kinds of narrative theories I am interested in (and there are many, I'll talk about some in just a second) are those connected with poststructuralist ideas and with what Foucault (1988a) described as the art (and/or) performance of the self. This is more of an invitation towards arts- and literary-based research methods than seems to have been taken up thus far.

Mr Gingey: Oh, so these are new ideas are they?

Jane: Well, maybe a new juxtaposition or constellation of ideas: all research is always part of a conversation, and ideas, like planets in a constellation, come from somewhere and are always fluid and on their way somewhere else. Narrative forms of inquiry have been emerging over the last thirty years or more. This book represents a contribution along the way and an introduction to a meeting place that I have found quite useful and hope that other people might.

There have been quite a lot of books about narrative research and narrative therapy practices, but very few are situated at the crossroads between them. Angus and McLeod's (2004a) handbook is a very comprehensive overview of existing narrative research and therapy traditions, but not so much concerned with the ways these traditions might merge with the other more arts-based research genres. A narrative turn invites our actual minds into other possible worlds (to paraphrase Bruner, 1986a) but also speaks to fictionalised, imagined and impossible worlds and perhaps hints at the languages of the unsaid and the unsayable (Rogers et al., 1999).

The crossover between research, fiction and other arts-based genres is becoming more of a consideration within educational and other applied 'social science' fields (Clough, 2002; Sparkes, 2002a) and is well established within anthropological, ethnographic traditions (Mathiessen, 1962; Harris, 1985; Van Maanen, 1988) but has not impinged very much upon psychotherapy research. This book contains some of what Van Maanen (1988) calls 'realist' tales of actual conversations (with Donald, for example, in Chapter 4, and Gina et al., in Chapter 6), as well as some poetically represented accounts of conversations that took place (as with Morag and Hyatt in Chapter 5) in both therapy and research. It also contains fictionalised accounts and even magical realist tales (as in Chapters 8, 9 and 10).

Narrative therapy practitioners are beginning to conceive of many of their practices as legitimate, non-traditional ways of co-researching their own therapy but they have not really begun to consider how ways of working such as definitional ceremony (more of which in Chapter 6) might sustain new developments in collaborative and participatory research across a variety of domains. Poststructuralist and postcolonialist writers have produced, in combination with literary, feminist and queer studies, a whole gamut of transgressive, experimental and emancipatory research genres. As a narrative practitioner and researcher with a love of new kinds of writing I find myself stepping into a space that juxtaposes collective biographies with definitional ceremonies, auto-ethnographies with experimental poetics, and that my practices of both therapy and research are as much sustained and enriched by works of fiction and poetry as they are by more professional and academic treatises.

Mr Gingey (rubbing his forehead fiercely):   Whoa!! Hang on dearie; I'll go and make us another nice cup of earl grey and then perhaps you can take me back to how you got started on all this. You have to bear in mind that the last time I had an extended conversation with you, you had just fallen off your trike and hurt yourself quite badly and the world wasn't post-anything, except post-war of course. I feel suddenly like a bit of a relic.

*   *   *

I went off to the kitchen, made a proper pot of tea and laid out a tray with cups, saucers and milk in a proper jug. The ginger nuts seemed to have mysteriously disappeared, leaving just a crumpled empty packet, but I found some nice shortbread fingers and took the tray out onto the deck in the back garden. It was one of those unusually warm and sunny autumn mornings with clear blue skies. Jane was sitting out on the deck, beneath the tree ferns. She had added a blue woollen robe and soft slippers to the pyjamas.

*   *   *

Mr Gingey: Let's get back to this book. How did you end up at this 'crossroads' in the first place?

Jane: Well, it was through an interest in narrative inquiry methods that I stumbled across narrative therapy practices (see Crockett, 2004, for a 'reverse' version of this story). I was a counsellor educator exploring and researching ways of undertaking research interviews. There seemed to be some information within the research literatures, particularly from anthropology and ethnography, about the curious, unknowing 'position' that a discovery-orientated (as opposed to interrogative and hypothesis investigating) researcher might take up (Coffey 1999; Kvale, 1996; Mishler, 1986, 2000), but nothing about actually *conducting* research interviews (Chapter 4 discusses these circumstances more fully). I gained considerable amounts of information about narrative theory from literature searching, but almost the only interest in the *practice* of narrative interviewing came from the narrative therapies.

The links between narrative therapy and poststructuralism, feminism and literary metaphors for discerning the world, made sense to me and I really liked these 'practices' of identity as a social achievement. Narrative therapy practices of definitional ceremony, of re-membering conversations, of de-centred therapist positions, were all *social* practices of conversation. This was very different from the group therapy practices of the more traditional psychologies.

Initially, I began working in a style akin to 'narrative therapy' from my position as a research interviewer. Then, when it seemed to me that my research interviews were more effective and more therapeutic than my counselling sessions, these ideas began to seep into my therapeutic practice as well. I began to travel the globe, soaking up narrative approaches to therapy wherever I could.

It was the politics of narrative therapy practice that fitted, for me, the commitments to social justice and the stated intention to place therapeutic endeavours outside 'special relationships' with specialist people, and back within people's everyday lives and communities. At the same time, I was working in a leading international research university, which provided the ground to position narrative therapy alongside a whole collection of poststructuralist, discursive and 'critical' ideas. This included emerging narrative research practices like collective biography, the 'new' ethnographies, the collating of 'local' knowledges advocated by cultural anthropologists and sociologists, writing as inquiry, auto-ethnography and so on. These all seemed quite familiar literary genres and ways of working to me, as I had grown up amidst a world of collective action and on a diet of postcolonial and feminist fiction and poetry.

Poststructuralist experimental texts, when I came across them later, described a world I was already immersed in. What struck me as something of a gap in communication within all this was that although narrative therapists and some narrative inquirers were drawing on the same body of poststructuralist/critical ideas (including those from literary theory) to inform their work, neither of these groups seemed as much informed by each other as they might be, or by the fictional or arts-based genres that had in many instances preceded them.

Mr Gingey: Okay. I think I need to try and understand these cross-ings over one at a time, over many biscuits. First of all, are you the only person standing at this crossroads?

Standing at the Crossroads between the 'Narrative Turn' and 'Postmodern' Uncertainties

Jane: Not at all, this is a multidisciplinary and very busy crossroads in several dimensions. My overarching description of this crossroads would be the place where the 'narrative turn' (a turn towards 'story' as a metaphor for how human beings make sense of their lives and their world) meets the postmodern condition of uncertainties and increduli-ties towards universal truths. There are many people working at the interfaces between these intersections, and each brings a different (and shifting) emphasis and contribution.

From the work of Myerhoff (1980, 1986) onwards there has been a crossover between anthropology, the 'new' ethnographies, and narrative therapy practices. Gremillion (2003) and Epston (2001), for instance, are both situated at this interface, the former bringing understandings from narrative therapy practice into a feminist anthropological research domain and the latter advocating the use of ethnographic imagination and remaining attuned to anthropological writing in relation to the ethics and politics of representing 'others' within therapeutic domains.

Similarly, Drewery and Winslade (1997), Parker (1999) and Besley (2001) are amongst a group positioned within the space between 'the academy' and 'therapy'. This territory crosses the borders and extends the conversations between poststructuralist philosophies (the work of Foucault, Derrida and others) and the more discursive, narrative and socially constructed therapy practices that interrogate power relation-ships between counsellors and clients.

Some narrative therapists (Epston, 2004, and Bird, 2000, for instance) actually describe the work they do as 'co-research': a form of research alongside people, into matters that are of concern to them in their lives. Bird (2004a) speaks of researching the resources that people have or might have available in their lives. This lends itself to a blurring of research and therapy practices, as does the work of some social-sciences researchers who are beginning to realise the value of narrative practices such as reflecting team work and compassionate witnessing, which extends beyond therapeutic conversations and into wider research domains (see Gergen, 2004).

Mr Gingey: So you are wanting to show us what's transferable between these fields, and question the differences between them?

Jane: Well yes, that's part of it, but this is not just a one-dimensional crossroads between therapy and research. There is another dimension, not so much a crossroads, but rather a 'blurring of genres' (Geertz, 1980) between ways of thinking about and re-searching the world. This is the crossroads where arts-based methods meet 'the social sciences'. I was talking about fiction and poetry just a moment ago, but there are also people researching and describing their social world and those of others in experimental and creative ways, such as Richardson (2000a, 2001) and Clough (2002) in writerly and poetic ways, and Trinh (1999) and Ruby (2000) in terms of cinematic and visual narratives. Somehow, therapy researchers have embraced personal narrative as researcher reflexivity, and poetic stanza as transcription of their clients' words (Etherington, 2004; McLeod and Balamoutsou, 1996; Speedy, 2001), but have been more tentative in relation to experimental and fictionalised accounts of their work with others and of moving between fiction, imagery, fantasy and life story in ways that reflect the layers of meaning and genres that are often apparent in therapy sessions. These are borders Mair (1989) has long since transgressed. They are waiting to be crossed by others:

> To live in a world of personal vision
> Rather than conventional vision
> Is perhaps to live in a desert
> Or in a world of dwarfs
> Demons, pygmies and elves
> A place of fear with flashes and sparks
> Of love and beauty.
> (Mair, 1989: 132)

Mr Gingey (hanging upside down from the lowest branch of the old pear tree, yet somehow still remaining the consummate toff): Mmm, now you're talking. Miller Mair sounds like a man with an appropriate appreciation of the little people. Does he have any imaginary friends? Okay. So this is not so much a crossroads then, more like a multiple meeting place. Any more border crossings?

Jane: Well yes, for me there are. These literary spaces may have been opened up by the novelists and poets I talked about earlier but they are also inhabited by poststructuralists, particularly feminists (Lather and

Smithies, 1997, and Davies, 2000a, for instance) and those engaged in queer, feminist and postcolonial studies (such as Tierney, 1997; Chaudry, 1997; Ifegwunigwe, 1999).

Poststructuralism is not of itself a philosophy of the margins, but in drawing attention towards the discourses and discontinuities governing sexual norms (Foucault, 1981) or the many different readings of any text that might be available to readers from different positions (Derrida, 1978), poststructuralist ideas resonate particularly strongly with the life experiences of those outside contemporary 'regimes of truth' in society.

These ideas also place counselling very much within a political arena with its own regimes of truth, ways of describing itself and also ways of researching itself. It seems to me that most people seeking therapeutic support in their lives are doing so because they have found themselves, sometimes inexplicably, at the margins. Thus, the 'unassuming geeks', the group of young, mostly white, European men thinking about suicide whose account appears in Chapter 7, found the writings of Ntozake Shange, an African American woman, highly evocative. They were a predominantly heterosexual group, but also found Butler's (1993) explorations of 'critically queer' identities connected very closely to their own experiences.

There has been a growing critique of mainstream research methods from those at the postcolonial margins (see, for instance, Tuhiwai-Smith, 1999) and this often seems to bring us back full circle towards more 'storied' accounts of people's lives. Sarris's (1994: 5) conversation with Mabel McKay, the Native American Indian who was the subject of his research, illustrates some of these cultural tensions between people's stories and the research cultures and conventions that constrain and dissect the ways they might be told:

GS: A theme is a point that connects all the dots, ties up all the stories.
MM: That's funny. Tying up all the stories. Why would somebody want to do that?
GS: When you write a book there has to be a story, or idea, a theme
. . .
MM: Well, theme. I don't know nothing about. That's somebody else's rule.

Mr Gingey: I'm with Mabel. She sounds a fine woman. Let's have that cup of tea now, seeing as how you've finished off all the biscuits . . .

Jane (sounding outraged):   Excuse me!! I haven't had one . . . You just took them up into the pear tree and chomped your way through the lot.

Mr Gingey: **Nothing's changed around here in fifty years I see. I still get the blame for what you get up to. Now getting back to this book, I'm a bit at sea. Is all this jargon really necessary? How is it going to help the rest of us make sense of our world? Or are you just trying to make yourself sound clever because you've got a job at a university?**

Postmodern Times, Poststructuralist Ideas and Socially Constructed Worlds

Jane: Well 'new jargon' has a range of purposes that may not have anything to do with cleverness. I think that these ideas – poststructuralism, for example – are new and difficult to get an initial grasp of, but are worth struggling with, especially for counselling researchers. In the 'developed' world we have had such individualistically constructed notions of people's life spaces up until recently, often based on very structured (or structuralist) models of what it means to be a human being. I also think that therapists should have an interest in ways of interrogating that which is excluded, that which is outside the mainstream and that which is 'other' than dominant in society.

I lack clairvoyance and cannot tell you which of these notions is going to endure and which is passing contemporary jargon, but my sense is that in the future this period in the history of ideas will be looked upon as the postmodern era. Perhaps it will even be the space in between eras, but we do not know what it is in between yet. I can give you my take on this, although the distinctions between how some people use these words vary considerably and have also changed over time.

Mr Gingey: **Well go ahead, dearie, go ahead.**

Jane: **The postmodern era** or condition (Currie, 1998; Lyons, 1999) describes a growing sense within western societies following the Second World War and the end of empires in the traditional sense (although not of western imperialism), in academic disciplines, throughout popular culture and across political, religious and geographical borders, that there is less certainty and universality in the world. This worldview inculcates less sense of adherence to one overarching truth or belief system, but rather, aspires to an acceptance of many possible truths, many ethics to live by, muliple cultures, various forms of social organisation and so forth.

This has become at the least an acceptance, and at best a celebration, of diversity and has led to an academic interest in 'local' rather than universal knowledge. People have also become less sure of the twentieth-century 'progress myth' in relation to economic expansion and technological development and are not only less certain that we know the answers, but are also perhaps more questioning that 'the right answers' (as opposed to several possible, contingent solutions-in-the moment) are out there waiting to be found. There are links here, too, with theories that expand beyond human experience and out into the complexities, chaos and interconnectedness of the world's ecologies (see Cilliers, 1998; Lewin, 1993).

Lyotard, who first coined the phrase, describes postmodernity as 'incredulity towards metanarratives' (Lyotard, 1984: xxiv) – hence an interest throughout this book in local, personal and culturally contingent stories. This is not to say that modernity has been replaced, any more than modernity, in its heyday, replaced traditional religious and folk accounts, or that they in their heyday replaced magical versions of how the world worked, but rather that whilst all these modes of thought and practice co-exist, postmodernity is enjoying a certain currency. Postmodernity refers (Lyons, 1999: 9) 'above all to the exhaustion – but not necessarily the demise – of modernity'.

Mr Gingey: **Yes, okay, but what about all those other terms? Are postmodern, 'socially constructed' and poststructural absolutely necessary distinctions, or are these lots of ways of saying the same thing, again?**

Jane: Well, 'social constructionism' (Burr, 2003; Gergen, 1999) is a term used almost exclusively by psychologists as a way of positioning themselves outside the traditions of mainstream psychology. In a way, social constructionism represents 'psychology' acknowledging ways of knowing that are already familiar to sociologists and anthropologists and that are more routinely described by them as 'socio-cultural theory'. Social constructionism heralds a recognition that people construct their lives and identities socially and culturally, through language, discourse and communication.

Social constructionism also represents western, particularly post-cold-war North American, psychologists catching up with the work of Soviet theorists such as Bakhtin and Vygotsky, who described creativity and meaning-making as collaborative activities and 'reality' as the space between people engaged in conversation. Bakhtin (1986) argued that there was always an invisible third party that conversations were addressed to, an imaginary 'super addressee'. Vygotsky was interested in learning and in how people's learning (particularly children's learning) took place within a 'zone' between them and the adults they were learning from. Adults (often parents) stretched or 'scaffolded' their explanations and conversations with children across what Vygotsky (1978) described as the 'zone of proximal development', between the child's grasp of ideas or meanings and their own, moving back across the zone towards what was meaningful to the child if their conversation had stretched too far. Vygotsky saw the shared meanings and ways of learning that parents and children generated as socio-cultural constructions, rather than (for example) innately developmental phenomena.

Mr Gingey: **Well we seem to be zoning in on Gingey here. I'M GETTING QUITE A GRASP OF THIS. But you don't seem very keen on all this. In fact you are beginning to sound bored, a bit like a textbook. What's the problem?**

Jane: Not a problem, exactly. I find collaborative constructs of creativity and dialogic understandings of meaning-making extraordinary contributions. I do, however, sometimes detect a certain determinism from social constructionism, almost as if socio-cultural factors, albeit contextual and contingent, have become the new structuralism or the latest 'grand narrative'. Our socio-cultural saturation of 'selves' (Gergen, 1992) may have become a new certainty, leaving little space for different, local knowledges or personal agencies.

Perhaps it is sometimes to do with my arts-based, literary tendencies, or my feminist experience of 'resistance from the margins', that draws me more towards poststructuralism. Poststructuralism, quite simply a move away from structuralism or essentialism 'concerning the relationship between human beings, the world, and the practices of making or reproducing meanings' (Belsey, 2002: 5), maintains that, as words have no absolute meaning, any text (body of work, group of ideas or conversation, for instance) is open to an unlimited range of local interpretations. This opens up the space for Geertz's (1983) emphasis on the legitimacy of local, partial knowledge and local, contingent stories. This sense of the infinite possibilities in conversations, stories and other text and Derrida's (1976) invitation to regard this muliplicity of possi-eanings as a 'chora' (the Greek word for 'womb') or fruitful, limi-ce seem to stand on the side of hope and in a place of agency.

Deconstruction has frequently been regarded as a somewhat nihilistic contribution, so perhaps I should unpack my sense of hope and excitement (particularly in relation to the talking therapies) a little more. Derrida's (1976) emphasis was not only on 'difference': the way the meaning of the words we use refers (and defers) to their dualistic opposite (e.g. transparency's dependence on opacity for its meaning). He was also interested in intertextuality: in the many traces of other words and other meanings in the space in-between these words ('see-through', 'frosted', etc.) and in the trail of other meanings, from other contexts, that might become available ('see-through', 'leading towards', 'sham', and so on). For Derrida, and subsequently for narrative therapists, the language people used became an archaeological site, with conversations open to an infinite variety of possible meanings and histories that might engage therapists and clients (and/or co-researchers).

Mr Gingey: So deconstructing what people say is like *taking apart their meanings*?

Jane: Well, yes, putting what people take for granted as the story of things 'under erasure', having a look at the assumptions behind it and the possible other meanings contained therein. Michael White (1997a) described this process as searching for the 'absent but implicit'. Take the phrase 'imaginary friend' for instance. This is a particular category of friend, but is 'imaginary' more or less 'real' than other kinds of friend. If you have an imaginary friend, does that mean your friend doesn't 'exist'?

Mr Gingey: Well you tell me: do you think I exist? Am I real?

Jane: Well, there have been times when I've thought I made you up, and other times when you've surprised me, or even appeared out of nowhere . . . and then you seem to exist in a very real way, but I'm not so interested in whether you exist or not in any absolute, universal sense, as I am in the meaning and significance of an imaginary friend to me. Bird (2004a) describes in some detail her ways of 'escaping from the binaries', which is a poststructuralist conversational practice that I have become very interested in, both as a therapist and as a researcher. Let's take the binary opposites of real and imagined friends, for instance. Bird (2004a) would be interested in what she calls the space in-between these opposites, not in whether you were real or imagined perhaps, but in what holding to the idea of an imaginary friend means to me now and perhaps what it might have meant to me as a child, and what the differences are (if any) between having conversations out loud with an imaginary friend and with a real friend and whether this difference speaks in similar ways to senior lecturers at leading universities and to little girls. I could go on . . .

Mr Gingey: **Please don't. So there's no truth any more? Sounds like anything goes . . .**

Jane: Well it sounds to me like there are multiple truths and that deconstructing meanings by putting what people say about themselves under close scrutiny, either as a therapy or as a research process, or both, might lead to greater verisimilitude (truthfulness) and a sense of undermining the dominant discourses that can overshadow marginal versions of life.

Mr Gingey: **Mmm. So is this Derrida the main 'ideas man' behind poststructuralism?**

Jane: There's a whole bunch: Derrida, Bourdieu, Barthes, Deleuze, the 'French feminists': Kristeva, Iragaray and Cixous, many that came later and are applying these ideas in various ways, like Butler in terms of queer theory, Spivak in terms of postcolonialism and feminism. I'll tell you more about the work of some of these people as this book progresses. Another big 'ideas man' would be Michel Foucault. Foucault's (1980a, 1980b) early work on dominant and other discourses within cultures puts forward the contention that all regimes of truth or dominant discourses also open up the space for acts of resistance. (The term 'discourse' is used by poststructuralist writers to describe the 'language in action' – the ideas and practices with which we shape, and are shaped by, our world and that allow us to both see and make sense of things. Danaher, *et al.* (2000) is a clear introduction.)

Thus, as Foucault showed in tracing the genealogies of sexuality, the construction of homosexuality through its categorisation and condemnation, for example, also opened up the space for a gay-rights movement. There could be no 'rights movement' for gay people before this category of people had been so specifically established and condemned. Thus, between the historically relatively new 'dominant' discourses and violent exclusions of heterosexuality and its opposite 'homosexuality', the space emerges and grows for queer theorists like Butler (1993) to speculate about the instability of clear cut categories of gender and sexuality. Just as queer theory moves from the commonly held view of heterosexuality as the 'original' category and other categories as differences from this, poststructuralist feminists move from views of women's differences, to excavations of the way genders have been constructed (see Weedon, 1997, and McNay, 2000, for the dance between poststructuralism and feminism). Postcolonial and critical race theories (such as Gunaratnam, 2003; J. McLeod, 2004a) also move towards viewing all such categories (like race and class) as overlapping discourses and identities, and as ongoing sites of power and knowledge in relation to each other. Thus 'whiteness' becomes not just the original, unexamined racial opposite of 'blackness' in society, but the (dominant) product of complex distorting discourses of race and ethnicity that often prevent people from seeing their 'scattered' and contingent postcolonial sense of belonging as a contribution to a diverse society (see Ifegwunigwe, 1999; Richards, 2006). All of these ideas have in common a move away from the binaries of either/or thinking, towards explorations of the 'space in between' and to explorations (and perhaps celebrations) of difference.

Mr Gingey: So poststructuralism, or at least this business of having a careful look at the discourses that prevail, sort of gets underneath the surface and exposes what is really going on, right?

Jane: Well actually it's a bit of a move away from the idea that if you get to the bottom of things and figure out how they work (or are structured) you will find out what is really going on. It's a bit of a move away from saying 'everything is socially constructed' or that 'everything is in the hands of the gods and the ancestors'. It's more a group of ideas that would sustain the practice of continually noticing that there's a lot really going on (to quote Harraway, 2004), but that some of what's going on has more current power and meaning attached to it. Poststructuralism is a move away from the metaphor of 'depth' (and underlying causes and structures of how things are), towards what Geertz (1973b) would describe as 'thick description' – excavations of meanings (in relation to each other) and power relations and the deconstruction of competing and possible stories we might tell ourselves and have been told about ourselves.

Poststructuralist writers have responded to these invitations with regard to the way they represent their research. They have experimented with transgressive and rhizomatic texts: texts that have moved away from linear report-writing genres, texts that disappear under the surface and then burst up in unexpected, yet connected, ways, to 'frame

narratives that work against the terrain of controllable knowledge'
(Lather, 2000: 221)

Mr Gingey: **Blimey. I can't believe that you just came out with
that lot off the top of your head. Do you need a little lie down, or
can we just zig-zag back for a moment.**

Jane: No, I'm fine thanks. I might just have another half a cup of tea
. . . Where do you want to zig-zag?

**Mr Gingey: Well, I wondered where we were going with all this
in relation to narrative inquiries about people's lives? Can you
connect this all up a bit more for me with counselling research,
now I've got a bit of a handle on the terminology (not to mention
feeling somewhat reinstated as one of the infinite possibilities in
the conversation)?**

Researching People's Life Stories

Jane: Well, maybe only up to a point. I think that that part of this
process of 'messy text' production is a move away from neatly
connected and completed work that has had inconsistencies and
contradictions and non-commensurate stories 'smoothed' away. There
are some connections. The poststructuralism illustrated by Derrida's
experimental texts, the 'revolutionary poetics' of poststructuralist feminist writers (such as Kristeva, Iragary and Cixous, see Chapter 5) and the
sense of caring for ourselves in everyday living by creating and performing our selves as 'works of art', described in Foucault's later work
(Foucault, 1988a, 1988b, Linnell, 2004), are all possible connections
and interplays between these ideas and more literary and arts-based
research practices.

The kinds of rhizomatic research practices that Lather describes are
similar to the practices of 'doubly listening' (White, 2003, more of which
in Chapters 4 and 5) developed by narrative therapists – practices of
listening to the 'talk that sings', the unsaid, the unsayable and the absent
but implicit meanings in conversations. The open or liminal space in
people's talk suggests possible entry points towards alternative meanings
or traces of forgotten, or unacknowledged, stories. These stories, too,
have been running sideways under the surface like interconnected
rhizomes, just needing the space to burst forth into somebody's life. But
people don't routinely tell the stories of their lives to themselves . . .

Mr Gingey: Well they might if they were an imaginary person that no one had bothered to communicate with for years . . .

Jane: They might indeed, and the particularities of everybody's lives, local circumstances and 'everyday epiphanies' (to quote James Joyce) are different, but if we were to consider meaning-making relational, and identity a social achievement, then that would invite us to consider 'talking to ourselves' and/or to others as a social activity. Who are you talking to, when you tell yourself the stories of your life?

Mr Gingey: Well you, of course, and your brother and other people, sort of shadowy figures in the background, sort of . . . So you are looking to explore the stories of people's lives are you, in relation to the other people that make up their context?

Jane: Yes, the people, the context and the histories and social and other circumstances they find themselves in . . .

Mr Gingey: And you think this kind of research and therapy is better than other traditions?

Jane: Well I don't necessarily find this kind of research or therapy is better, but rather, that it is of the moment and fits with my values. I am well placed to conduct and facilitate it and it describes and theorises different aspects of life in different ways. As I was finishing writing this book the British government was publishing statistics on the lowest suicide rates for 20 years and claiming the withdrawal of large packs of painkillers and related pharmaceuticals from 'over the counter' sales as the cause (Dept of Health, 2003, 2005), and linked this to the current 'suicide prevention strategy'. This is significant information. The collective biographies produced by the 'unassuming geeks' group (a group of young men who have contemplated suicide) in Chapter 6 tell a different story. These are stories written poetically and metaphorically, without cause and effect, that give a different kind of insight into suicide. I am interested in encouraging people to create more of these kinds of texts. When these are placed alongside the statistics of suicide, huge gaps and cracks appear. None of these young men did, or would, consider suicide by taking painkillers. They had all envisaged other versions. Another story emerges.

Mr Gingey: And you prefer that other story?

Jane: No, but I like the fact that this way of working allows those other stories to emerge. Some therapeutic and research conversations create the space for people to rehearse the stories they already know. This way of working is about moving towards the spaces where untold stories lurk, and that interests me more. Also, in this book, I have deliberately described the chapters as different kinds of stories, rather in the slightly 'folksy' way that Sparkes (2002a, after Van Maanen, 1988) has described his sections as tales. This language is quite deliberate. The world of research, like the lives it is describing, is full of incomplete, non-commensurate stories, some based on themes and categories, some on statistics, some on the narratives people construct that shape and are shaped by their lives. Narrative inquiry attempts to describe the stories of people's lives and how they change over time, according to the spaces and contexts they inhabit.

Mr Gingey: So, why not just write a novel? Make it all up, isn't that what Charles Dickens did? He wasn't a poststructuralist was he. I bet he hadn't heard of half of these ideas, but his books really made a difference didn't they?

Jane: There are many genres of narrative inquiry, and I suppose that Charles Dickens might be described as one of Britain's earliest and most influential ethnographers, but he was also a popular writer selling his stories to national newspapers, and a product of his times. Perhaps, if he were alive today, he might tell those stories with more ambiguity. As a matter of fact I have made some of these research studies up, in the sense that this book does include some 'fictionalised' accounts.

Mr Gingey: So, why make everything so hard and complicated? Why not just tell us a few good stories?

Jane: Well, you know what, Mr Gingey? I do think that we live in a complex and multi-storied world that is sometimes quite hard to unravel and make sense of. At the same time I also hope that I've told you a few good stories here. If you want more of my take on those kinds of questions, you are going to have to get down out of that pear tree and read some of this book, because it just won't all fit into one conversation. All I can do for now is introduce some of these ideas – set the scene, as it were. I think that the literatures of poststructuralism and their applications within postcolonialism and queer studies and feminism (each of them big projects in their own right) should be lightly worn in relation to the arts and crafts of counselling and research, sustaining rather than constraining, you might say . . .

They also have a great deal to offer psychotherapy research because they are each exploring identities and identity claims being made at the margins and in new ways, and people seeking help from counsellors, regardless of gender or sexual preference or of their relationship with colonisation, tend to find themselves at the margins of their own lives. Narrative inquiries that are cognisant of the dominant discourses within society and the habitual well-rehearsed stories we tell ourselves and ways of telling them, but do not focus on or end with these thin descriptions of our lives, seem to be at the richer and more troublesome end of the spectrum. Irigaray urges us to 'analyse very rigorously the forms that authorise' (1993: 172) and to challenge the so-called neutrality of certain forms of speech. She argues that those not privileged within these authorised discourses will not even be seen, and that the other widely available, but invisible and illegible languages, need to be listened to 'with another ear' and represented subjectively, poetically, experimentally and tentatively since:

If we go on speaking the same language together we are going to reproduce the same history.   (1985: 205)

Counselling practitioners and researchers are also in the 'invisible and illegible languages' business and interested in ways of listening with another ear. These ways of knowing can enrich psychotherapy research conversations. All of this has a bearing on the position of the researcher and people being 'researched' in the text and in relation to different forms of narrative integrity, but the next two chapters have a great deal more to say about that. If this has really captured your attention you might like to engage in some further reading – not just my book, I mean, but some of the texts that take these ideas much further than I can in the space we've got here . . .

Mr Gingey: Oh, homework. Hmm, well, maybe you've forgotten about me and homework, but I was always a little careless around homework. I was the one who tended to drop it on the way home, that kind of thing. I'm not so great with homework as I am at climbing trees.

Jane: Well, yes, but its just that these are complex ideas, especially as most of us around these parts have been brought up with a much more structuralist and certain view of the way human beings work. I'm not speaking for or against tree climbing or homework as a resource here. I certainly wouldn't be keen to decide which of these practices informed my current skills as a therapist or as a researcher more. Predicting the load-bearing qualities of a branch seems to me to be very much part of my day-to-day repertoire. A strange capacity for hanging upside down from branches has informed both a resilience to 'hang in there' with people's life stories and an eye for an interesting angle on the world. All the ideas and histories I have spoken of here, alongside my life experiences, are part of the archive that informs my work. I bring them alongside me into the conversational space I negotiate with people. They do not sit between us, but they are there by my side to draw on.

Mr Gingey: Well it's always good to spend part of your day hanging upside down, just to keep your brains and your toenails apart from each other. I'm not sure I want to read any really hard books though. I think I left school when you were about seven.

Jane: Mmm. I'll just make you a little reading list, no pressure, and then . . .

Mr Gingey: My Goodness, are we out of biscuits again? How did that happen? I tell you what, I'll just hop over the roof and across the park to the post office on Derby Road and . . . I'll be right back . . .

*   *   *

And with that, I was gone. I flew straight on up and right out of town without even pausing for biscuits. I left her happily composing her 'no pressure' booklist and of course I never went back. I felt a little mean about that, but I've always had a bit of a mean streak. I dare say she wasted a bit of time and energy out there in her garden, trying to 'imagine' me back into existence when it suited her, but I also felt I needed to challenge the dominant version of just who imagines who around here. I am not here just to be 'constructed' when it pleases those in authority. Power relations cut at least two ways. Besides which, it seemed to me that it was time that she stopped obsessing with all this 'women's literature' and remembered her William Blake:

> He who binds to himself a joy,
> Does the winged life destroy;
> But he who kisses the joy as it flies
> Lives in eternity's sun-rise.
>   (Blake, in Stevenson (ed.), 1989)

A 'no pressure' booklist for Mr Gingey

Narrative approaches to research and therapy
Much of the rest of this book explores the relationship between narrative therapy and narrative research in more detail. Further readings about both these are suggested in Chapters 3, 4 and 5. For overviews of narrative, discursive and postmodern takes on therapy practice and research, I would recommend:

Parker, I. (ed.) (1999) *Deconstructing Psychotherapy* (London: Sage).

And, the rather expensive and expansive, but very comprehensive:

Angus, L. and McLeod, J. (eds) (2004) *The Handbook of Narrative and Psychotherapy Practice, Theory and Research* (London: Sage).

Also:

Strong, T. and Paré, D. (eds) (2004) *Furthering Talk: Advances in the Discursive Therapies* (New York: KA/PP).

Poststructuralism
The 'original' texts of poststructuralism are quite difficult for people who are not steeped in the traditions of European philosophy. Some good starting points are:

Belsey, C. (2002) *Post-Structuralism: A Very Short Introduction* (Oxford: Oxford University Press).
Danaher, G., Schirato, T. and Webb, J. (2000) *Understanding Foucault* (London: Sage).

Social construction
Burr, V. (2003) *Social Constructionism*, 2nd edn (London: Routledge). (This is a really clear introduction to social construction and sociocultural theory.)

See also:

Gergen, K. (1999) *An Invitation to Social Construction* (Thousand Oaks, CA: Sage).

Feminism, queer studies, postcolonial studies
For clear introductions, I would go to:

hooks, B. (2000) *Feminism is for Everybody: Passionate Politics* (Cambridge, MA: South End Press).
Young, R. (2003) *Postcolonialism: A Very Short Introduction* (Oxford: Oxford University Press).

And:

Filax, G., Sumara, D., Davis, B. and Shogan, D. (2005) 'Queer Theory/Lesbian and Gay Approaches', in Somekh, B. and Lewin, C. (eds) *Research Methods in the Social Sciences* (London: Sage).

Putting these ideas together, some examples
Weedon, C. (1987) *Feminist Practice and Poststructuralist Theory* (Oxford: Blackwell).
Bloom, L. (2001) *Under the Sign of Hope: Feminist Methodology and Narrative Interpretation* (New York: State University of New York Press).

2

Reflexivities, Liminalities and other Relationships with 'the Space between Us'

The opening lines of J.D. Salinger's (1951) novel *Catcher in the Rye* lay down the gauntlet at the feet of those who require a biographical account of narrators and authors in order to make sense of their texts. Salinger eloquently critiques these requirements, demonstrating within his opening lines:

> If you really want to hear about it, the first thing you'll probably want to know is where I was born, and what my lousy childhood was like, and how my parents were occupied and all before they had me, and all that David Copperfield kind of crap, but I don't feel like going into it. (1951: 5)

that describing such events and situations in detail, or according to a tried and tested tradition, is not always necessary or appropriate, particularly in work in which the imaginative mind's eye of the reader is being called upon.

I have had these kinds of conversations quite often, as an audience member in relation to performances and works of art. Should we 'just listen' to the opera; should we listen to the opera and then refer to the programme notes, as and when we need to, or at some later point, or should we get there in good enough time to have read and digested the programme notes before the performance begins? I recently became as fascinated by the visitors to a retrospective of Frida Kahlo's work at the Tate Modern gallery in London as I was interested in the exhibition itself.[1] Visitors could opt for the support of an audiotaped talking curator

---

[1] Frida Kahlo, Tate Modern, UK, 9 June to 9 October 2005, curated by Kathy Battista.

to take them through the galleries. Some wandered around galleries by themselves, absorbing the artists' work; some set off around the galleries, occasionally stopping to glance at the briefer curator's notes on the walls; some acquired headphones and walked around slowly listening to the curator's commentaries; others sat in the foyer, listening to substantive accounts of Kahlo's life and relationship with Mexican history before venturing forth into the exhibition; yet others (myself included) whizzed around once by themselves and then acquired some headphones and whizzed around again, before departing to the café to contemplate their postcards.

Art is curated, operas are directed and produced and books are written. Within these arts-based genres there are a range of legitimate ways of traversing the liminal (or threshold) space between audience and text or artefact. People can choose to a certain degree where to place the 'I' in their text and equally whose 'eyes' the text is seen though on first or second or subsequent viewings. Salinger (above) also makes explicit artifice that might be used by the artist or writer to further enter into the spaces between writers, characters in the text, and readers.

Within social-science research contexts, positions are also taken up around these ideas, but the space between writers, participants in the texts and readers is referred to in the main as a 'reflexive' space. Judgement calls about texts are made, in part, according to different reflexive stances (or lack of them). The amount of time and space given to the issue of how transparently the text is 'curated', so to speak, is determined in advance by the author, although readers, of course, can skim and skip those bits. Indeed, it may be that some readers of this chapter have already whizzed on to Chapter 3.

Both reflexivity and liminality and the interplay between them seem particularly pertinent to counselling research and practice, wherein we are continuously engaging in the spaces between that which is known and that which is not yet known. In his later works, Foucault (1988a, 1988b) outlined this space in which aesthetics and ethics conjoin as the art of continually creating the self, which in turn has been extended by Butler (1997) and others into a performative space. As soon as we enter this 'space between' us, we are entering relations of power. Reflexive/liminal spaces are, therefore, highly political, personal, imaginative and social spaces.

In this chapter I hope to 'unpack' constructs of reflexivity and liminality and to suggest that different genres of research clearly lend themselves to different ways of writing and perhaps different reflexivities. I would also like to consider how we might best position our 'selves' as researchers in our texts, given that the texts themselves and the 'characters' or participants in them might have some say in this, and that like Lather and Smithies (1997: 41) we might find ourselves immersed in 'a text that is as much trying to write me as the other way round'.

There are, it seems, multiple reflexivities and liminal spaces to hand and it is surprisingly easy to get lost amongst all these words. To reiterate, thus far: within the social sciences reflexivities represent the relationships between researchers and researched, between researchers and texts, between researchers and the 'stuff' of their research and vice-versa (Hertz, 1997, gives a good overview). Within arts-based research, the space between artist/creator/performer and text/artefact is more usually described as 'creative' or 'liminal' and represents the 'threshold' relationship between performer and audience, or artist, medium and audience, and a kind of stepping into unknown places (Broadhurst, 1999, embeds these ideas historically).

Unpacking Reflexivity

Reflexivity (often singular) seems to be perpetually acclaimed as an element in shaping the integrity of qualitative research, but is nonetheless a hotly contested construct. In addition to its inclusion in many introductions to research methods (such as those within the counselling field emanating from John McLeod, 1997, 2001a, 2003a), there is a growing body of work within the social sciences specifically exploring researcher reflexivity (Alvesson and Skoldberg, 2000; Davies et al., 2004; Etherington, 2004; Hertz, 1997; Lynch, 2000; Macbeth, 2001; May, 1998; Steier, 1991). Similar works explore researcher subjectivity (Ellington, 1998; Ellis and Berger, 2003; Ellis and Flaherty, 1992) and yet others explore researcher and/or ethnographer 'positions' (Davies, 2000b; Davies and Harré, 1990; Fine et al., 2000; Harraway, 1988, 2004; Ruby, 1982; St Pierre and Pillow, 2000).

Much of this research literature concerned with reflexivity is still a 'literature of justification' in that, despite Denzin's (1997) robust claims that reflexivity was now unavoidable in social science research, substantial space is given to the exposition or deconstruction of the 'myth of silent authorship' (see Charmaz and Mitchell, 1997), or writing as if positioned as someone 'neutral and absent' from the text, in what Harraway (1988) famously described as the 'voice of god' position within traditional, social science texts. Many of these texts are written in critical relation to this 'voice of god' style rather than in contrasting and divergent ways.

What is interesting about the literature of reflexivity within the social sciences is that many of the writers do not seem to have noticed, as Salinger (above) so acutely and immediately does, that all these positions are literary devices to be taken up or put down, according to the purpose of the text. Critics of the 'god trick' (see Hertz, 1997, and Charmaz and Mitchell, 1997) are drawing attention to a dominant cultural practice that they (rightly) suspect often goes unnoticed by readers and writers alike. They nonetheless appear sometimes to have forgotten, as Macbeth (2001) points out to them, that 'researcher neutrality' in a text is merely a device and the deployment of a tried and tested academic convention. They seem to have forgotten, in their desire to 'out' the writer's authentic voice in the text, that the **myth of neutrality** represents the taking up of a position and that somebody has had to bracket off 'all that David Copperfield kind of crap' (Salinger, 1951) in order to write themselves into a 'god' position. It is surely the lack of transparency about taking up a position, that they take issue with, rather than the number of times the author has used 'I' in the text?

Similarly, the defenders of 'proper' research conventions, holding out against the opening floodgates of biographical and reflexive studies from the margins (see, for instance, Atkinson and Delamont, 2005), seem equally taken in by the **myth of authenticity**, as if to imply that aspects of reflexive research texts not written from the 'I' position have not also been written by the same authors as a different and equally vulnerable performance of that 'I', by using a different literary convention.

For my part, I find that I do not much want to enter this fray, let alone the further foray that might ensue from taking up different kinds of reflexive positions of either personal embodiment or cultural embeddedness (positions that seem to be partly circumscribed by academic discipline and partly by worldview: mainstream counselling and psychotherapy substantially favouring personal positions, and sociology (for example) preferring culturally situated texts).

My navigation of these choppy waters has led to an engagement with the ideas of **discursive positioning** usefully outlined by Davies and Harré (1990). My emerging preference, still lightly worn, is for a poststructuralist 'constitutive and exhaustive' practice of reflexivity, whereby we experience ourselves 'like being held in a hall of "mirrors"' (Davies et al., 2004: 386). In this way, culture and agency are constantly reinventing and reproducing each other, inscribing our lives-as-lived and our texts-as-written on each other. Thus everything we do and everything we write is reflexive (i.e. it takes up a discursive position). Sometimes writers choose what to **make transparent** or decide what is representative of their position, and sometimes the positions they take up are implicit, forced upon them, if you like, through the discourses and regimes of truth that they inhabit. As Macbeth (2001: 55) comments in his critique of studied, over-emphasised writing from the 'I' as reflexivity:

> A constitutive reflexivity has no use for non-reflexive worlds and makes no sense as a demarcation exercise.

In other words, everything we write is part of a reflexive cycle of meaning-making whether we choose to specifically acknowledge and mark out certain textual territories as indicative of this process or not. I can see that it is useful to understand both the tacit and intentional positions we are negotiating for ourselves as researchers and that there may equally well be positions that we are forced into and/or excluded from (see Drewery, 2005, and Winslade, 2005), in relation to what Foucault (1989: 27) describes as the 'great anonymous murmur of discourses'.

I am much less interested in favouring a particular version of marking out this territory than I am in closely reading the research texts, of all kinds, that **generate liminal spaces** or thresholds to other ways of seeing, acting, working and or meaning-making and that actually make a difference to the lives people live. I am interested in the texts that describe life transformations in ways that make such possibilities available to others. So what do I mean by a 'liminal' space?

Exploring Liminal and Creative Places

It is in the more writerly and fictional accounts that liminal (or threshold) spaces seem more readily to appear. I have some commitments to these kinds of accounts and a not inconsiderable determination to encourage their proliferation amongst psychotherapy researchers. The novelist David Malouf (1998: 35) reminds us that 'we possess the world we inhabit imaginatively as well as in fact', and it seems to me that counselling practitioner-researchers, spending as much day-to-day time as they do engaged in conversations about possibilities, hopes and dreams as yet barely imagined, are well positioned to bring these kinds of accounts more to the forefront of research studies.

Our work as therapy practitioners (of whichever 'school') commits us to a daily practice of multiple listening: a practice of listening to what is being said, to what is not being said, and to what is being referred and deferred to. It is within the gaps and cracks that exist between these different stories that the liminal or threshold spaces in the conversations, the points of entry to 'other' sites and identity performances, begin to appear. The interplay between culture and agency and the significance of the space between them is only one such gap or fissure. If we were (following Derrida, 1976, 1978) to look more closely at the space between culture and agency and to place these meanings 'under erasure', we would find ourselves excavating the traces of other discourses contained therein, deconstructing not only the 'binary opposites', but also the multiple other meanings that exist within the 'chora', or open space between these opposites. The spaces between culture and agency (or indeed researcher and researched, and author and text) become not only reflexive, but also open and liminal.

This process (of deconstruction) has been radically transported into therapeutic practice through Michael White's (2000, 2003) use of 'doubly listening' for the absent but implicit in client's stories. This situates client and counsellor alike as curious co-researchers and invites them into:

stretch[ing] their minds and imagination; think[ing] beyond what they would otherwise be thinking; connect[ing] with their histories in new ways and rais[ing] possibilities for action in the world that would not otherwise have occurred to them.   (White, 2004a: 55)

Researchers, therapists (or co-researchers), poets and novelists alike then, have an interest in opening up spaces in conversations and texts where that which has not been previously thought, imagined or acted upon might emerge. Bachelard (1971, 1986) considered that poetry and dreams (particularly day-dreams or reverie) were the landscapes to inhabit in order to evoke liminal spaces. In Broadhurst's (1999) detailed exposition of liminality, she advocates performance spaces as creative thresholds, citing the spaces between audience and performer and author and text. Research genres involving creative fiction and/or writing as a form of inquiry seem to meet at the interplay between the discourses of reflexivity and creativity/liminality. Richardson (1997a, 2000a) uses creative and imaginative writing to help her to think differently as a researcher. She also considers this a reflexive process and, indeed, cites thinking reflexively as a 'liminal space', commenting

(1997a: 17) that 'the process of re-reading one's work and situating it in historical and biographical contexts reveals storylines, many of which may not have been articulated'.

This interplay between **reflexive knowledges** (relational knowledge about how meanings have come to be articulated and understood) and **liminal spaces** (imaginative sites in which to extend, provoke and create knowledge in new ways) is surely somewhere in the ball park if not at the heart of all rigorous research, regardless of discipline, and yet for me at least, it is the arts-based genres that currently have the edge over others in seeking out and shedding light upon these territories. Perhaps this is because they are less 'mediated' forms that allow us a more 'hands on' connection with the tools and materials of our trade? I am reminded of Barbara Hepworth, the sculptor, who had a great deal to say about shedding light on forms, but also said of her hands (1985: 79):

> My left hand is my thinking hand. The right is only a motor hand. This holds the hammer. The left hand, the thinking hand must be relaxed, sensitive. The rhythms of thought pass through the fingers and grip of this hand into the stone. It is also a listening hand. It listens for basic weaknesses of flaws in the stone; for the possibility or imminence of fractures.

I have 'shown' some of Barbara Hepworth's insights into her practice here, but I have not 'told' you the places that these metaphors invite me into in relation to my work or suggested where you might place them in relation to your own: the space is open, inevitably reflexive and multi-storied, possibly liminal.

Different Purposes and Practices of Reflexivity and Ways of Generating Liminal Space

In terms of my own work, an exhaustive nomadic practice of reflexivity, informed, but not limited, by poststructuralist ideas and a literary/participatory narrative style, fitted my current purposes, but I am jumping ahead of myself here. I did not come upon my own current positions through surveying the literatures of the research field, although I'm sure these discourses were informing my work to some degree. I came upon them through various apprenticeships in therapeutic conversations and through my own writing practices. As I engage in my therapeutic work, I have conversations, which I record. I also engage in what has been described (Geertz, 1973a) as 'deep hanging out' with people. In addition, I read a lot of other people's work, but what I mostly do, to make sense of my world, is write. I write alone, I write with others, I have conversations with other people, with imaginary characters and with myself that lead to re-writings and yet more re-writings of re-writings. I write myself into and out of corners and I write until I've written myself some spaces in which to find a place to stand. To quote Geertz (from Van Maanen, 1988: 73):

> If you want to understand what a science is you should look in the first instance not at its theories or its findings; and certainly not what its apologists say about it: YOU SHOULD LOOK AT WHAT THE PRACTITIONERS OF IT DO. (*My emphasis*)

Where Did I Stand?

I realised during the course of writing this chapter that this depended very much upon my purposes and that these could be determined or made transparent by my choice of writing tools and techniques. In particular, by the relationships between my purposes, the writing spaces that I inhabit and the tools of the trade I am using. I am grateful to Andrew Wojecki (2004) for drawing my attention to Foucault's (2000) use of the Greek term *Hupomnemata* to describe the keeping of a kind of intertextual account book, which caused me to reflect on my own accounting system with regard to memories, conversations and 'that which is culturally available'. I am offering a brief outline of my own notebook-keeping here for the consideration of readers, not as a template or paradigm for others, but rather to *show* others how I work, thus offering them opportunities to notice and consider their own ways of working. I had not realised, until I started overtly examining my working practices, that I gave quite different meanings to work crafted in dissimilar ways. We often get to 'know' other people's work, but rarely get to see 'how' they work. In placing something of my own day-to-day process of text-making up for scrutiny, perhaps I might also encourage others to ponder on their own working process (which perhaps does not come about by chance) a little more.

NOTEBOOKS OF PERSONAL NARRATIVE

I have a love of expensive italic fountain pens and green and purple inks and softly covered notebooks filled with good quality writing papers, which are dotted (extravagantly) all over my house and my office at work. I also have a weakness for fine-tipped coloured gel pens, particularly in pink, purple and green. Certain writings always begin in this way, in my notebooks: sometimes notes from conversations and talks, but more frequently, notes and fragments of writing from my own experiences and imaginings. These are embodied writings that lend themselves to the scratch of pen on paper, that seem to have more urgency about themselves. They are not always beautifully written and the books or journals often contain post-it notes and stray pieces of paper. Those that have lurked, for all or part of their lives, beside my bed, invariably end up in complete disarray.

'There is something unique and uncompromising about green ink,' it says in broad green italic, on cream parchment, next to my computer.

These writings from my life have often emerged with a certain urgency, concerning, for instance, my relationship with my brother, or my times sitting in the kitchen as night falls across the garden. They contain all sorts of words, phrases, snatches of bus stop conversation, fragments from dreams and mad moments of poetic reverie, as well as things I think Derrida might have meant if only I could understand him, and so on. I still see them as collaborative and social achievements and wish to locate them culturally, but nonetheless they feature prominent chunks of personal and poetic narrative. These are the writings in which I, at least in part, have emerged as the field of study. My identity claim in relation to these notebooks is that of 'writer'.

FIELD NOTES AND THERAPEUTIC DOCUMENTS

I also have stacks of A4 writing books and folders, mostly, but not exclusively, containing lined yellow paper. My writing books are filled with doodles, draw-ings, notes and spider diagrams (or maps of the landscapes) of sessions with clients and groups, which contain only the words of others, not my own words at all, as well as field notes that I have taken from observations or reviews of tapes of my work.

There are lots of these out in use, also many more locked away with the past tapes. They go back years. These accompany what Riessman (2000) would call my 'holy transcripts' of therapy and research interviews (of which I only transcribe parts as I also have the videotaped or digital recordings).

The A4 books often contain 'translations' of the tapes and transcripts along-side the maps of the conversational landscapes I have been engaged in (more of which in Chapter 4). The field notes are partly my observations, but mostly contain the words of other people. Most of all they contain the 'talk that sings' (Bird, 2000): the words, phrases, images, metaphors and expressions of life that have struck a chord in the space between me and the people whose expressions they were and whose lives I am co-researching. I feel less inclined towards personal narrative in relation to these stories, notes and carefully recorded words of others and more inclined towards 'positioned ethnography'. My reflexive practices in relation to this work tend towards political and cultural embeddedness and issues of accountability and responsibility towards life story tellers with less power in the world in this moment than myself (the work of the 'family centre' from New Zealand offers some clear accountability frameworks to ponder, see Waldegrave et al., 2004). My most strongly held identity claim in relation to these documents is 'co-researcher'.

POWERBOOK, PILES OF PAPER AND POST-IT NOTES

I wrote about my office at home towards the end of my PhD (Speedy, 2001a: 267/273):

> *In one corner a large pine table is stacked with computer equipment and papers that are spilling over onto the floor. A cardboard box under the table is stuffed with electrical wiring, audiotapes; computer discs and abandoned electronic gizmos. There are a few chairs scattered haphazardly about, including an old wing-backed armchair piled with books . . . It is late at night and the author is sitting at her computer in the small ground floor office at the front of her house. The only free floor space is entirely taken up by a large, old, golden retriever, sprawled across the papers.*

I regret to report that, despite my having retreated to the attic, this is still my preferred method of gathering together the published and scholarly work of others that informs, questions and is placed under scrutiny in relation to my own. Piles of highlighted papers and books with many pages folded over and many post-its protruding are spread across the floor (currently 25 piles) with the occasional book slide creating a serendipitous interdisciplinary merger.

Citations from and references for this work are entered into a software package on my portable computer. I make notes and write critical comments directly

onto my computer from and about other people's books, already set down in a
certain order on the page. Indeed, many journal papers are now available to
me electronically and are downloaded directly onto this machine. My princi-
pal identity claims in relation to this literature are that of scholar and
archivist.

Embodiment, Embeddedness and Conversation

These are the three main groups of sources that I gathered together as I
produced this book. My constructions of writer, co-researcher, scholar
and archivist positions are different. These positions lend themselves to
different written genres and perhaps represent different purposes in
relation to reflexivities as embodied, and/or culturally embedded,
and/or ambivalent practices. These categories are not as neatly divided
as I have suggested, of course; there is much crossover and a certain
messiness about the ways all these genres are woven into the 'final text',
but I am talking about the sources here and about the constitutive
process of text production.

I am reminded of Elliot Mishler's (2000) storylines of craft artists'
strong commitments towards working against the grain of manufac-
tured goods, and towards working with their hands, as I think, with
affection, of my fountain pens, inks and notebooks. I am also reminded
of Hélène Cixous's passion for handwritten notebooks that:

> allow for a free arrangement of words and phrases on a page. Lines
> can be written at angles to each other, new ideas can be signalled or
> inserted in the spaces between words, or points developed by extend-
> ing into the margins, in a manner that is alien to the pre-established
> order of word-processed text. Crucially, crossed out thoughts can be
> left alongside the passage that stands.   (Sellers, 2004: x)

My writing notebooks are written in experimental ways, in portrait, in
landscape, sometimes dancing across the page, sometimes in careful
italic pen, sometimes in fast urgent pink gel pen. As Cixous comments
(above), these texts are produced outside the constraints of 'word-
processed text'. The writing notebooks in particular are more of a play
space than any of the other sites.

My word-processed comments and post-it notes on other people's
texts are routinely in conversational form. I have conversations down
the sides of texts. I paste quotes from their writings into my computer

and then have conversations with them about our different ways of constructing knowledge. To quote Josselson et al. (1997: viii):

> good social science evolves from people coming together to talk and listen and learn from one another. Conversation makes more demands than a single authorial voice.

My field notes and therapy notes are taken whilst I am in conversation; they are drawn in 'mind map' (see Buzan and Buzan, 2003) form across time within the dimensions of various landscapes, which I will discuss in more detail in Chapter 4. I could not possibly sit talking with people, co-researching their lives, behind a computer. The paper notebook on my lap rarely gets between us and when it does I discard it.

The point that I am trying to make here is that by the time I am at the point of bringing these sources together to engage in the process of creating a text they are already positioned as 'other' than they were. The 'research' texts are produced from tapes, transcripts, notes, writing notebooks, fictionalised accounts, quotes and references to other works. They emerge from artefacts and not from 'my' words or the words of other people. There is also a certain messiness and shape shifting between these sources as they are in the process of 'translation' into the final text. The reflexive genre emanating from the writing notebooks tends towards personal embodiment (see Chapters 8, 9 and 10) and, from the field notes, towards cultural and social embeddedness (see Chapters 4, 5, 6 and 7), but even as I attempt this binary moment of clarity, it is washed away within the temporariness and ambivalence within the interweaving and dancing and space that opens up between the two. Identities such as scholar, co-researcher and writer are lightly worn and quickly shift shape to give way to new, equally temporary performances such as author, ethnographer, or critic.

LITERARY ACCOUNTS

It has been hard to write my way into the constitutive fluidities of poststructural thought and even harder not to stay trapped in the culture/agency binaries of 'modern' thought. It seems easier to stay tentative, partial, open and nomadic in my thinking when I am writing in a more literary style. I am supported in this observation by many poststructuralist feminists, including Kristeva (1974: 439), who suggests that poetic [creative/experimental] language speaks to that which is not fixed or known and that which 'moves or escapes' and appears to defy the confines of conventional language. In these traditions, as in literary fiction, there is no question that the text, however intertextual or saturated with previous meanings, has been shaped by (and also shapes) the author.

I would suggest, for instance, that in your readings of Chapter 1 of this book, you assumed quite readily that 'Mr Gingey' was constructed by Jane Speedy and situated within her social and imaginative world. You also co-constructed your own images, personalities and qualities of imaginary friends and also, perhaps, of Jane Speedy. Thus this text, once published and in your hands, becomes other than the one that I wrote.

PARTICIPATORY ACCOUNTS

Displays of position and reflexivity become more troublesome within narrative inquiries that include representations of the voices of 'others'. The ghost voice (Langellier, 2001) of the principal researcher is still constructing the text, so how do we pay due honour to the voices of our participants? How do we describe and theorise and give space to the life stories of others and, given that we are creating the whole book or paper or thesis in any case, how much attention should we give to declaring personal positions?

There are several inquiries into the lives of others contained in this book. This may be a multi-storied, polyphonic text but some stories definitely have more power than others and in the case of this text, I have the power to frame and juxtapose other people's stories. This has nothing to do with 'informed consent' (a necessary but insufficient requirement) and everything to do with power relations, narrative transparency and integrity. My writings with Gina, Morag, Hyatt, Margie and Gregory were all collaboratively constructed, but in all but the conversations with Hyatt, the writing was a translation, produced and edited by me, of taped conversations. The conversations with gargoyles and other 'fabulous' characters came from my own imaginings and those with and about my brother come from my memories and are my versions and not his.

I do not have any glib answers to these concerns about representation and the balance of voices, other than to persistently interrogate and seek out my own and other constructions of ethical know-how and constantly and tentatively navigate the landscapes between competing sets of ethical and aesthetic principles (of which, much more in Chapter

A further step towards negotiating balanced representative texts is to engage in close readings of other people's work, both within and outside the counselling and psychotherapy field.

Constructing Reflexivities: Various Practices

As mentioned earlier, this book is not in the least intended as an exhaustive or comprehensive overview of the literatures of narrative research. It would appear from the texts that have captured my attention and/or have some resonance with my own fields of inquiry that there are many places to stand. In my extensive excursions into the field I have come across several, very differently constructed exemplars of texts in which researchers are clearly positioned. The research texts that stand out for me are written within the **transformative spirit** of making a difference. Paul Willis's (1977) vivid and chilling account of young working-class people 'learning to labour' within the classrooms of the English school system, for instance, has probably influenced my understandings of power relations and my subsequent work within a variety of educational and organisational settings more than any other text (yet Paul Willis 'the person' does not feature in the book). By way of contrast, Ruth Behar's (1993) portrayal of Esperanza's border crossings between Mexico and the United States continues to inform my current research projects, co-constructing the narratives of Somali women in Bristol, because the book concentrates so much on the experience of the privileged, white author and her sense of belonging in her country, in relation to Esperanza, the incomer.

In some narrative studies researchers are **situated lightly, in relation to the context** of the research. They are *there* in their texts, transparently engaged in their work in particular ways, but the central narratives are those of the people whose lives are being 'told'. Luttrell's (2003) work with pregnant school students is a good example of this, as is Riessman's (2004) ongoing struggle to give an account of Burt (a man suffering from multiple sclerosis) and the ways the resonances from his story have stayed with her, or indeed, Langellier's (2001) account of one woman's performance of identity following treatment for breast cancer. Such studies might be described (to quote Riessman, 2004: 321) as 'positioned ethnography'. They are situated and partial accounts that make no universal claims about pregnant school students or chronically ill men or women with cancer, but rather describe the particularities of certain lives and social worlds.

In other studies (particularly within counselling research), the author's **personal narratives are positioned more vigorously alongside the stories** of the people whose lives are being researched. Wosket's (1999) explorations of herself and with her client Rachel, and Etherington's (2000) explorations of her work with sexually abused men, demonstrate this more auto/biographical and interwoven way of working. In these studies, reflexivity requires the personal narratives of the researchers in process to be made transparent. In a later work, Etherington (2004: 31–2) goes on to claim this genre of reflexivity as a form of 'rigour' and ventures a definition of reflexivity as:

> The capacity of the researcher to acknowledge how their own experiences and contexts (which might be fluid and changing) inform the process and outcomes of inquiry. If we can be aware of how our own thoughts, feelings, culture, environment and social and personal history inform us as we dialogue with participants, transcribe their conversations with us and write our representations of the work, then perhaps we can become closer to the rigour that is required of good qualitative research.

In yet other studies **the ongoing conversations between the co-researchers and/or between the co-researchers and their excavations in the 'field' are presented** as a parallel text to the participants' stories. Josellson et al. (1997) present us not with their research, but rather with a series of conversations constructed as the lenses through which various readings of their research may take place, and Lather and Smithies (1997) have recorded an ongoing researcher conversation which transparently locates their theorising-in-process across the bottom third of their text. Here the reflexivity is both positioned and conversational. These texts exhibit innovation and experimentation. They are densely written and hard to read. They are 'pushing the envelope' on realist definitions of personal awareness and authenticity, such as those put forward by Etherington (above) towards more 'slippery ambivalent ground' (Davies et al., 2004: 364) wherein:

> The self who carries out the research and the self who is the subject of the researcher's gaze, is [thus] not denied in this model, but neither is it made central or separate: it is there as an effect of discourse, and is an important presence in any research (and thus important too that it be acknowledged).

Each of these studies, whether predominantly 'positioned', 'authentically' reflexive or 'discursive' in style, is vibrant and engaging. They all have flaws, capture attention in different ways and are transparent about their reflexive balancing acts. Etherington (2004), a text favouring 'personal embodiment', Ruby (1982), an edited work, way ahead of it's time, meticulously exploring 'positioned ethnography', and Davies et al. (2004), a densely argued collective biography of the 'ambivalent practices of reflexivity', are amongst the few that **show** (as well as justify and tell) their ways of working to us. I found these works more engaging than most, since, as a general rule, finding out how other people work gives me more opportunity to find my own places to stand.

Reflexivity as an Inexhaustible Invitation towards Liminality

To regard reflexivities as invitations towards liminality and towards constructing our identities not as 'nouns' and thus fixed, albeit open to change, but as 'verbs' and as discursive processes may lead us into more creative (and messier) research conversations. These might be conversations about the tensions and slippages that arise as we negotiate our way around the confusions that still abound (see Lather, 1993, for a more detailed discussion of these tensions). They might also be conversations concerning the interplay between reflexivities and liminal spaces.

This nomadic (see St Pierre, 1997), reflexive process of always travelling and never arriving is hard to sustain. It requires not only tentativeness, but also tenacity and resilience. The temptations to pitch camp and 'settle' are many. Firmly held commitments towards uncertainty and messiness may well be misread as a lack of 'authority'.

I have not found a way of working that fits for all occasions, and have some concerns about the proliferation of complex literatures of justification within the social sciences arena that draw me more towards the sometimes riskier, but often sharper and clearer arts-based practice of constructing a position and seeing where it takes us. I do seem to have found different reflexive styles that are (in as far as this is possible) transparent, flawed and ambivalently practised. I have some sense of that which remains at times unsaid and why, and slightly less sense of what remains unsayable. I remain at the threshold of that which I do not know.

Further reading

Reflexivity
Davies, B., Browne, J., Honan., E, Laws, C., Mueller-Rockstroh, B. and Bendix Petersen, E. (2004) 'The Ambivalent Practices of Reflexivity', in *Qualitative Inquiry*, 10(3): 360–89.
(This is not an easy read, but gives a compelling account of reflexivity as a 'hall of mirrors'.)

Etherington, K. (2004) *Becoming a Reflexive Researcher: Using Our Selves in Research* (London: Jessica Kingsley).
(A very accessible text within the genre of 'reflexivity as writing from the "I" position'.)

Hertz, R. (ed.) (1997) *Reflexivity and Voice* (Thousand Oaks, CA: Sage).
(Still the only overview of the various current approaches to reflexivity.)

Liminality
Broadhurst, S. (1999) *Liminal Performance* (London: Cassell).
(This text is borrowed from 'performance studies' and provides a historical account of the different spaces between audiences and performances.)

Richardson, L. (1997) *Fields of Play: Constructing an Academic Life* (New Brunswick: Rutgers University Press).
(A sociologist/performance poet exploring the liminal space that opens up in writing.)

Other spaces
Sellers, S. (ed.) (2004) *Hélène Cixous: The Writing Notebooks* (New York: Continuum).
(A detailed look at the processes of free writing and keeping notes for a novelist.)

Artography: arts-informed research association:
http://m1.cust.educ.ubc.ca:16080/Artography/ (a website with superb reading lists and links, exploring arts-informed research practices).

3

Narrative Ethics: Trustworthiness, Accountability and 'Writing Good Stories'

So what *is* narrative inquiry, why are we doing this kind of research and how do we know when it is done well and ethically? In her essays *In Search of my Mother's Gardens* (1984) the African American writer Alice Walker describes her mother's petunia – growing as an act of resistance to the day-to-day racism she experienced in the Southern United States. Her increasingly vibrantly coloured and voluptuous array of blooms stood as an unexpected and revolutionary testament.

> Rebellious. Living.
> Against the elemental crush.
> (Alice Walker, *Revolutionary Petunias*, 1988: 70)

Similarly this research genre is about taking people by surprise, capturing their attention, their hearts even, and providing different spaces from which to ponder the world or ponder the same spaces with different eyes. But I am starting in the middle as usual here. First I should probably establish what I mean by 'narrative inquiry' before going on to discuss the ethics, aesthetics and transgressions that might accompany such a journey.

Describing Narrative Inquiry

There are as many versions of narrative inquiry as there are people engaged in it, some of which, such as Riessman (1993), Lieblich et al. (1998), Wengraf (2001), McAdams (1993) and Ellis (2004), have been offered as templates or models to other researchers. Equally there are various positions taken on the meaning of 'narrative'. Sarbin (1986) speaks of 'living in a storied world' and of a 'grand' integrating frame-work or worldview, as do Polkinghorne (1988) and Bruner (2002). Angus and McLeod (2004a: 373) believe the concept of narrative is:

> so fundamental to human psychological and social life, carries with it such a rich set of meanings, that it provides a genuine meeting point between theoretical schools of therapy that have previously stood apart from each other.

Others (see Currie, 1998; Bennett and Royle, 1999) view narrative as a very specific aspect of literary and linguistic theory.

For myself, although I am clearly interested in a narrative practice that moves beyond the literary, I am wary of worldviews and 'funda-mental' claims, particularly those currently made by the dominant west for the rest of the world. There are some powerful commentaries on these claims. Speaking for indigenous and colonised peoples, for instance, Linda Tuhiwai-Smith (1999: 1) comments:

> It galls us that Western researchers and intellectuals can assume to know all that it is possible to know of us. It appals us that the west can desire, extract and claim ownership of our ways of knowing.

The Narrative Invitation

I do not know what a storied world might look like to people from very different cultures and life experiences than my own. It certainly rings true, in my own experience, that 'we engage in narrative often, with unconscious ease' (Abbott, 2002: 1). I have found the narrative invita-tion a useful means of making sense of things. Human identity as a social achievement, contingent on audience, culture, history, memory and agency (that which is available to us and what we make of all this at any one moment), seems a helpful metaphor. As I mentioned in Chapter 1, the 'narrative turn' is both enjoying a postmodern currency and is part of an age-old tradition in many cultures. As Pinkola Estes (1993: i), a Mexican-American 'cantadora' or traditional storyteller, points out:

> Among my people, questions are often answered with stories. The first story almost always evokes another, which summons another, until the answer to the question has become several stories long. A

sequence of tales is thought to offer broader and deeper insight than a single story alone.

This makes for a very accessible research paradigm, almost (to quote Bruner, 1986a, and White, 2004b) a folk tradition of researching people's lives. The notion of telling stories about our lives is readily available to people and the distinction between 'narrative' (a literary/academic term) and 'story' (a more everyday term) becomes blurred. There are many ways in which, as Gerrig (1993) suggests, they 'write themselves', loosely, in overlapping ways. These words seem to jump into particular positions in a more literary context, and others in more academic contexts. *Webster's Dictionary* describes narrative as 'a discourse or an example of it, designed to represent a connected succession of happenings' (1966: 1503). In his descriptions of a more literary version of narrative, Abbott (2002) distinguishes between 'stories', which exist within the ether as folk stories, virtual stories, latent stories and untold stories, and 'narrative' as in the telling of stories. 'Story' (he suggests, 2002: 32) 'is something that is delivered by narrative but seems to pre-exist it', whereas 'narrative always seems to come after, to be a representation'.

Certainly I would wish to concur with the distinction between life stories (the way people's lives have gone, or are going, regardless of the telling of them) and narratives (the business of what happens when stories are told by a narrator). Stories are no use to us when they are languishing out there in the ether; it is the telling of them that has us all in its grip.

My understanding of 'narrative inquiry' is broad, messy and inconclusive and I have opted in this text for showing you some of the ways I have conducted such inquiries rather than to offer a model. I have been most readily sustained in this work by Clandinin and Connolly's (2000) similarly 'loose' three-dimensional construct of **narrative as a form of discourse taking place over time, within space** (although I prefer the landscape of people's lives) **and in a context**. I am uncomfortable with culturally fixed notions of 'archetypal' stories, but it also seems useful to explore the different narrative domains that people are engaging with. The ways, for instance, in which narratives are performed within the **dominant discourses** of their cultural or social milieu; or are **habitual narratives** that are well rehearsed; or appear as more **local or personal narratives** that are peculiar to circumstances and life spaces, and/or as **alternative, emergent narratives**, co-constructed in the moment (see Angus and Hardtke, 1994, for an exploration of habitual narratives, and White and Epston, 1990, for the other narrative domains discussed here).

It is not just the theoretical existence or naming, but the *performing* of narratives (see Langellier and Peterson, 2004: 72–112) that reveals the relationship between different discourses and exposes the cracks, fissures and possible sites for transformation. Thus narrative, when performed: 'transmits and produces power, it reinforces it, but also undermines and exposes it, renders it fragile and makes it possible to thwart it' (Foucault, 1980b: 101). Chapter 8 in this text, for instance, offers an exposition of the dominant discourses of bereavement in British society, together with Margie's 'habitual' narratives about normality, the personal and local narratives that she explores and the alternative versions that emerge for both Margie and myself.)

I am drawn towards Frank's (1995) definition of 'story' as being a narrative, not necessarily told chronologically, but containing such a chronicle and told in a particular 'voice', with an audience in mind:

> Storytelling is for another just as much as it is for oneself. In the reciprocity that is storytelling, the storyteller offers herself as guide to the other's self-formation. The other's receipt of that guidance not only recognises, but values the teller. The moral genius of storytelling is that each, teller and listener, enters the space of the story for the other. (Frank, 1995: 18)

Storytelling, whether written or spoken, is primarily an 'everyday' tradition (see Langellier and Peterson, 2004: 7–33). I have a particular interest in the stories or episodes (and fragments, snatches and traces that might become such stories) that are transformative as well as descriptive endeavours. I am also aware that unless co-research relationships are carefully navigated and continually and transparently negotiated:

> Narrative research, based on the real lives of people made public, converts what is private into public; can violate privacy and can cause mental, legal, social and financial hurt and harm. (Bakan, 1996: 3)

Not just petunias then: transformative and even emancipatory petunias that make a difference, but that also require careful tending and watering.

Research Integrity within Counselling and Therapy

The British Association of Counselling and Psychotherapy (BACP) has recently produced some useful and flexible guidelines for researchers (Bond, 2004a) based on an ethic of trust and trustworthiness between researcher and researched. This ethic refers to the skills and practices of the researchers, their ethical know-how in terms of risks to participants and the management of research processes (such as safeguarding any data collected). These guidelines are a great improvement on the previously fixed 'one size fits all' codes of ethics. The previous ethic of 'doing no harm', although not something that could be argued with, did bring with it an atmosphere of mistrust and suspicion, and concern with 'is it allowed' or not (Bond, 2004b: 8) rather than an atmosphere of constant negotiation and navigation between the people and within the territories being researched.

One of the difficulties involved in producing guidelines to encompass the breadth of research in any given field is that of doing so with sufficient clarity without excluding any of the range of ethical principles that people might live by. These sets of ethical principles, in my experience, do not so much compete with as 'bump up against' each other in unexpected and sometimes fruitful ways. Postcolonialists and indigenous researchers (J. McLeod, 2004; Prowell, 1999; Tuhiwai-Smith, 1999) have critiqued traditional western ethical codes for not attending to ethics of community, collaboration and interdependency. Traditional western research ethics have also been critiqued by feminists for their 'patriarchal' focus on truth and justice, as opposed to a more female 'ethic of care' (Gatens, 1995; Gilligan, 1982). In relation to this study there are also narrative ethics and aesthetics of 'what makes a good story' to consider, and of what happens when the principles involved in writing a good story bump up against the principles of caring for people or of not betraying communities we have had access to.

It seems that research guidelines based on the recognition of inequalities and the development of trustworthiness between people (Bond, 2004b) might go some way towards addressing some of these concerns and allow locally and culturally appropriate research methods and practices to emerge. Indeed, in researching other people's lives we are, in some sense, apprenticing ourselves to their vast wealth of insider knowledge and to the everyday ethics by which they live their lives (see Linnell, 2004). This apprenticeship requires more than a little modesty

and humility (words often missing from ethical frameworks). S\
do these 'big' words, ethical know-how, trustworthiness, re,
modesty and integrity, actually mean? As nouns they are slip₊ery
customers with complex histories that are valued differently in different
currencies. As Trinh (1989: 7) comments:

> words empty out with age, die and rise again accordingly invested
> with new meanings, and are always equipped with a second-hand
> memory.

As contingent-practices-to-be-going-on-with-and-reviewed, they offer
us hooks on which to hang our ongoing conversations, either as
researcher and researched (as with Donald, in Chapter 4) or as co-
researchers (as with Gina and others, in Chapter 6, or the Jones family,
in Chapter 8), but are they sufficient?

In his fictionalised accounts of 'theft and ethics', Peter Clough
(2002) creates powerful images of the seductive pitfalls and moral
perils that await narrative researchers mining for rich stories at the
expense of other people's personal dignity. Readings of 'Lolly: the
Final Word' (Clough, 2002: 54–9), or similar, should, perhaps, be on
the syllabus of all research training courses. Chapter 4 of Meera Syal's
novel (1999: 152–82) *Life Isn't All Ha Ha Hee Hee*, provides an equally
unsettling account of the betrayal of trust displayed by a central character, Tania, when she makes a short documentary film that merci-
lessly ridicules and humiliates the married lives and cultural practices
of her closest (Asian) friends in order to achieve critical acclaim from
Europeans.

Perhaps the scene in Meera Syal's novel (1999: 178) is all the more
chilling for the fact that 'Tania' remains oblivious, certainly unaf-
fected by the damage and mayhem all around her that her film has
caused:

> Beroze and Suki nodded briefly. 'Good work, Tania, much better
> than any of your other stuff.'
> Tania nodded. She said thank you again.
> Suki leaned into her. 'How do your friends feel about the film
> then?'
> Tania paused, 'I just told the truth,' she said.

Varela (1999: 4) describes a wise or virtuous person, the sort of person
who exhibits ethical know-how, as a person 'who knows what is good

and spontaneously does it'. As Tania demonstrates, not all of us know spontaneously what is 'good' (as opposed to good for our careers), 'the truth' is a slippery and multi-storied customer and few of us know what is deemed to be good and what is deemed to be the 'telos' or ethical substance of other people's lives, except those with insider knowledges.

We will not know this unless we take the time and trouble to find out what really matters to us and what really matters to the people whose lives we are (briefly) apprenticed to, learn to navigate and interrogate these (and other) competing regimes of truth with ethical mindfulness and then tell our research stories accordingly.

Clough (2002: 57–8), in a totally fictitious account, describes an unexpected visit from the very angry older brother of one of his research participants, a young Italian/English boy nicknamed 'Molly':

'Hm', he [the brother] nodded at me, and turning back to the page started to read again from my account:
'When I visit Molly's home to meet his mother, I am amused by the identical downy moustache that they share.'
Again he paused, maybe some 10 seconds.
'Does your mother have a moustache Doctor Clough?'
I was silent, immobile, not sure of it was a real question or not.
'I said: does your mother have a moustache, Doctor Clough?'
I tried to say, I muttered: 'No'.

Trustworthiness, justice, care, respect, integrity, modesty, humility, ethical substance, mindfulness and know-how in relation to people, communities and their interdependencies: this is quite a list, already, of words emptied out of truth and risen again (Trinh, 1989). I have offered no 'codes' for their practices, other than my own partial and contingent conversations with participants and with myself, and with the literatures of the field (see, for instance, Josselson, 1996a; Varela, 1999; Welch, 1999; Bond, 2004a) scattered throughout this book. I do not know what matters to you (the reader) and the people whose stories you might wish to tell. I suspect that there is a 'Tania' in most of us and I have certainly woken up in the middle of the night in a hot sweat, wondering like '*Doctor* Clough' what would happen if my client's older brother (as it were) had come across my account. There is much written about these issues, but they also need constantly revisiting in light of the different circumstances we find ourselves in.

Ethical Practice in Narrative Inquiry – a Reciprocal and Relational Space

One of the almost universal omissions in the traditional literatures and guidelines for human science research (including within counselling and psychotherapy) is that of the reciprocity of power relations between researchers and researched (which is well illustrated by Henry, 2003, and Thapar-Björkert and Henry, 2004). It is assumed throughout the BACP ethical guidelines (above) that it is counsellors and not clients who are researching therapeutic practice and that this research is carried out by individuals, not collectives or communities. (This sort of assumption is probably inevitable. These guidelines are not intended as exhaustive but rather as a broad brush stroke sweeping across a wide field.)

The language used in these guidelines (and others written for teachers, nurses and social workers, for instance) speaks of the fragility and vulnerability of clients. Clients' 'vulnerabilities and sensitivities' need 'adequately protecting' (Bond, 2004a: 12). Few would argue with this stance. Children, young people, health and welfare system users and others seeking therapeutic support are not routinely amongst the most powerful groups in society. Even when groups such as children and young people do come from the most powerful sectors of society, they are likely to be encountering fragile rather than robust moments on this earth if they are consulting counsellors and therapists about their lives.

As the *only* stance, however, this seems a rather thin description that does not take into account collaborative and/or critical research in this field undertaken by its consumers. Is this counselling research endeavour always such a one-way track? What about issues of accountability to caucuses of client groups, and what about communities of clients researching us (see Sands, 2000, for a consumer's story, or Calgut, 1999, 2005, for a robust critique of counselling from lesbian consumers within the UK).

I would endorse Thapar-Björkert and Henry's (2004) observations that research participants even in quite traditional studies often exercise considerable agency. Gina (Chapter 6) had considerably less overall responsibility for the completed text than I did; nevertheless she undertook to negotiate and renegotiate the written content. The unassuming geeks (Chapter 7) are, in some ways, anonymous research participants. Nonetheless, the passages of collective biography that they have chosen to include in this book out of our extensive collection would not remotely have been the ones that I would have chosen. I was (quite rightly) not included in the discussions. Conducting research with young men like the unassuming geeks, who have had a considerable interest in suicide, might be considered a 'high risk' activity with vulnerable people. Whilst I did regularly consult with supervisors during this project, the most rigorous and sustaining support for this work was through constantly consulting with my consultants (Epston and White, 1992), that is to say, the geeks and their families and friends, to whom I consider myself permanently accountable. The language of accountability and responsibility towards the people consulting us offers a very different emphasis and positions researchers very differently from thin descriptions of participants as vulnerable people. Accountability structures perhaps speak to an ethic of 'political' action and emancipation that is not as familiar to some counselling and psychotherapy researchers as an ethic of care and protection, but either of these alone would offer an equally thin description. Trustworthiness, integrity, modesty, accountability, care, justice, sensitivity towards community, interdependency, agency and reciprocity: the list goes on and on – we haven't even got to 'narrative ethics'.

Telling a Good Story

In providing evocative and literary rather than literal texts to illustrate ethical dilemmas (such as those of Clough and Syal, above) we have traversed the fuzzy borders and (sometimes) liminal spaces between ethics and aesthetics and have perhaps also come across a different practice of trustworthiness and accountability, wherein:

> There can be truth in madness, dreaming, poetry, or prophecy, which is higher than literal truth, this we might describe as a **narrative ethic**, whereby: a metaphor or a fiction might open a door that cannot be opened by approaches that are too weighed down by duty to literal truth. (Bakan, 1996: 7)

Narrative ethics then, position us differently in relation to ethics of care, justice, accountability and so forth, not by telling the literal truth (which in the case of ethical dilemmas and issues may not be possible to tell) but (like Clough and Syal, above) by creating the space for us to imaginatively feel our way into the experiences described, whilst remaining accountable to the spirits and values of the original storytellers. In describing the synthetic creation of his texts, Clough (2002: 9) talks of drawing on 'data as well as dreams, hunches and histories, causes and cases, transcriptions and transgressions, morals and meanings'. This then is a different kind of truth, the 'verisimilitude' of a story that is well crafted, that works, that provides liminal space for resonance and for the co-creation of our own stories as readers and also has some purpose to its literariness. Van Maanen (1988: 135) warns us of the possibility of writing 'fluff – merely zippy tales on inconsequential topics', which for me moves the accountability conversation towards an ethic of making a difference: surely our research should be of a greater purpose than 'mere fluff'? Surely it should make a difference to people's lives?

With regard to well crafted, substantial and transformative texts, narrative researchers who are claiming aesthetic merit for their work have to be counted (and accountable) alongside some stiff competition. In many cases, unless they can write with the evocative power of Carolyn Ellis's (1995) account of living through her partner's death and of their 'final negotiations', counselling and psychotherapy researchers might do better to leave the telling of evocative tales of bereavement, illness and mother–daughter relationships to the likes of Alice Walker (2004: 38).

It was a sultry summer day, the day we buried my mother. The night before, at the wake, I stood over her body and tried to peer straight into her brain. She was shrunken from the cancer she'd battled the last years of her life; her mouth was twisted from the suffering she had endured. The flowers arrayed around her coffin smelled heavy and wet. I felt desperate for fresh air. Why were you so dissatisfied with me? I asked her.

An ethic of accountability towards the people we are representing in our life story telling is as 'slippery' as any ethic and people may find themselves differently positioned in relation to the stories that have been told, once they find themselves in print. McLeod (2001a: 181–210) and Josselson (1996b: 45–60) reflect usefully on these issues. Hyatt, for instance, whose poetic exchanges feature in Chapter 5, came to hear me give an earlier version of our work together as a presentation at a Narrative Therapy conference in Liverpool, in the UK. We had spent a long time agreeing what I was going to say, but it was only when she got to the conference and saw the audience that Hyatt realised people might think she was white and European (as most of them were) unless her African-Caribbean origins were directly mentioned. We amended the text. Similarly the Jones family were delighted to finally see a version of Chapter 8 in print in a counselling journal (Speedy, 2005a) but had not expected an editorial introduction (Buckroyd, 2005) to our work that asked questions, in a critical tone, about the way in which our work together had been represented.

Having endured the ethical discomforts of research projects for my own Master's and doctoral qualifications, wherein generous participants were taking part in *my* chosen topic, I have come to infinitely prefer research projects that emerge from, and are of intense interest to, the people consulting me about their lives (not that this is easily determined in a reciprocally constructed and storied world; this depends very much on the positions taken up and constantly renegotiated between co-researchers). Indeed, the therapeutic co-research we have engaged in, which in many cases has already involved a lot of writing, has often been followed quite fluidly by collaborative research projects such as those, published in this book, emerging out of the ideas and concerns of Gina, Gregory and the unassuming geeks. This is not to say that I no longer wish to conduct research led by my own interests, but rather it is in those instances that I have been more drawn towards fictionalised, rather than literal accounts of events.

I seem to go back and forth in this work fuzzying the edges between therapy and research, and indeed, research participants have experienced participation within a wide range of projects as therapeutic (Etherington, 2000; Hart and Crawford-Wright, 1999; Ortiz, 2001; Speedy, 2004c). The narrative therapies, given the position of the therapist as curious, unknowing, de-centred and influential, have often described practitioners and people consulting them as engaged in 'co-research' (Bird, 2000; Epston, 2004). Equally, these edges are not completely blurred and distinctions can be made between positions as participant in a project and as co-researcher. I am differently positioned in a co-research project that negotiates the day-to-day landscapes of my life compared with a co-research project that describes that life to others, even though both may contain therapeutic elements. Crockett et al. (2004), engage in a useful discussion of the different positions taken up by people consulting therapists/undertaking research projects that moves beyond primary and secondary ideas of research into people's lives. They suggest that:

> If we work to practice research . . . out of the same concern for relational ethics as the therapy itself, what is primary and what is secondary might be thought of as fluid.   (Crockett et al., 2004: 63)

There are, I would venture, important distinctions between what I might describe as primary and secondary co-research projects within therapeutic relationships. In the primary or initial relationships, we are researching issues that have been intensely troubling and often distressing for people (such as my initial relationship with Gregory, who came to see me to find a safer place to speak about his thoughts of suicide).

In the subsequent or secondary projects we are devising ways of disseminating some of the findings of this research to a broader audience (such as the collective biography initiated and produced by the 'unassuming geeks' group). Either of these projects might be initiated by 'clients' as much as therapy practitioners, although there may be an inequality of experience in relation to the management of the secondary research process, such as the risk-taking and exposure that comes with publication. I had quite lengthy discussions with Gregory and the geeks, for instance (see Speedy, 2005c), about their pride in and ownership of their writings, versus their desire to limit repercussions for their families by using pseudonyms. When an interest in disseminating stories of my work as a therapist emerges from me in the first instance, I seem to want to follow Yalom (1991, 2000). Creative fictions, fictionalised accounts and magical realisms often seem attractive alternatives to the inequalities and issues of power relations that would otherwise ensue.

Evaluating this Kind of Work

Much of the above focuses on ways of *doing* research and on relationships with the people you might be undertaking research with, but there are also myriad ways of *reading* research texts. As Sparkes (2002a: 191–224) points out, different research tales require different 'judgement calls'. The kinds of research described in this book that inhabit and trouble the borderlands between narrative therapy and research, between arts and social sciences and between private troubles and social landscapes are going to seek out different criteria to be judged by.

Although I have listed, in the table below, some of the criteria that have already been suggested by writers across the disciplines (such as Bochner, 2000, 2001; Clough, 2000; Denzin, 2000; Ellis, 2000; Ellos, 1994; Freire, 1982, 1998; Heron and Reason, 1997; Hertz, 1997; hooks, 2000b; Humphries, 2000; Humphries et al., 2000; Josselson and Lieblich, 1999; Lather, 1991, 1993; Lather and Smithies, 1997; Mienczakowski, 2000; Richardson, 1993, 2000a, 2000b, 2000c; Ronai, 1998, 1999; Smith and Deemer, 2000; Speedy, 2001a; Trinh, 1989; Tuhiwai-Smith, 1999; Waldegrave et al., 2004; White, 2000) there are sure to be more to come.

I list some current thinking in table form, not as an exhaustive list, nor as a checklist, and certainly not in any order of priority, but rather to enable myself and other readers to consider the criteria they wish their work within a particular context to be judged by. There are, for example, a range of ways of negotiating the space between researchers

Some criteria to support readings of creative narrative research

Transparency	How did the author(s) come to write this text? How was the information gathered? Does the writer make the purposes, perspectives and positions that have informed the construction of the text available?
Trustworthiness	Does this text seem 'truthful' – a credible account of a cultural, social, individual, or communal sense of the world? Are claims to verisimilitude (truthfulness) and knowledge embedded in multiple criteria that address 'lived experience'?
Aesthetic merit	Does this text succeed aesthetically? Does it use creative practices that open up the text and invite interpretive responses? Is the text artistically shaped, satisfying and (above all) *not boring*? Does the writing make my heart sing?
Reflexivity	Does this text include a sense of personal embodiment and/or cultural embeddedness on the part of the author(s)? Is this text partial, situated and contingent?
Accountability	Which community's interests does this text represent? In what ways are researchers accountable to those people? Are ethical issues and issues of collaboration/participation and power relations discussed? How is the space between researchers and researched navigated? Does the contribution made outweigh the ethical dilemmas/pain for participants/writers and readers? Is the separation of private and public spheres transgressed?
Substantive and enduring contribution	Does this contribute to our understanding of social/cultural life and what it means to be a human being? Will this text endure and be of some lasting value in the field?
Impact and transformation	Does this resonate with me? Does this affect me emotionally/intellectually/spiritually/politically? Does this generate new questions? Move me to try new research practices? Move me to action? Transgress taken-for-granted assumptions? Transform/make a difference? Implement an emancipatory agenda?

and researched within different contexts and from the different positions of participant, co-researcher and fictionalised character. This list is not foundational. It represents the fruits of my investigations thus far. Readers are invited to pick from and add to this list according to context, as I have and continue to do for myself. Research has different purposes, for instance, and some studies may be more suited to capturing attention or making a short-term impact rather than making the 'substantive' contributions suggested in this table.

Different aspects of these criteria wear their cultural history differently and will fit different researchers and their purposes in different ways at different times. There will be constant discussion about relativism and fluidity (Sparkes, 2002a: 191–224), the legitimacy of particular criteria (Richardson, 2000a, 2000b, 2000c), or indeed of any criteria (Bochner, 2000; Clough, 2000), and the tensions between producing good, relevant research within a constantly changing landscape (Humphries, 2000; Smith and Deemer, 2000). In navigating my way through the projects in this book in the company of co-researchers and the writers that have gone before me I am drawn towards different criteria at different moments, through attention to purpose and style. I can only set these down lightly, but set them down nonetheless.

The tyranny and limitation of word-processing tools has resulted in a somewhat linear depiction of these suggestions and I am grateful to a group of doctoral students (Cindy Gowen, Christine Bell, Jenny Yuen, Eve Dolphin and Dione Mifsud) for kicking up quite a fuss about 'having as much of a problem with "the new ruler" as with the previous criteria of validity, generalisability, authenticity, etc.' (see Atkinson and Delamont, 2005). My various inadequate attempts to produce creative, rhizomatic and/or spiralling images of these criteria, however, failed to generate an equivalent, reproducible A4 sheet. I have remained, for the moment, with 'the ruler, which is not one'.

Perhaps the hardest of the tasks suggested within these attempts at evaluation is to identify that which is aesthetically pleasing, a vital criterion that not only lacks universality, but may also change over time and with the 'mind's eye' of the reader.

For myself, the most compelling criterion is that of transformation and emancipation, both of others and of myself. My interest as researcher is in creating a climate for co-researching unheard-of stories and in discovering, both for myself and for others, the possibilities that lurk beneath the surfaces of the 'statues' that have been made of them. As Hurston (1942: 34) so shrewdly observed, more than half a century ago: 'I did not know then as I know now that people are prone to build a statue of the kind of person that it pleases them to be.' Richardson (1999b: 665) suggests that we face a 'continuing task' in the creation, choice and (presumably) competent performance of criteria. In this respect our responsibilities and visions are shared with those who went before us. As Welch (1999: 26) asserted in her search for ways of presenting an ethic of power, chaos and social change:

> We are not ushering in a new age.
> We are not part of a grand cultural revolution.
> We are not fighting the war to end all wars.
> We are, quite simply, like all the generations before us, and all the generations that will come after, learning to walk.

Further reading

Forms of narrative inquiry
Clandinin, J. and Connelly, P. (2000) *Narrative Inquiry: Experience and Story in Qualitative Research* (San Francisco: Jossey-Bass).
(A clear overview of the work of one group of narrative inquirers that shows us in some detail what they did, but does not tell us what to do.)

Langellier, K. and Peterson, E. (2004) *Storytelling in Everyday Life: Performing Narrative* (Philadelphia: Temple University Press).
(A careful and well written unpacking of narratives as performances of our 'selves'.)

Bumping up against ethical principles
Bond, T. (2004) 'An Introduction to the Ethical Guidelines for Researching Counselling and Psychotherapy'. In *Counselling and Psychotherapy Research*, 4(2): 4–10.
(An account of the BACP's process of changing from fixed to relational ethics.)

Clough, P. (2002) *Narratives and Fictions in Educational Research* (Buckingham: Open University).
(An exploration of the aesthetics and ethics of fictionalised accounts.)

Josselson, R. (ed.) (1996) *Ethics and Process in the Narrative Study of Lives* (Thousand Oaks, CA: Sage).
(Lots of examples within the only edited volume of its kind.)

4
Constructing Stories in Narrative Interviews

I have always been a private person. I have shared my life with a few special friends only. The first session felt intrusive. You knew so much about me and I knew nothing about you. My shell was broken open and the vulnerable meat of the clam was splayed to the sun, to the world. Yours remained tight and impenetrable.

(Olivia, in Bloom, 1998: 22)

Much is made, now the world has turned its narrative turn (Denzin and Lincoln, 2000), of the co-construction of our world and of the constitutive nature of the stories we tell ourselves about our lives. Much is also made about the reciprocity of this process and of the power relations inherent within narrative (see, for instance, Clandinin and Connolly, 2002; Josselson and Lieblich, 1993, 1995, 1999; Josselson et al., 2003; Langellier and Peterson, 2004; McAdams et al., 2001; Riessman, 1993; more of which in Chapters 5 to 9). There now exists a considerable literature of narrative interviewing as a postmodern process (see Gubrium and Holstein, 2001; Kvale, 1996; Mishler, 1986, 2000) wherein:

> the text is read for its unconscious silences and unspoken assumptions. A deconstructive reading makes use of drawing, artistry, literary practices, and blurs the fact/fiction distinction. . . . These different readings . . . involve different questions posed to the text and lead to different answers about the meaning of the text.   (Kvale, 1996: 227)

And yet we still know very little about how poststructuralist, co-constructed interviews with people might have been, or might yet be, ethically and engagingly carried out *in practice*. There is much written about the age of the postmodern, media-savvy 'interview society' (Atkinson and Silverman, 1997; Fontana and Frey, 2000, 2001, 2005), about different types of interview, interviewee and interview contexts (see Gubrium and Holstein, 2001: 55-486, for an overview) and about polyphonic forms of analysis, transcription and representation (see Ellis and Berger, 2001; Etherington, 2004; Langellier and Peterson, 2004; Lapadat and Lindsay, 1999; Richardson, 2000a; Riessman, 2004). There are various versions of semi-structured interview manuals (Wengraf, 2001), accounts of narrative interview cycles and protocols (Lieblich et al., 1998) and suggested ways of producing interview questions (Chase, 2003), eliciting stories (Johnson and Weller, 2001) and producing narratives from ethnographic fieldwork notes, including interviews (see Clandinin and Connolly, 2000).

Perhaps for fear of appearing to produce too definitive or 'manualised' an account, few researchers have given much sense or flavour of the actual interview process, as opposed to the completed narratives that eventually emerged. Phrases such as 'from my accumulated wealth of fieldwork notes and interview transcripts' or 'a series of semi-structured interviews took place over a period of nine months' or 'I conducted open, unstructured interviews with all the staff' litter the literature of qualitative research and it is extremely hard to know what meanings to attach to them.

The Literatures of Narrative Interviewing

Mishler's work (1986, 2000), extended by Kvale (1988, 1996), gives some sense of the position of the researcher as a curious, unknowing and tentative participant in an unstructured narrative interview in which 'interview schedules' are abandoned in favour of conversations wherein one question might lead to a 'one thousand page text' (Mishler, 1986; Kvale, 1988). Subsequent analysis of the 'storylines' that might emerge from such an unstructured conversation (see Mishler, 2000; Bamberg and Andrews, 2004) describes rich texts containing multiple narratives and counter-narratives of the co-construction of people's identities in research interviews as (for example) craft-artists (Mishler, 2000), mothers (Andrews, 2004a) and older women (Jones, 2004). These detailed readings speak to complex understandings of the position of the researcher in producing the final text, readings and writings both with and against the grain of 'the expected storylines of inter-view-based narrative research' (Andrews, 2004b). They acknowledge the compliance of research participants with interview cultures, but also highlight their resistance towards dominant discourses within the tales they tell. These readings of dominant discourses and narratives of resistance fit with those from narrative therapy (see White and Epston, 1990) and both are sustained by the poststructuralist ideas put forward by Foucault (1980b: 82), of discourse opening up spaces for resistance and counter-narrative:

> it is through the re-emergence of these low-ranking knowledges, these unqualified, even directly disqualified knowledges . . . that criticism performs its work.

The difference, however, is that as therapy practitioners, White and Epston are concerned with immediate, tangible, life-transforming access to these alternative stories for the people consulting them. White and Epston are not conducting interviews and wanting to get better at holding narrative conversations, in order to collect data to analyse *at some later juncture*; they are wanting to support people in noticing they are making a difference to the stories they tell about themselves *there and then*, in the conversation, and thus, the way they live their lives. So do I. This is a big difference between therapy (and other) practitioner researchers who are permanently involved in what might be described as 'participatory action co-research' and researchers who are more interested in 'describing and theorising our social world' (Riessman, 2005).

The researchers above (Mishler, Kvale, Andrews, Jones, Bamberg and others) are able to access and represent all these openings to what White (2000, after Derrida) would describe as the 'absent but implicit' meanings in the complex texts they create after their participants have departed, but do not give much information about the 'live' production of these stories through conversation, as this is perhaps not so much of a priority as the representations that unfold in the written text that is subsequently constructed.

My own interest in narrative research is very much as a collaborative co-inquirer, first in relation to the problems that have come to overshadow and shape peoples lives, and secondly in terms of re-telling these stories in writing. It is very useful to read the work of other researchers who are in the business of creating narrative theories, but I also suspect that quite a number of researchers might benefit from more 'showing' what happens in narrative conversations, as well as the final written representations. Paying attention to the more ephemeral art of narrative research conversations might lead to less repetition of 'expected tales' (Andrews, 2004b) and to more transformative research conversations. To reiterate, many have argued convincingly that the research interview is not a neutral exchange (see Fontana and Frey, 2005, for a comprehensive overview) and have demonstrated multi-storied, multi-intentioned, multi-positioned facets of these exchanges in their subsequent analysis of interview texts, but few have demonstrated an active interview practice consistent with these ideas.

Therapy/Research Interviewing Overlaps

There is some discussion about the overlap between therapeutic and research interviewing, a process which might go some way towards nurturing future 'Olivias' (see the beginning of this chapter) and avoiding their experience of interviews as intrusions. Many have found the process of being interviewed by social inquirers therapeutic (see Hart and Crawford-Wright, 1999; Ortiz, 2001) or experienced research as an extension of therapy (Etherington, 2001), and yet others have advocated the psychoanalytic interview, at least, as a form of research (Kvale, 1999).

Perhaps the most thoughtful and extensive current text from the therapy/research crossroads or threshold is Hollway and Jefferson's (2000) account of free association as a from of narrative inquiry. This text explores the use of free association as a means of narrative interviewing that taps into the unknown and unsayable spaces and stories underneath conversations, rather than eliciting that which is already known and readily available. In a very different form from that of narrative therapists, these researchers are listening for 'talk that sings' and for the use of metaphor and poetic language as forms of expression that chisel away beneath 'taken for granted assumptions'. This way of seeing relies heavily on the metaphor of what lies beneath (of inner and outer worlds) rather than what might be placed alongside (as other possible stories within a multi-storied world). What is not offered so readily within this paradigm is a way of exploring the spaces in between agency and culture or of distinguishing between dominant stories or regimes of truth within society and more local, personal, habitual or preferred accounts. For a more poststructuralist interview practice we have to look towards the more discursive therapy practitioners and feminist researchers.

The Contribution of Feminisms

Feminist researchers have opened many doors on multiple positions and power relations whilst researching people's lives. Postcolonial and queer researchers have continued to push out the envelope of possibility made available by feminisms in relation to what constitutes a legitimate research conversation (see, for instance, Gunaratnam, 2003, a critical postcolonial feminist, on the ways in which the current trend for generating race and ethnic categories in interview research has also extended opportunities for racism).

Feminist researchers have been at the forefront of critiquing unexamined assumptions and dominant forms of knowing (in this case in relation to gender) and of contesting ideas about 'uninvolved' professional researchers (see Harding, 1987). They openly promote an interest in giving 'voice' to a range of women's experiences. Feminist researchers have troubled established definitions of biographical/autobiographical, self/other, object/subject in research, not just in terms of the reciprocal nature of storytelling, but also in making the personal (or private) political (or social/public) not only 'by' but also 'for' women (see Evans, 1999; Stanley, 1992).

A range of feminist projects have explored and made transparent the complex relations of power in research conversations between 'the perceived' and 'the perceivers' when social and other locations differ dramatically (such as race, see Collins, 1990; Phoenix, 1994; and class, see Luttrell, 1997; Richardson, 1997a). Contemporary feminist researchers can no longer assume as Rogers did (1998: 1), that all women 'face the same odds that put us in the same "big boat"'. What they do share, is: 'a commitment to reflecting on the complexities of their own and participants' social locations and subjectivities' (Reinharz and Chase, 2001: 232).

This gives rise to Bloom's (1998) commitment to transparency in unpacking the parameters and pitfalls of her interview relationship with her colleague 'Olivia' and to the myriad versions of what constitutes a legitimate site for feminist research conversations (such as gossip and friendship, see Tillman-Healy, 2003). Feminists have challenged the 'one-off' social-science interview culture and have sought to extend responsibilities towards participants beyond interviews into 'chat' and beyond research projects into 'life' (see Ellis and Tillman-Healy, 1997, and Oakley, 1981).

Much of what follows below in relation to narrative therapy practice as a form of 'transformative interviewing' owes its genesis not only to feminist therapists such as Hare-Mustin and Maracek (1990) and Laird (2001) but also to the ethics of the entire feminist conversational project of telling stories about women's ways of knowing.

In breaking out of binaries such as male/female, masculine/feminine and lesbian/heterosexual and opening up the possible alternative spaces around and between these constructs (see Davies and Gannon, 2005; Lather, 1991; Weedon, 1997), poststructuralist feminist researchers have been working similar territories, sustained by ideas similar to those inhabited by narrative therapists. There is consequently considerable overlap (and space to gain from, and sustain, each other) between post-structuralist feminist practices of 'collective biography' and the narrative therapy practice of working with 'outsider witnesses', for example (see Chapters 6 and 7). Continued feminist interest in regimes of cultural truth, discourses of resistance and constantly shifting power relations has led to experimentation with ways of representing women's stories and investigation of the hidden spaces that women have inhabited. See, for instance, St Pierre's (1997) nomadic excursions into inquiry and Gremillion's (2003) critique of prevailing assumptions surrounding anorexia nervosa.

Feminist scholars, then, have much to offer psychotherapy researchers in relation to questioning and disrupting the boundaries of 'legitimate' research, exploring ways of positioning ourselves as collaborative researchers and continuing to develop innovative ways of representing research findings.

Narrative Therapy Practices

This chapter cannot provide an exhaustive overview of what have come to be known as the 'narrative therapies'. It is intended as an exploration of the ways in which such practices might support a range of collaborative researchers in the conversations they have with people and to *show* examples of the two-way process of such conversations rather than the routine convention (in research texts) of analysing the outcomes of such conversations for particular, possible or even universal meanings. There is a rich and growing literature sustaining developments within the narrative therapies and I would recommend Alice Morgan (2000), White and Epston (1990), White (1997a, 2000), Freedman and Combs (1996), Monk et al. (1997) and Payne (2000, 2006) as good introductory texts. Johnella Bird's (2000, 2004a, 2004b) work on using relational language, albeit focused very clearly towards therapy practitioners and the people consulting them, also has much to offer narrative researchers.

Narrative therapy contributes a conversational practice that positions people alongside each other, as emotional (and other kinds of) ethnographers and archaeologists. There are myriad ways in which these practices might be explored and made manifest. The elements that stand out for me are:

- The collaborative relational and conversational position taken up by the interviewer (and the spaces that this position makes available and diminishes).
- The commitment to deconstruction, in other words to exoticising the domestic assumptions, habits, rites and spaces people inhabit (and the excitement of discovery and intrigue that this evokes in people).
- The focus on intentional states and local, partial knowing (rather than inner or essential states and/or expert or analytic knowing).
- The sense of movement across the conversational landscapes (over time and context and in relation to other people) that is constantly attended to.
- The practices of doubly listening in to the 'spaces in between' people's expressions of their lives, and drawing attention to this space through:
  - (a) relational use of language that 'deconstructs' and highlights these spaces;
  - (b) attending to 'talk that sings' in people's expressions of their lives (use of evocative, lyrical, local and poetic words and phrases).

INTERVIEWER POSITIONING AND THE EXOTIC DOMESTIC

Narrative practitioners take up a position of co-researcher in relation to the issues of interest and concern that have been established with the people consulting them. White (2004a: vii) describes this as a process of exoticisation (quoting Bourdieu, 1988) whereby:

in the context of inquiry shaped by this sentiment, therapeutic conversations that might otherwise reproduce the known and the familiar become journeys to destinations that cannot be specified or predicted in advance of arrival.

This kind of conversational practice, then, is of no use to researchers who have specific goals in mind, but is clearly of interest to people who want to co-research neglected, forgotten and possible stories.

Narrative interview practice explores alternative and possible stories that might interest people. It also explicitly recognises the reciprocal nature of conversations between storytellers and audiences. Perhaps, for example, Olivia's (Bloom, 1998: 22) grievance, quoted at the beginning of this chapter, that 'You knew so much about me and I knew nothing about you,' might have been avoided if her interviewer had taken up a more reciprocal position as she approached the interview and had also included some of her own responses to the stories that unfolded during their research relationship.

EXTERNALISING ISSUES AND CONCERNS

The process of 'excavation' of unknown territories that has come to characterise the narrative therapies might begin with a conversation externalising or richly characterising their concerns (see Rusell and Carey, 2004: 1–19). This rich characterisation allows people to gain a degree of what might be described as 'altitude' on events within their own lives and become intrigued by them, as co-researchers, rather than remaining overwhelmed. Such an excavation might comprise an 'unpacking' of the descriptions given to, and meanings attributed to, the issues that concern people. It might include the histories and contexts of such concerns and the extent of their influence (or not) in people's lives and how that influence might be diminished or enhanced.

Perhaps the most (in)famous example of an externalising conversation is White's (in White and Epston, 1990: 38–75) account of Nick, his family and their encounter's with 'sneaky poo', and its relative influence in their lives. This account reveals much about the lightness and availability with which postmodern irony can be used (as Nick and family resist sneaky poo's attempts to 'outstreak' them) within narrative conversational practice.

Instead of describing this concern as Nick's encopresis (a version which collapses Nick's person together with 'his' problem and in so doing also implicates his family), White encourages the family to come up with their own definition: sneaky poo; and then supports Nick and family in charting the history and relative influence of sneaky poo in their lives, within a range of contexts as well as moments when 'Sneaky poo' is less dominant or even outwitted.

Johnella Bird (2000, 2004a) is another practitioner in the field who describes her own use of 'relational language' as a conversational process that opens up the space for 'the language in between' the 'single stories' of people's lives, in order not so much to externalise as to create the possibility of movement between the more limited binary opposites available to people.

I have found Johnella Bird's (2000, 2004a, 2004b) *relational* use of language, extremely helpful in supporting me in engaging with the complexities of people's lives. Bird's movement has been away from binary constructs and this has been supported by her attention to 'talk that sings [that] brings us closer to the experience of poetry' (Bird, 2000: 30). Bird speaks of the need to develop a 'feeling for words' that she likens to Hoeg's (1983) novel *Miss Smilla's Feeling for Snow*, in which Miss Smilla, a Greenlander, has multiple words and phrases to describe the various textures and types of the phenomenon known within the English language only as 'snow'. She also has myriad and complex feelings towards, about and in relation to snow. In my own listening for, and co-construction of, talk that sings, I have found myself increasingly positioned as if 'at a poetry recital' whilst engaged in both therapeutic and research conversations.

One of the distinctive features of this way of working is that the conversation moves back and forth continually between people's meanings and intentions and their context and history (see White, 2001, 2004b, for introductions to **intentional** state or 'folk' psychology). Thus, in the conversation that follows later in this chapter between myself and Donald, explanations of events as out of the blue or innate are put under some scrutiny and the intentions, histories and social contexts of these traits and events are explored. Certain 'outside of the box' personal characteristics turn out not to have evolved by chance, but to have had quite a social and cultural evolution and to have influenced later decisions about choice of workplace; in other words: what appeared to have been accidental was in fact intentional and spoke to some important values that have been held to and developed by Donald over a long period of time. A differently constructed research interview might have 'reflected back' or paraphrased the interviewee's words (see Fontana and Frey, 2005; Kong et al., 2001).

TRAVERSING THE CONVERSATIONAL LANDSCAPE

Narrative therapists have defined narrative as the stories we tell about events, in sequence taking place over time, organised into a plot (see A. Morgan, 2000; Russell and Carey, 2004a: 19–45). These might be the 'dominant' stories of the times, more personal or local stories and/or the traces of less familiar 'alternative' stories. Borrowing from Bruner (1986a, 1990, 1991), White and Epston (1990) have used a landscape metaphor (including landscapes of both meaning and action) to describe the storied space that people inhabit. Thus the stories we tell ourselves and others about events in context, over time (the landscape of action), are given or take on specific meanings and values (the landscape of meaning). They have also borrowed from Vygotsky (see Bruner, 1986b, and Vygotsky, 1978) to encourage therapists to ask 'scaffolding' questions, stretching out across these landscapes towards the edges of people's zones of proximal development (and expanding the conversation from that which is known and familiar towards that which it is possible to know: aspects of the landscape where discoveries can be made and/or forgotten, or 'subjugated' knowledges can be reclaimed).

There are many versions of conversations explicitly mapping and illustrating the journeys back and forth across these landscapes over the time available (see White, 1995, 1997a, 2005a, 2005b; Russell and Carey, 2004a: 19–63). This is not intended as some kind of foundational conversational protocol or technique to follow. The metaphor of 'narrative landscapes' and of inhabiting certain terrain over time, does nonetheless provide co-researchers with some useful tools for excavating difficult or uncharted terrain together, and with ways of bringing to mind events or the meaning given to them that might otherwise have been overlooked or left out of the story altogether. This 'geographical' metaphor of landscapes also speaks to and draws our attention towards the spaces between the stories that we tell, or to the gaps in the stories where different meanings or points of entry to alternative, contradictory, non-commensurate and/or multiple narratives might lurk.

Interviewing Donald in Context

Let me first place the extracts from my interviews with Donald, which follow shortly, in context. These are two brief snatches from several hours of conversation with Donald, during much of which I was almost completely silent, whilst he held forth. There were also periods, particularly at the beginning of both conversations with Donald, where there was much scene-setting chat between the two of us and I had much to say about the background to our meetings, and he asked about the outcomes of my conversations with others (Donald knew that he was the last of a group of sixteen interviewees). There were also several moments when I paused in the conversation to check that I had understood what he had said, or to produce short summaries of the conversation as I seemed to have heard it, thus far, or, most importantly, paused to check that the way the conversation was going was still of interest to Donald.

The pieces I have chosen are both moments when I am 'interviewing' Donald as co-researcher. We are both very engaged in this process. I am asking questions about his experience that appear to interest us both and I am clearly not just asking a 'one thousand page text' question, but asking questions that engage us, that have to be thought about and that are uncovering new territory.

It is not my contention that all interviews should take place in this way, but I aim rather, to show how attending to the relational and contextual aspects of the positions that Donald is taking can create the space for him to reconsider and reflect on what he has said and might say. I have deliberately chosen extracts from an interview conducted some years ago when I was new to these conversational practices. An experienced narrative practitioner would no doubt see many more openings for inquiry and might have asked very different questions. What I hope to demonstrate, however, is that any researcher with a strong commitment to conversations as collaborative research endeavours can fairly swiftly learn how to position themselves alongside people as de-centred and influential co-researchers. All of this makes a crucial difference to the research process. As soon as researchers are positioned in this way, with these commitments and this ethic of collaboration they are positioned for a voyage of mutual discovery within the conversation. This is a very different stance to take up from that of a researcher who is positioned to sit back and 'listen' to stories that they are later going to 'analyse' (even when they theoretically recognise the reciprocity of this endeavour).

Donald Placing Himself as Someone with a History 'Out of the Box' . . .

I have chosen this particular interview from my doctoral thesis as it illustrates the effectiveness of this way of working in research as well as in 'therapy' interviews, and equally with people who do not themselves subscribe to narrative approaches to therapy. My thesis was concerned with therapy practitioners' relationships with research and with 'the academy'. All the participants in my study were colleagues and thus each conversation began with a fair amount of two-way chat about what had gone before and about the ideas that were beginning to form in my mind. In the first extract, from talk fairly early on in my interview with Donald, who is a psychodynamic therapy practitioner, we are talking about the fact that he found himself working on a training programme producing 'person-centred' counsellors, despite this not being his preferred way of working. At first he had implied that he had just ended up 'out of the box' by chance, but as the conversation below illustrates, between us we uncovered quite a history – possibly a lifelong commitment to taking up these 'out of the box' kinds of positions. In this case, the ways in which he was most perceived by others as different, were ways of working that he especially valued and that he had come by, not by chance, but through considerable practice and experience, through what he later came to describe as his own research.

This interview was nothing like the kinds of 'therapeutic' conversations that Donald was familiar with, but this did not seem to get in the way of a fruitful exchange. Donald seemed quite fascinated by the exchange and by the kinds of questions that I was asking. Towards the end of our interview (Speedy, 2001a: 253) he remarked:

> You asked some very interesting questions in very interesting ways. We've gone down quite unexpected avenues, not new avenues exactly, but we seem to be traversing them differently. What did you just ask and how did you decide what questions to ask?

My quite lengthy answer to the second part of this question was something of a description of the landscapes I had in my mind and that I saw us both inhabiting and traversing together. I also listed some of the questions that I had put to him towards the end of our discussion and described some of my sense of a relational way of using language, but let's get back to the earlier extract from our explorations together.

Just before the piece of conversation I have chosen, Donald was talking about the difference between 'thinking types' of people (academics for instance) and 'feeling types' (such as therapists). Equally, he perceived a division between thinking and feeling institutions, and regarded universities as 'thinking institutions'. This is the point we join the conversation. I have written my interventions in bold, in order to be able subsequently to refer to the relational language, and the traversing of landscapes and histories. Donald's replies are in italic script. The boxed texts refer to my (unvoiced) thoughts, speculations and critique of my part in the conversation.

It is quite clear from this part of the conversation (in which I am speaking quite a lot), that although I am wearing my theories lightly and asking questions into the spaces that Donald leaves open, I do have values and beliefs that are influencing the way I am talking. Despite the very definite way that Donald has been speaking about people who are 'naturally' thinking or feeling types, for instance, I start by placing his sense of himself in a 'relational' rather than a 'natural' or general context through my use of language. At times I switch the way language is used around into what Bird (2004a) would describe as the continuous present, suggesting movement and tentativeness rather than closed down meanings. The expression to 'be in different camps', for instance, led to a question about 'this joining different camps', and 'I value groups' evoked a question about 'this valuing of groups' and what it linked with.

Although Donald later became interested in these questions, I don't think either of us would have been able to identify this change of tense as it was happening, but it did perhaps make a difference to the possibilities within Donald's storyline that a mere reflection back from me about his valuing of groups, without any reference to context, history and other people, might not have done. I was not so interested in his general, habitual and overarching sense of himself, as in how he found himself 'positioned' in relation to the university and how this had come about. This 'relational' version of events was clearly not how Donald routinely described the world he found himself in, but he was nonetheless curious, as I was, to discover his answers to these kinds of questions.

*   *   *

JS: So how would you describe your sense of yourself in relation to the university?

Donald: Well it's a sense of being a feeling type

this real sense I have
about being a feeling type,
and being marginalised in institutions,
not being valued

and feeling that that was,
at the same time
that I felt my training also affirmed that side

and . . .

> Am I moving out of Donald's zone here? Why didn't I ask him if this interested him?

JS: So your sense of the university is that it is a 'thinking' institution, the sort of institution that might marginalise 'feeling' types, and your sense of yourself is of a feeling type, is that right?

Donald: (Nods)

JS: So would you be interested, for the moment, in just taking a look at your coming to work here?

Donald: (Nods vigorously and laughs)

> So this does interest him, but I wish I'd checked

JS: It's just that I'm interested in this move. Was it a move away from 'feeling' sorts of institutions? Was this a move towards something, something else?

Donald: I wanted to be,
I wanted to be there,
because I felt my . . .
my type was equally as valid,
and so I wanted to be there and found a niche for myself.

JS: That's an interesting development . . . to find a niche for yourself within a 'thinking institution'. Is that something of a surprise to you, or is it the kind of 'out of the box' position you were talking about earlier, the kind of position you regularly put yourself in?

Donald: In terms of my motives.
I've had it all my life really,
this ability to be able to cross boundaries
*   and cultures . . .*
and be in different camps at the same time.

> 'All my life' . . . that's a long time . . . that interests me, has he taken this for granted . . . does this have a history?

JS: This joining different camps . . . can you remember other times in your life, then, featuring 'different camps' at the same time?

Donald: I did that in the church, in my family, at school,
it's not something I planned to do, it's just . . .
a place I tend to find myself.

JS: You tend to . . . is this an accidental tendency would you say or is it a move in a particular direction?

> Not accidental:
> intentional?

Donald: It's not accidental,

It's not accidental
that I, as someone who describes myself as having a psychodynamic approach,
will be working in an institution, which describes itself as 'person-centred'

I don't know if this is true,
but I know it's my perceived view of it,
and that is that somehow I'm seen as different here,
by the people I come into contact with . . .

JS: Does this 'being seen as different' speak to anything about your work or anything else that you especially value?

Donald: I think it's to do with how I run the groups here,
especially the skills groups and supervision groups,
and they're to do with my group training; I think that's my group side of me,
because I enjoy groups enormously,
I value groups.

JS: This 'valuing of groups' on your part, does it link with any particular practice or processes?

Donald: I love it when groups make discoveries,
and when the group feels proud of something and feel good about themselves . . .
and that happens not because I'm wise,
or because I can tell a student what's happening in their counselling relationship,
but because suddenly the group comes alive and sees things.
My task to facilitate that is what I enjoy.

> Warning bell: I have a strong preference for loitering in the landscape of meaning, I need to remind myself to ask questions that scaffold us back to the landscape of actions too.

JS: So have you always liked working in groups and enjoyed facilitating these discoveries that people make or is that a more recent development in your work?

Donald: Oh god, I used to sit in groups and when people made insightful
    remarks
I'd feel terrible . . .
I felt [that] I, as the supervisor, should be making all these remarks . . .

**JS: What's your sense of the process
of how this changed?**

Donald: Well, fortunately, in my advanc-
    ing years,
this is no longer a problem . . .

> Out of the zone.
> Not a clear enough
> question, although
> Donald kindly
> answers.

*   *   *

This short exchange forms the prologue to a lengthy monologue about
Donald's relationship with research, researchers and his own supervision practice. Interestingly, he starts that conversation by saying:

> *Research, I've never done it*

but goes on to discuss his interest in reading the research that other
people conduct and eventually to reconsider this 'thin' description of
his own relationship with research and to construct the ways he uses
supervision as a form of co-research into his own practice (see Speedy,
2001a: 249–53), but I am getting ahead of myself again.

From the conversation outlined above, it is evident that I am wanting
to extend Donald's stories beyond his day-to-day assumptions and his
habitual characterisation of the feeling type 'ending up' in the thinking
institution, as if by chance. This is not to disregard or replace that story;
it still stands, but has been expanded to reveal some further intentions
and commitments behind the 'chance', which provide alternative
meanings that were interesting to both of us. There is clearly an extensive history to being 'in different camps at the same time', peopled by
Donald's family and others. Later in the conversation we went back to
some of these stories and discussed his different religious affiliations in
relation to his family, and his different positions in relation to ordina-
tion and the different denominational 'camps'. On reflection, this
history of boundary and culture crossing, which had roots within
Donald's family and its traditions, also stood Donald in good stead in

relation to different 'schools' of therapy and schools of research, not least finding himself working on a programme ouside his own familiar zone, 'not accidentally' but in fact 'wanting' to be there.

These actions, together with Donald's groupwork practices, clearly spoke to past meanings and intentions but also to more recent and current shifts that had occurred in relation to Donald's work with groups in his 'advancing years', whereby he no longer felt that it should be him, as supervisor, making the 'insightful remarks' in groups, but rather, he enjoyed facilitating groups that came 'alive' in insightful ways.

These events were clearly more than just the after-effects of 'accidental ending ups', and a few questions elicited current and past histories, meanings, intentions and values.

I have no way of knowing how this conversation might have gone between two other people. It was the particular histories behind 'tendencies' that moved the conversation from current 'ending ups' into the arena of intentions towards different ways of working, and values, and commitments from past experiences of being in more than one camp. Thus questions delving into what sounded like a very well rehearsed story about feeling and thinking types led the conversation from a thin description of current 'out of the blue' occurrences towards the landscapes of past events and meanings and thence back into current practices informed by similar values and commitments. Much could have been expanded that was left unsaid and never returned to. The 'side' that Donald's training affirmed was never explored, nor did we go into how many other possible sides or types of person and/or institution there might be (only two are talked about – 'thinking' and 'feeling'). Looking back on this conversation, there was much that we could have gone back to, but never did. It might have been interesting to explore the contexts in which Donald found himself a 'feeling type'; I remain curious to this day about whether there were other situations or contexts in which he had already found himself or might imagine finding himself, in which he would have identified more as a thinking type or as some other kind of type altogether. I have no idea whether any of this would have interested Donald, but suspect it might have.

The reason I am not drawing attention here to possible points of entry that were missed in this conversation and that might have interested Donald, is not that I think the conversation 'went wrong'. I am trying to show the infinite possibilities that were available to us as we co-constructed this narrative. A more experienced practitioner might have thought to ask Donald more frequently about the direction he wanted to go in. There were, nevertheless, many trajectories available. Later in our conversation Donald extended the (partly) tongue-in-cheek explanation of 'advancing years' and referred to the supervision and research practices that sustained him in his shift in position from the kind of supervisor who had felt he should be making insightful remarks, to the kind of supervisor who supported the group to do this. It transpired that he was also encouraged into making this shift by the mutual 'research' climate that was being created within his supervision groups between his students and himself. Having initially declared that he had 'never' done research, he went on to describe his supervision groups almost in terms of action-research settings, commenting:

I do it in my own way in terms of my own supervision
and supervision groups
and so on,
we look at things,
and test them out.
If someone, for example, if someone says in my supervision group,
'Well, I suddenly had an intuition that . . .'
I say, 'Where did that intuition come from?',
and I'll say, 'Was there any other evidence to back up your intuition?',
in other words, how can that be tested?
So that might be an approach I would take in the supervision,
which I think is a research model,
in fact, it's not just accepting something at face value,
it's saying,
how can you support that in doing . . .?

It would have been interesting, I imagine, to excavate a little more about the history of this shift, not only in terms of the ethics of these different ways of working, but also in terms of the history of Donald's relationship with these ideas, and to find out what connections there were, or could be, with the people (living and/or dead) that had influenced the ethical substance within Donald's work with groups.

Donald and I met again about four weeks later, to revisit our first conversation and consider anything that had emerged in the interim. This second meeting mostly consisted in Donald reflecting on our previous conversation. This second extract is taken from the last few minutes of that exchange, when once again, I became much more active in the conversation and asked him quite a lot of questions.

*   *   *

JS: So this sense of your thinking about 'research' shifting during our conversations, tell me a bit more about that?

Donald: that's very important,
isn't it,
really very important,
the way in which the process affects you,
changes you,
and its what's happened.

JS: Are there other contexts in your life in which the process of the conversation changes you?

Donald: I don't know if it's true of researchers,
it's certainly true of my counselling,
it's not to do with what I do with my clients,
it's what my client does to me,
and I can never foretell what that will be.
But if a client does something to me to get him better
mind you, I want to qualify that all to you . . .

JS: How do you mean? Which bit do you want to 'qualify'?

Donald: I used to say that,
if a client had changed,
the counsellor has to change.
If the client sees the counsellor change,

then they can change themselves,
or something like that.

[pause]

well, I wish you well,
. . . it sounds fascinating . . .

> Donald's speech is slowing down here, is he bored with all this, or is he ruminating about it in his mind's eye . . . or something else?

JS: Do you want to stop there, or can I ask something else . . .

Donald: No, no go on I'm fascinated . . .

JS: Well, you started by saying you'd never done research and we explored that a bit. . . . You've now gone on to list at least three ways

in which you would describe yourself as a researcher and yet we have still been talking all this time about the discrepancies and differences between researchers and practitioners. Given that you are, in many ways, a 'researcher' in your work, what are these differences I wonder?

Donald: What's occurring to me
it's quite different from what I said before really,
is about the nature of research

JS: That's interesting, could you say a little more about the nature of research in the practitioner's context and the nature of research in the researcher's context?

Donald: we [practitioners] don't go on to write,
write it up
and I'm wondering
if that's actually the academic's preoccupation
with writing it up
that's the interest of the academic . . .
where it's
not the interest actually,
of the pure practitioner,

> Talking as if in a state of 'reverie' about these concerns

JS: I'm interested in your use of words there. You've shifted from the more general 'researcher' to specifically describing 'academic's preoccupations' here . . . are you saying that 'academic researchers' as distinct from 'practitioner researchers' have different interests and preoccupations?

Donald: Yup (nods)

JS: So do you have any sense or any hunches about the history or purpose of these different preoccupations, has this just come about by chance, this difference do you think?

Donald: it's the interest the academic brings
to it as well,
and it's also become
in academic terms
as far as I understand from my knowledge . . .

the writing up of our papers has become an obsession,
because the whole thing
about research
is being marked on,
institutions get money for it . . .
and so you have to be producing
paper
   after paper
      after paper,

and after a while,
your own status is made
in a number of papers

[pause]

or not . . .

JS: Mmm, the 'regimes of truth' of the academy, that's spot on, I reckon. We're running out of time AGAIN. Shame, I'd like to go on all morning, there's tons more I'd like to ask about, not least about how 'status is made' amongst practitioners. You spoke earlier about the process of change and about counsellors and clients witnessing each other changing, but that's a very private sense of 'success'. How do we 'make status' I wonder in the therapy world? Still, I guess we need to finish there. Is there anything you were left curious about or that you'd like to ask me?

Donald: *you asked some very interesting*
questions
in very interesting ways.
We've gone down quite unexpected avenues,
not new avenues exactly . . . but we seem to be traversing them differently.
What did you just ask . . . and how did you decide what questions to ask?

JS: The questions I asked you when we started again were . . .

*   *   *

We went on to look at the sorts of questions that I had asked and how this was informed by a metaphor of a 'storied world' in which events took place over time, in a context, and might inhabit different land-scapes: landscapes of actions and landscapes of meanings ascribed to those actions. We looked at the ways that attention to the particularities and contexts of people's meanings opened up the space for people to 'exoticise' the everyday stories they told themselves about their lives and find new possibilities, meanings and stories. In many ways, although apparently differently positioned within the discourses of therapy, these ideas were a good fit with Donald's own therapeutic practices, particularly his sense of himself as a researcher who was as much changed himself as he was engaged in the process of supporting others to change during therapeutic exchanges. We talked about the fit and 'not fit' between psychodynamic and narrative ideas and the different practices of 'not knowing' these engendered.

In the second conversation, Donald embraced some of the alternative versions of his relationship with research that he had touched on previously. He also explored the idea that researchers and counsellors might operate in similar 'process' ways (a conversational process in which everyone involved is changed) but that the process and possibly the people would have different relationships with writing, different outcomes and different discourses and political positions in relation to 'professional status'.

In this short extract Donald traversed some of the territories he visited in the first conversation, but was now more curious about the many meanings that the word 'research' might have and how these meanings might have shifted for him over time, and might also be different in different professional contexts. In the first conversation the 'gap' between research and practice started to become a more complex site for multiple meanings. With further reflection, this 'liminal' space between therapy research and practice became considerably more multi-storied and there turned out, for Donald at least, to be more of a difference (possibly personal, but certainly professional and political) between practitioner research leading towards people (therapists and clients) making changes, and academic research leading towards an outcome of writing for publication.

Note Taking 'In the Moment'

I have not specifically 'plotted' these conversations in relation to the questions that I asked or to maps of the landscapes of action and meaning over time, nor do I work or would I personally advocate working in such a prescribed way 'in the moment' in co-research conversations. I sustain my commitments to opening the spaces in the conversations through scribbled notes or ongoing 'mind maps' of the conversations that we have. I jot down the expressions, words and phrases that captured my attention and that I wanted to remember. As I have mentioned in my commentary, we did not have the time to give further consideration to all these possible openings and Donald may not have been interested in pursuing them all.

By roughly dividing my page vertically into landscapes of meaning and action, and horizontally across time (neither of which I necessarily stick to rigidly in the moment), I can look at the kinds of terrain our conversations are focusing on and the kinds of territories we have not yet explored. I find this useful. I have a tendency, with regard to my own interests, to want to ask questions about meanings and purposes and histories, and the way I 'map' my notes is often a useful reminder to invite people to consider the practices and actions and events that emanated from, have sustained or might sustain their meaning-making processes. (See Figures 1 and 2, diagrams of 'Traversing the landscape' and 'Notes on my conversation with Donald', on pp. 82 and 83.)

The notes I took during the first part of the first conversation show a number of expressions from Donald's life that particularly caught my attention; these are plotted roughly on the page as an 'aide' and joined up loosely across the landscapes with a series of squiggly lines and arrows. I have underlined 'WANTED' in the phrase 'wanted to be there' several times and have scribbled rings around a number of expressions that obviously sang out to me in some way in the moment. There are also various question marks dotted about, which suggest to me that these were issues that I found particularly engaging for some reason (often because of the ways they were spoken about, tone of voice, etc.) and that I might have invited Donald to explore further if we had had the time and he had had the inclination. 'Not accidental' (ringed several times) received something of an excavation, as did 'different camps'.

My sense from these notes and my recollections of the tenor of the conversation, as opposed to my later reflections, outlined above, is that the group 'coming alive' was really interesting and engaging to Donald, and that would have been quite a potent space to explore. Similarly, as mentioned above, it seemed likely that more than 'advancing years' was informing and sustaining his shift to a different position within his supervision groups. I was quite keen to come back to exploring some of this further and, as it happens, so was Donald, which he did subsequently.

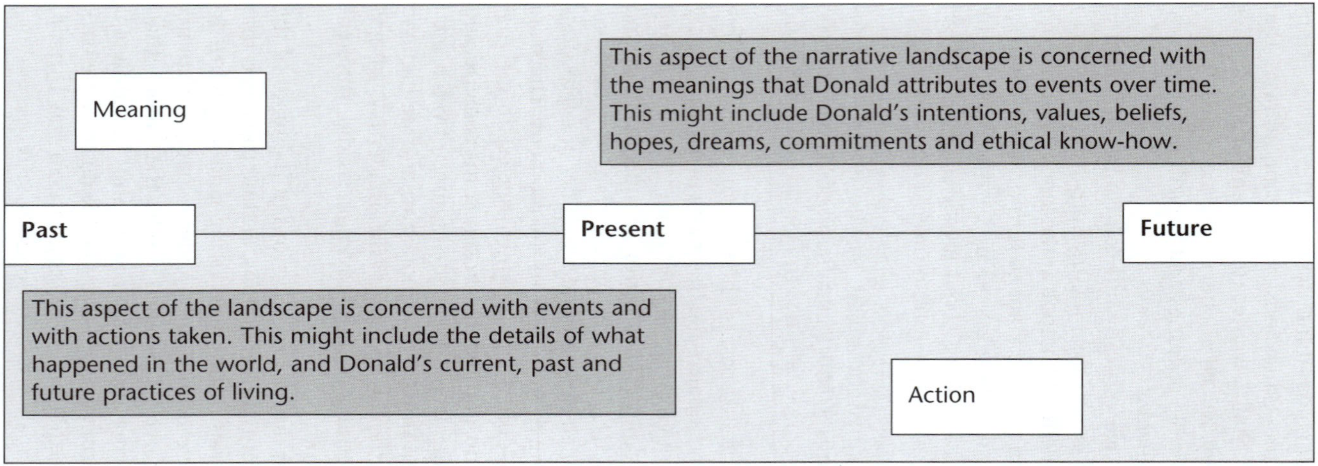
Meaning
This aspect of the narrative landscape is concerned with the meanings that Donald attributes to events over time. This might include Donald's intentions, values, beliefs, hopes, dreams, commitments and ethical know-how.
Past
Present
Future
This aspect of the landscape is concerned with events and with actions taken. This might include the details of what happened in the world, and Donald's current, past and future practices of living.
Action

Figure 1 Traversing narrative landscapes of meaning and action

The diagram presented here is not exhaustive and is intended not as a 'template', more of an 'aide memoir' to have in the mind's eye, or on the page in front of you, as conversations progress. I often take notes on conversations in the form of a mind map or spider diagram. The phrases that I capture on paper are loosely and untidily placed across time from left to right and across the landscapes from top (high ethical altitude) to bottom (things that happened, or might). Other people take notes in different ways or not at all. This 'map' of conversations was generated by Michael White, who has radically adapted and combined Bruner's narrative landscapes, Vygotsky's ideas about 'scaffolding' conversations from within zones of proximal development, Foucault's work on the discourses and power relations that both stalk and constitute the landscape, and Derrida's ideas about deconstructing people's expressions of life. (See White, 2007, for a more current and complex version.)

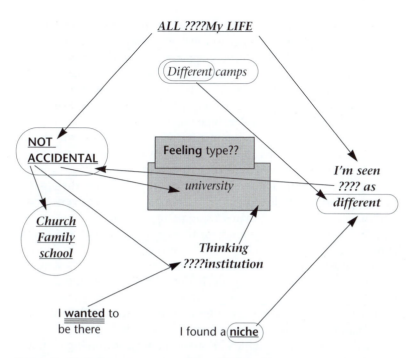

Figure 2 Notes on my conversation with Donald . . .

In Summary

Researchers and/or therapists do not just 'have open conversations', or 'conduct semi-structured interviews'. People conducting interview research with narrative intentions are anticipating and intending to give particular attention to the stories people tell themselves and others about their lives and worlds, and this does not happen by chance.

In the main, narrative inquirers 'show' us extracts from interview transcripts and often discuss at length issues of selection, positions and stances taken by researchers and co-researchers, representation, transcription and analysis, but very rarely discuss or 'show' the particular ways in which the conversations took place. The language used to describe narrative research interviews classically interrogates the power relations between researcher and researched but very rarely offers different ways of conducting research conversations, although we subsequently learn a great deal about how researchers have analysed these conversations. We might anticipate that counselling researchers and or narrative researchers would have made a rich archive of transformative interviewing styles and strategies available to researchers positioned in a range of ways (and this may yet happen). The contribution of discursive therapy practices to the technologies of co-research remains unique and extraordinary. I have focused on the formulations that have come to be known as the 'narrative therapies' for a number of reasons: first, these are the best known and recorded of the 'post-psychological therapies'; secondly, I have some familiarity with and enthusiasm for this approach; and lastly, this approach maintains ethical commitments to the transformation as well as the description of people's lives.

Unlike most narrative research frameworks, narrative therapy (an approach, not a model) offers us a transformative **conversational practice**. There are now many accounts of these kinds of conversations available between a variety of therapy practitioners and people consulting them, including some conversations on videotape (www.masterswork.com distributes a wide range).

The conversation with Donald is not offered as a narrative interviewing 'protocol' to be followed, and is quite deliberately presented as brief snapshots or sketches, in order to 'show' one way of negotiating the terrain of narrative conversations.

What I hope these examples illustrate is a way of working that does not just present research participants with an opportunity to re-tell their well rehearsed and habitual stories. It also pays close attention to the language people use, the meanings they give and the assumptions they make, in order to excavate unexpected knowledge about their own lives. I hope that this gives other practitioner researchers food for thought about research and about the differences between an ethics of description and an **ethics of transformation and emancipation**. Each of these (description, transformation and emancipation) is, of course, unstable, overlapping and ambiguous. Like Donald, I am more interested in engaging in co-research that imagines the world differently than in meticulously recording the stories that people have told many times before. Who knows where such excavations might lead?

Further reading

Narrative interviewing

Gubrium, J. and Holstein, J. (eds) (2001) *Handbook of Interview Research: Context and Method* (Thousand Oaks, CA: Sage).
(Very expensive, but a great overview. Alternatively, the more pertinent half of this volume has been reissued in paperback as *Postmodern Interviewing*).

Kvale, S. (1996) *Inter Views: An Introduction to Qualitative Research Interviewing* (Thousand Oaks, CA: Sage).
(Thought-provoking on ethical positions.)

Mishler, E. (2000) *Storylines: Craftartists' Narratives of identity* (Cambridge, MA: Harvard University Press).
(Meticulously constructed from interviews: interviews themselves not included.)

Narrative therapy

Bird, J. (2004) *Talk that Sings* (Auckland: Edge Press).
(Complex, but gripping on relational language.)

Payne, M. (2006) *Narrative Therapy: An Introduction for Counsellors* 2nd edn, (London: Sage).
(This is very clearly written and relates to UK counselling cultures.)

White, M. (2004) *Narrative Practice and Exotic Lives: Resurrecting Diversity in Everyday Life* (Adelaide: Dulwich Centre Publications).
(Examples of different conversations: interviewer's contributions included.)

White, M. and Epston, D. (1990) *Narrative Means to Therapeutic Ends* (New York: Norton).
(The core text from two founders of narrative therapy.)

5

Re-presenting Life Stories

The great function of poetry is to give us back the situations of our dreams.

(Bachelard, 1986: 15)

Having recorded people's words as part of a research and/or therapeutic conversation, issues of transcription and selection (processes with overlapping and blurred boundaries) start to emerge if all or some of that conversation is going to be re-presented either to them, or to the world at large, in written form. Therapists routinely write notes either with or about their clients. They are often asked to write reports about (and/or with) their clients and this often requires the selection and/or transcription of elements of their conversations. Narrative (and some other, see Bolton et al., 2004) therapists frequently write therapeutic documents as part of their work, either with or to the people consulting them. Counselling researchers also record moments and fragments of conversations. As Ochs (1979) attested more than 25 years ago in her paper on the transcription of oral conversations with children 'as theory', transcription is a form of translation. Once we are engaged in translation we are engaged in negotiations in which there will be both losses and gains. Transcription is a research method that is 'a selective process reflecting theoretical goals and definitions' (Ochs, 1979: 44). Riessman (1993), Mishler (1991), Denzin (1997), Kvale (1996) and C. Bird (2005), as well as Lapadat and Lindsay (1999) in their useful overview of transcription practices, all refer to the construction of a transcript as a re-interpretation, re-telling or reconstruction of the text. 'Translation', maintains Eco (a much-translated author):

> is always a shift, not between two languages, but between two cultures – or two encyclopaedias. A translator must take into account rules that are not strictly linguistic but, broadly speaking, cultural.   (2003: 5)

It is a highly political process, then, involving editorial powers and distillations of conversations into shorter written texts for the purposes of publication, or report writing, or therapeutic document making. These powers may be in the hands of those being represented, or shared with co-researchers, or these tasks may be undertaken by the principal or professional researcher, who subsequently consults those being represented. In many cases, although there is much discussion about ethical considerations and the representation of 'other' voices within the literatures of narrative inquiry, it remains unclear how transparent and/or collaborative the processes of selection, transcription and translation have been (see Clandinin and Connolly, 2000; Josselson, 1996b; Josselson and Lieblich 1999; Lieblich et al., 1998; Josselson et al., 2003).

The work of narrative analysts like Mishler (1986, 2000) and Riessman (1993) has been highly influential in drawing researchers' attention to the more 'storied' sections of conversations. The work of ethnographers like Ellis (1995) and Ellis and Bochner (1996), Denzin (1997) and Richardson (1993, 1997a, 2001) has also encouraged researchers to use evocation, resonance and poetic-mindedness in their selection and transcription processes, all of which seem to be criteria reminiscent of Bird's (2000) 'feeling for words' and ear for 'talk that sings' when working as a therapist.

Whatever the process of selection and whoever is involved in it, a point will be reached when the text will need to be translated into written form (although this procedure may disappear or change radically over the next few decades, as I indicate within the 'Afterwords' of this book, with the introduction of readily available digital recordings and the possibility of the single click of a button within an electronic research document leading into entire recordings of conversations).

It is this current and contemporary process of transcription, in particular into poetic forms, that I want to focus on in this chapter: a process where once again I have a strong sense of a threshold or crossover space between transcribing and writing for therapeutic and research purposes.

Poetic Representation

The poetic representation of speech is not a new idea. Poetry is an intrinsically oral tradition, whereby:

> What your eye sees on the page is the composer's verbal score, waiting for your voice to bring it alive as you read it aloud or hear it in your mind's ear. (Ferguson et al., 1996: lix)

The tradition of 'found poetry' has experienced a considerable recent revival. This is a form of poetry that has been co-constructed from words and phrases found or overheard in particular contexts.

Contemporary researchers, particularly ethnographers, are increasingly using poetic means to represent material from interviews, field notes and research conversations. Gee (1991) has described the interrelationships between poetic and conversational narratives in terms of meaning-making, rhythm, textual space and implicit intonation. This work has been used by a range of human-science researchers (notably Riessman, 1993), who have transcribed sections of spoken language into stanza form, including some transcribing therapeutic conversations or conversations concerning counselling and psychotherapy research (see Danchev, 1998; Etherington 2000, 2004; Leftwich, 1998; McLeod, 2001a; McLeod and Balamoutsou, 1996; Telling, 2004).

Laurel Richardson (1992, 1997a, 2000a, 2001) has used poetic methods to produce evocative texts from everyday conversations. Here are the words of Louisa May, transcribed by Laurel Richardson (1992: 128):

It was purely chance
that I got a job here
and Robert didn't. I was mildly happy.

After 14 years of marriage, that was the break.
We divorced.
A normal sort of life.

From Research into Therapy Practice

I have found Richardson's poetic distillations particularly moving. I was at first drawn to this style of transcription as a means of 'representing' people's voices, but I later came to consider the possibility of poetic documentation as more of a generative and transformative than a representative space and to speculate about the therapeutic value of these ways of working. Much of the thrust of this book has been towards the ways in which therapeutic practices might cross over into the research domain, but in the case of poetic transcription and document writing the crossover, certainly in terms of my own working practices, has been the other way around.

By the time I came to transcribe the texts that I had been listening to for my doctoral thesis I had many of the 'story moments' that had resonated with me powerfully ringing in my ears. The intonation, uses of silence, repetition and different dialects were all part of the texts as I 'read' them, but were hard to reproduce in accessible ways. Take this opening moment from Morag's text about finding herself working as a therapist within a university setting, 'translated' (by me, in consultation with Morag) into standard prose:

> I mean I always think there are reasons why people are at particular places. Mine is to do with unresolved stuff around my intellect and to do with having . . . Oh, I felt a censor then. Having a breakdown when I was at university and losing a sense of . . . losing my mind. And that had very kind of physical . . . it had effects on me. Like every time I started to walk into the University I sort of . . . I became very clouded. I stopped being able to read. So very powerful. I had very powerful associations with the University, and with not being able to function. I also come from a family of intellects and felt very inferior when I was growing up, and felt very stupid, and really only in perhaps the last 10–15 years have I begun to feel as if I have a brain. That I can think logically and I can make sense. I can understand things.

Gee (1991) has argued that an idealised 'poetic' transcription of speech is more akin to, and evocative of, oral language than prose. He argues (after Aristotle, 1932 edn) and alongside Mair (1989), Rimmon-Kennan (1983) and Katz and Shotter (1996), that a poetic sensibility towards language, a sensibility towards the gaps and pauses that are evocative of meaning (as used in ancient Greek poetry and drama, both originally oral traditions), is the written form most akin to spoken language. Gee advocates a poetic style of transcription of speech, in stanza form, that follows closely the pauses, silences and emphases of speech and in this way evokes richer and more accessible meanings than in the 'cleaned up' or smoothed prose of most transcriptions, wherein: 'language is used as a transparent medium, useful primarily to get to underlying content' (Riessman, 1993: 31).

This highlights a contested aspect of narrative inquiry, between those who view language, storying and/or discourse as *representative* of meaning, and those who view language, storying and/or discourse as *constitutive* of meaning (see Richardson, 2001). Re-presenting the core texts for my thesis in stanza form evoked powerful and enthusiastic responses from participants, who found this version a far thicker description than the smoothed prose versions.

I found that the stanza form also seemed closer to the voices that I had singing in my head. Here, for example, is Morag's opening moment again, this time represented in stanza form:

I mean I always think there are reasons
    why people are at particular places,
            mine is to do with
                unresolved stuff around my intellect
and
to do with having,

oh I felt a censor then,

having a breakdown when I was at university
and losing a sense of
losing my mind

and that had very kind of physical,
it had effects on me

like every time I started to walk
into the University

I sort of

I became very clouded,
I stopped being able to read,

So
very powerful,
I had very powerful associations
with the University, and with not being able to function

I also come from a family of intellects
    and felt
            very inferior when I was growing up
            and felt very stupid
and really only
in perhaps the last 10–15 years
have I begun
        to feel as if
        I have a brain.
That I can think logically and I can make sense
I can understand things.

This is not just a verbatim translation, attending to paralinguistic features. It seems to create a richer, more meaning-laden text.

Poststructuralist Feminist Contributions

I have found further creative sustenance for the extension of my own poetic writing practices within the writings of what have become known as the 'French feminists' (something of a misnomer since Kristeva is Bulgarian, Irigaray is Belgian and Cixous was born in Algeria; Cavallaro, 2003, gives brief biographies) on intertextuality and poetic/experimental language as revolution. These writers merit further study and, apart from their own works, I would recommend the introductions by Robbins (2000) and Cavallaro (2003) as well as those by Moi (1986, 1987), McAfee (2003), Oliver (1997), Irigaray and Whitford (1991) and Sellers (1994) as useful starting points.

As feminists these writers have explicitly extended Derrida's work on *differance* and Foucault's work on *discourse* in relation to gender. As a woman struggling within a language whose structures are designed by others, Irigaray (1993) finds herself and all women 'being spoken by' men. Her particular contribution to deconstruction has been to 'analyse very rigorously the forms that authorise' (1993: 172) and to challenge the so-called neutrality of certain forms of speech. She argues that those not privileged within these authorised discourses will not even be seen, and that the other languages that are multiply available, but invisible and illegible, need to be listened to 'with another ear' and represented subjectively, poetically, experimentally and tentatively.

Cixous also argues for a poetic, fluid use of language as a means of generating new ways of thinking. She has a particular interest in the ellipses between words and phrases that emerge in poetic writing, as, she contends, it is in these spaces between words, between 'binary opposites', that that which is 'left out, unthinkable and unthought of' (Cixous and Clement, 1986: 64) may emerge. She offers a critique of the binary opposites that have dominated western thought and language, frequently in poetic and experimental form, and offers her own female, Jewish subjective experience as 'a person between oppositions', as a means of occupying and writing into the spaces in between (see Cixous and Calle-Gruber, 1997: I-117). She characterises her work as a process of: 'reaching towards a place where knowing and not-knowing touch' (Cixous, 1993: 38).

Kristeva's intertextuality or deconstruction of the 'infinite possibilities of language' (1974: 2) traces the intersections of a multiplicity of competing discourses that constantly modify each other within a single word, phrase or text. In this way both the 'speaking subject' and the language being used are constantly in 'process'. She sees poetic language as a means of attending to the multiple 'complex, critical and contradictory' traces and meanings within our use of language and suggests that poetic texts are 'the most striking example of such a [multiple] practice (1987: 115). For Kristeva, poetic language is a way of writing/speaking that is distinct from the everyday, the commonplace, and the obvious. It represents a use of language that disrupts the relationship between words and that which is already known. She regards the use of poetic language, for women, as 'a matter of ethics' (in Moi, 1986: 117).

RELEVANCE TO POETIC DOCUMENT WRITING

Each of these writers has a particular focus on gender issues, but at the same time is writing into the fissures, where they appear, between privilege and oppression, between the known and seen and the unknown or unseen, and between authority and that which remains tentative and uncertain. These feminist descriptions of the spaces and opportunities in between what we know and what it may be possible to know have been of considerable assistance to me in my growing understanding of the use of poetic document making as a therapeutic endeavour.

Many of the people consulting me in therapy, both women and men, appear constrained by the limits of all that is everyday, obvious and transparent to them about their lives. They come into therapy with relatively thin descriptions of their lives and life circumstances and with very little leverage or room for life-performance space outside that which seems already possible. It would be true to say that they frequently arrive 'being spoken by' these constraints.

It seems to me that it is not only the conversations that we have that may open up richer possibilities for people's lives, but also, for many (albeit not all) of us, the poetic documents that we construct within, or as an adjunct to, these conversations. Opening up the space between us is a process actively supported by the cultivation of multiple forms of listening, listening with 'another ear', or what I would describe as 'poetic-mindedness'. It is *this* kind of listening that most consistently sustains me and those who consult me in not 'arriving' within the conversations we are engaged in, but rather in continually remaining as 'speaking subjects in process'.

Poetic Documents and the Narrative Therapies

Narrative therapists position personal agency firmly within social and political discourses. In this way the construction of preferred stories in therapeutic conversations, however fleeting or tentative, may be seen as something of an extraordinary achievement that warrants a written record in order to be more firmly captured and embraced. Documentary accounts of therapeutic conversations often follow on from the more ephemeral and transitory 'talk' that has taken place. David Epston, who first developed many of these ideas with Michael White, suggested that the use of therapeutic documents increased the impact of 'talking therapy' fourfold (see White, 1995: 199–214). Many narrative therapists send documents to clients as a supplement to face-to-face sessions, providing a permanent expression of what might have been key moments, asking supplementary questions that might be useful and, particularly with children, presenting certificates that acknowledge achievements. These documents capture words and stories from the more ephemeral, spoken, therapeutic conversations and put them into writing. Thus people can remind themselves about the ways their stories change over time and the ways in which they position themselves differently from how they might have done at the beginning of therapy (Payne, 2000: 127–57, explores this process extensively).

In all the examples above, the therapeutic documents can be seen to consolidate and to thicken stories that are only faintly held on to. Putting these traces into writing not only seizes the fleeting moments and gives them some permanency, but, given the power differential between spoken and written languages (and the higher status afforded to written text, outside of therapeutic exchanges, in modern society), it may also lend more authority to the stories being told.

I have found that the production of these documents has offered my clients and me opportunities to capture 'sparkling' images and metaphors, to loiter for longer in the open spaces that have emerged in conversations and (perhaps) to ask some of what might have been asked and say some of what might have been said. This might equally describe other kinds of therapeutic documents, such as therapy notes, letters and certificates (see White and Epston, 1990). Poetic writings, however, speak to other discourses, in British society at least, than notes, letters and certificates. Poetry is perhaps less 'official', more intimate, more succinct, and often presents a distillation of meanings that surprises and heartens people, when it emanates from the therapeutic domain. There are times when people are more supported in their lives by 'official'-looking documents and find it empowering to have reports about themselves transparent and in their own hands, not least as something of a challenge to the professional regimes of truth and authority that abound within the 'personal problems industry'; but equally, there are times when people are sustained by more subversive and creative poetic texts that represent the 'heart and soul' of their words and phrases. The receipt of poetic documents seems to echo some of the more radical traditions of 'poetry for the people' (see Jordan, 1995), to link with poetic writing as an act of resistance (see Kristeva, 1974) and to keep the words we use to represent our meanings 'under erasure'. The use of poetic documents also inspires two-way written exchanges to take place, particularly when these exchanges take place using email.

Perhaps this way of working has captured my attention because it is in these moments of receiving poetic documents, or in the experience of hearing poetic versions of their conversations read out to them, that I have *most consistently witnessed* the people consulting me stepping into a space that exoticises the domestic, the everyday, the taken for granted and the unquestioned in their lives. It is within this context that I have most regularly witnessed people positioning themselves as curious co-researchers or anthropologists, engaged in the pursuit of making 'the familiar' in their lives 'unfamiliar' (Myerhoff, 1986).

AN UNEXPECTED POETIC TURN

As with most narratives, this chapter has not given a chronological account of events, but rather, comprises a re-telling in relation to the context. Although the feminist poststructuralist ideas that I have outlined above increasingly shape my therapeutic practice, I came across them in much later, more recent excavations. The first tentative poetic documents that I produced with a client were something of a surprise to me. I stumbled into this practice by accident. At the time, I was immersed elsewhere, in my work in the transcription and distillation of the substantial number of conversations, such as those with Morag and Donald. I had become excited and moved by the poetic transcription practices that I had come across amongst contemporary ethnographers. I was influenced by Bird's (2000) descriptions of 'talk that sings', which struck a chord with my own excavations of liminal or betwixt-and-between spaces in conversations. Within narrative therapy practice, Denborough (2002) had described a similar process of finding the lyrics to co-written songs on community assignments and I was to discover later that Behan was also experimenting with co-writing what he described as 'rescued speech poems' with the people who consulted him, and found that these practices had:

> given birth to a more poetic practice with the people who consult me. These days my work is about finding the words and sharing them. (Behan, 2003)

Constructing Poetic Documents

The notes that I had been taking as I engaged in therapeutic conversations, my attempts to capture the words and phrases that caught my attention, were generally pretty messy. I had usually scribbled several circles around the expressions that really stood out, and had often joined these up to each other with squiggly lines criss-crossing the page and (in my mind's eye) navigating and peopling the landscapes of action and meaning across people's lives, histories and possible futures. One afternoon I was contemplating a sheet of scribbles, wiggles and words that seemed to capture some of the spirit of a conversation with Gregory that had really touched me. Gregory was a young man who was consulting me about the scale of his concerns for the future of the world. It occurred to me that I might send Gregory a therapeutic document in order to record our conversation, to more firmly embrace the traces of some alternative stories and to capture 'the said from the saying of it' and the 'told from the telling of it' (White, 2000: 6). Instead of writing a letter I began to connect some of the more vibrant expressions of life on the page, jotting them down in the order they had been uttered and then re-presenting them, not verbatim, but rather in 'stanza' form, making poetic use of space, rhythm and tempo. The short piece of writing that emerged was the beginning of a series of poetic exchanges with Gregory that has continued, off and on, until today. The first piece that I had co-written, using Gregory's words was:

I am apparent to
them all

I am 'suicidal'

I am willing to chat
about the suicidal state of this world,
which is very preoccupying and
concerns me, as

despair eats away at
the sides of my brains
and eats into all
aspects of my life

even asleep I dream of
rivers full of dying fish
and awake fatigue
stalks me like a hungry dog

I have loads of thoughts, snatches, glances,
moments of a more hopeful future
and I want to get some sleep,
to get some energy
to help it happen

but I need to stay
awake to keep those dogs
away

it is a lonely task, so
a team would be good

but not a team of dogs

I imagine a team of
quiet young men

unassuming geeks
taking their time
to get going

in this world.

Sending this poem off to Gregory was not a particularly radical departure from narrative therapy practice. Indeed, attention had already been
paid in the preceding session to what White (1995) describes as 'the
receiving end' of this kind of document in terms of a conversation about
feelings for poetry, about Gregory's interest in receiving such a document and about issues of privacy and safety. Nonetheless, the use of
poetic language made a striking impact. The juxtaposition of the 'suicidal state of the world' in relation to Gregory's 'willingness to chat' really
stood out for us both, as did the resilience he showed in 'staying awake
to keep those dogs at bay' and the visions he portrayed of a 'team of
quiet young men'. These vivid images certainly opened up considerable

conversational space and were the beginning of an intense poetic exchange that eventually led to the creation of an 'unassuming geeks' group that continues to meet, albeit infrequently.

This has not left me with any evaluative sense that this kind of document-making is better than others, nor with any fixed sense that this should be part of all therapeutic exchanges (Gregory had already expressed a feeling for poetry that I was responding to). It *has* left me speculating about different kinds of listening and about the value of multiply (an extension of 'doubly') listening. One of the original advocates of therapeutic documents, David Epston, spoke in a recent interview (2001) about his liking for the 'precise, the minute and the particular' and his current interest in questions of representation. It seems to me that the co-authoring of poetic documents also addresses these concerns. A poetic kind of listening may or may not lead to the co-authorship of any subsequent documents, but it does lead, in my experience, to listening for unexpected nuances and details – details that may, for instance, shift the climate of the conversation in the moment.

POETIC CONVERSATIONS AND EXCHANGES

The poetic exchange with Hyatt (shown below) started both face-to-face and on email and continued on- and offline across the globe, for over a year. The documents shown here are our first written exchanges. Hyatt is a young African-Caribbean woman, who was studying in Britain. She had a long, complicated relationship with food, her own body and 'anorexia nervosa'. At the time of our conversations she was keenly missing her two older brothers and mentors, one of whom was back home and seemed, to have disappeared, and the other of whom had died some years beforehand.

We had been engaged in what had seemed to be a particularly powerful conversation just before Hyatt left the UK. This was subsequently extended via email. The conversation explored Hyatt's relationship with the 'bones' inside the flesh that covered her body. We started with a detailed account of the feel of Hyatt's body at bonier and at not so bony times. There had been moments in the past when the flesh had been very thinly stretched across her bones. During one of these times she had been in hospital and in this context the prominence of her bones had been the cause of some concern.

In this conversation, however, Hyatt was excavating aspects of her bones that were not so much a 'danger' as a sustaining influence in her life. She spoke about the ways in which the physical feel of her bones, the sense that she could trace the shape of the bones inside her arms, legs and rib cage, was a source of comfort and safety. The feel of her bones reminded her of a shared ancestral bone structure with her much-loved brothers. Both her bones and her brothers were important to her and both were on her side when she was up against the forces that she struggled with in her day-to-day life. Hyatt's hopes and dreams included the possibility of a future when she might be able to spend more time alongside both her brothers, in different ways. Hyatt's bones had troubled the medical authorities frequently. There had been times, however, when they had seemed like life-saving bones to Hyatt since they had come to represent connections with brothers and other ancestors at times of loneliness.

The first document was:

The cruel inroads
of patriarchy
(and other animals)
into friendships, companionships
and secret alliances with much-loved brothers

brought you vividly
back in touch with that time
of being so lonely
lonely down to the whites of
your bones

yet now it seems those bones
those same authority-troubling bones
those 'alone bones'
were the very bones that kept you
safe and calm
and in touch with your ways

This led to many further email exchanges that we do not have space to include here (see Speedy, 2004a and 2004b, for a fuller account) apart from Hyatt's initial reply, which was:

Listening to our poem

Got me into remembering
Remembering those lonely old bones

They have more flesh on them now
And my women's bloods are flowing
Again

But it is those bones who know me best

I shall stay sailing close to my
Bones
Just to be on the safe side of any
Gales

The production of these documents was astonishing to Hyatt. She had particularly hated 'doing poetry' at school, which, to her, had represented the most incomprehensible of the languages of colonisation. She had previously described poetry as 'wordy, woolly and white' and yet, when her own words were represented to her in poetic form, she was inspired to contribute to these poetic exchanges. In my experience, an uncomfortable or ambivalent relationship with 'poetry' in the formal sense is quite common, and yet many of the people who consult with me seem to have stepped into similar co-authoring relationships with an unexpected ease and delight.

CO-AUTHORING POETIC DOCUMENTS

This way of working has clearly made a significant impact on Gregory, Hyatt and many other people who have consulted me about their lives. Like any of the practices that more permanently record people's stories, such as video recordings, re-tellings from witnesses or letter-writing, the construction of poetic documents is not universally applicable. As with all therapeutic documents, poetic writings will stay on a dusty doormat in some distant hallway if the 'receiving end' of these exchanges has been left to chance (see White, 1995). Written documents may, for instance, be better exchanged in the next face-to-face session than arriving in inappropriate contexts of people's lives. Given the power relations evident in therapeutic and research relationships, clients engaging in therapy and/or participants in research projects may well respond positively to the suggestion of poetic forms of writing out of politeness or other versions of deferring to the 'normalising therapeutic gaze'. Nonetheless, some people clearly do not respond to poetic documents, or indeed, to any writing forms, with any interest at all. The space available for and usefulness of poetic writing needs to be extensively and sensitively explored with people, including, for instance, their relationships with literacy, or with song lyrics, their feelings for imagery or the use of 'unusual' words and their sense of connexion with these kinds of expressions of life. Sometimes, as with Hyatt, people surprise themselves. For others this is evidently not a useful way of working, whereas the use of visual imagery or movement might be.

I have used the words 'co-writing' and 'co-authoring' intermittently throughout this text, terms which speak to the heart of this co-research process. There are times when it has worked well for people to review the notes that have been taken and for us to create a poetic document together, during our conversation. There have also been times when people have gone away with their copy of these notes and composed a poetic document out of the words I have captured and/or others of their own, and sometimes have posted or emailed these documents back to me.

For the most part I have produced the document after the session. The manner of representation might vary. Gregory's document quoted above, for instance, was written in the first person: his words, as if in his voice. Hyatt had just travelled to the other side of the world, and the document was written to her as if I was in conversation with her, reminding her of what she had said (which I was). In both instances, however, Hyatt or Gregory had generated all the notes taken and the words and phrases used.

This is not a 'hard and fast rule'. There are times when it might be entirely in keeping with the spirit of this work to consider, tentatively, what *might* have been said or asked, or even to acknowledge resonances, traces and rememberings from my own life, as long as the context of these words is made transparent and is clearly differentiated from the other people's words.

I have conducted workshops with both trainee and experienced practitioners on 'using poetic documents', throughout the United Kingdom as well as in Australia and Mexico (2001–6). I continue to compile an archive of practitioners' and researchers' commentaries and communications about this work.

What I have noticed, however, from my extensive experience of running therapy practitioner workshops exploring these ideas, both nationally and internationally, is that the power of this work evaporates in the instant that other words or phrases seep in, as if 'from out of the blue', to the documents produced. The moment that the document writer (often unwittingly) moves from their position as co-researcher to that of 'paraphraser' the process is transformed and reflections about this way of working change from descriptions of 'unexpectedly powerful' and 'moving and honouring' experiences to comments on 'somewhat jarring and disconcerting feelings' and being left with 'a sense of disappointment'. If nothing else, the practice of co-writing poetic documents does much to draw practitioners' and researchers' attention towards their habitual listening and note-taking practices.

Whilst not offering a 'blueprint' for such practices, I would like to offer some suggestions and safeguards that have worked well for the people consulting me, and have begun to re-shape the therapeutic and co-research conversations that I am engaged in. These are:

- Taking notes from the language of the people who consult us and/or our research participants, not our own words.
- Capturing words and phrases that are unforeseen, evocative and resonant, that link lives and that attend to 'particularities' rather than generalities.
- Attending especially carefully to 'talk' that seems hard come by, or that emerges out of moments of silence or reverie.
- Including 'talk' from all sorts of times and places – past and future times as well as the present, places of struggle, and difficulty and humour, as well as sparkling and joyful or more hopeful moments, but above all, evoking 'talk that sings': talk that surprises people, comes unexpectedly to their lips, shifts and/or exoticises their experiences of life's possibilities.
- Taking care to differentiate between poetic accounts co-authored from talk in conversations, and poetic rememberings and other retrospective exchanges and speculations on the part of researchers and therapists.

Future Directions

I am increasingly persuaded that attention to the 'poetics of the every-day', in the conversations that I have, is a fruitful means of describing and navigating the landscapes of our identities and actions. White (2003) talks of a form of double listening, listening not only to that which is said, but also to that which is absent but implicit in conversations. I am convinced that in attending to poetic language we are attending very particularly to 'alternative' metaphors, and that these represent Kristeva's (1987) 'intertextual intersections' and possible points of entry to more fluid and multi-storied accounts.

The co-authoring of poetic documents is a relatively new aspect of my therapeutic work that represents an interesting crossover from my work as a researcher. I am encouraged to explore these territories further through my discussions with Behan (2003) and through the interest in these practices that has been generated in workshops across a broad spectrum of therapists and researchers. I am currently interested in moments of stillness and 'poetic reverie' in conversations, and in pondering, alongside the people who consult with me, about the relationship between reverie and the spaces in between the said, the 'as yet unsaid' and the 'as yet unsayable'. I am also interested in excavating the particular properties of listening or co-researching, with literary intentions (whether or not 'poetic' documents are eventually produced). Conversations that explicitly contain the possibility of poetic writings seem qualitatively different from other kinds of therapeutic conversations. The notes taken, questions asked and spaces entered all appear to be shaped, to some extent, by these possibilities. I would suggest that this warrants further and closer examination.

I have no way of knowing what the outcome of these investigations will be. This co-research project, alongside other therapists, researchers and the people who consult them, is still in its infancy. These reflections on 'work in progress' are offered in a spirit of tentative and curious inquiry and as an invitation to others to enter this conversation. I have found that the co-authoring of poetic documents has brought different dimensions of spaciousness, playfulness and hopefulness into this work. It has extended my listening practices and has taken me, and the people who consult with me, into some unexpected places. In positioning ourselves *as if at a poetry recital* we seem to regard ourselves more consistently and creatively as poststructuralist co-researchers. Opportunities to exoticise that which we took for granted or considered mundane seem to emerge with greater frequency, as do excavations of the extraordinary from the 'poetry of the everyday', through: 'listening to the still unspoken words of the other' (Irigaray: 2004, p. xiv).

TROUBLE AT THE THERAPY/RESEARCH BORDERS

There has been blurring, in this chapter, of the boundaries between therapy and research. Indeed, co-research and co-researcher have been used interchangeably with therapy, therapist and client. This is something of an open invitation towards trouble. If it doesn't invoke trouble with the gods and goddesses of social science research, it may stir up trouble among the gatekeepers of professional therapeutic endeavour.

This is not an invitation to trouble for trouble's sake, however, but more of an invitation to question the guardians of borders that I have found myself constantly crossing over during the last few years without either a passport or visa. I find myself leaning constantly on the fences between therapy and research and seeking out the spaces where they give way and the other patches of ground where they hold firm. This is surely the kind of trouble that all therapists and psychotherapy researchers should be getting themselves into?

Further reading

Transcription
Gee, J. (1991) 'A Linguistic Approach to Narrative'. In: *Journal of Narrative and Life History*, I: 15–39.
(An important paper making the linguistic case for poetic transcriptions of speech.)

Lapadat, J. and Lindsay, A. (1999) 'Transcription in Research and Practice: from Standardisation of Technique to Interpretive Positionings'. In: *Qualitative Inquiry*, 5(1): 64–87.
(This is a great overview that explores the changing position of transcription processes for qualitative researchers.)

Poetic documents
Behan, C. (2003) *Rescued Speech Poems: Co-Authoring Poetry in Narrative Therapy* (http://narrativeapproaches.com)
(A very clear account of the work of another narrative practitioner who uses poetic documents in his work.)

Oswald, A. (2002) *Dart* (London: Faber & Faber).
(A long found poem that plays on the boundaries of overheard conversations and poetry.)

Richardson, L. (2001) 'Poetic Representation of Interviews', in Gubrium, J. and Holstein, J. (eds), *Handbook of Interview Research* (Thousand Oaks, CA: Sage).
(This chapter is a detailed and thorough argument for poetic representation. It includes the entire Louisa May text, cited above.)

6

Re-telling Stories in Reflecting Teams

Definitional ceremonies deal with the problems of invisibility and marginality; they are strategies that provide opportunities for being seen in one's own terms, garnering witness to one's worth, vitality and being.

(Myerhoff, 1986: 267)

In this chapter I want to illustrate some of the ways in which definitional ceremonies (a process of authoring 'defining' aspects of our life stories in the context of a reflecting team or audience of witnesses) can be 'borrowed' from the therapeutic domain and used by a variety of collaborative researchers. These practices have much to offer the wider world of research and can do much to usefully muddy the waters between so-called 'research' and so-called 'therapy' practices. I hope to illustrate some of the ways in which outsider witness practices and definitional ceremonies might contribute to collaborative research processes that sit congruently with collaborative feminist, postcolonial and other narrative research into the ways that people live their lives. I also hope to highlight outsider witness practices and definitional ceremonies, as valuable research tools that are easily accessible to both narrative practitioners and the people consulting them. I hope they might use these as a way of interrogating their own work, rather than turning to more traditional research models in their attempts to influence policy makers and shape future services.

Re-visioning Reflecting Teamwork

Reflecting teamwork as a 'not-knowing approach' (Anderson and Goolishan, 1992) has been available to family therapists for some years (see Andersen, 1987; Friedman, 1995) and has also been suggested as a framework for collaborative research by academics engaged in excavations of generative collaborative research methods (Gergen, 2003, for instance). Using the metaphor of the definitional ceremony, White (1995, 1997a, 2000) has developed these ideas to take a radical account of the power relations that abound within therapeutic conversations between 'professionals' and 'clients'. The family and narrative therapies alike present quite a challenge to therapeutic practices that focus primarily on individuals, their lives and potentials (see White, 2001, for a discussion of these differences). It positions personal agency firmly within social and political discourses and the cultural and historical traditions and 'local' stories that are available to people. In this way the construction and embracing of 'alternative' or preferred stories in therapeutic and other conversations, however fleeting or tentative, may be seen as something of an extraordinary achievement that warrants a witnessed acknowledgement or ceremony in order to be more firmly captured.

Definitional Ceremony

The term 'definitional ceremony' was coined by Myerhoff (1980, 1982, 1986) to describe the ways in which people (in particular the elderly Jewish population of Venice Beach, California) generated visible identities by creating opportunities for the witnessing of their life's events and defining moments. Myerhoff also came up with the idea of re-membering. That is to say, both accessing memories and introducing new 'members' to the team available to witness and sustain the performance of lives.

> When cultures are fragmented and in serious disarray, proper audiences may be hard to find. Natural occasions may not be offered and then they must be artificially invented. I have called such performances 'definitional ceremonies'. (Myerhoff, 1982: 105)

Michael White (1995, 1997a, 1999) and subsequently other narrative practitioners (Andrews 2001; Behan, 2002; Carey, 1999; Russell and Carey, 2004b; Speedy 2000a, 2000c; Trana et al., 1999) have used these ideas to create opportunities for the witnessing and re-telling of stories and re-membering of lives in therapeutic, workplace and community settings. Counselling and psychotherapy practitioner researchers, borrowing from Behan's (2002) work in particular, have begun to use these practices to engage in research with groups of people around shared themes and concerns (see Adair, 2003; Dale, 2005; Midwinter, 2004; Speedy, 2003a).

Re-tellings within definitional ceremonies offer the opportunity to engage with others in not only richly describing, but also re-shaping life stories. Outsider witnesses are then invited to listen carefully to and re-tell the stories they have heard. In particular, they are invited to notice what struck a chord for them and what expressions and images from the story resonated with events or images within their own life. The reflections from witnesses are followed by re-retellings from the original narrator, followed by a more informal discussion of the whole process by all concerned. It is anticipated that this process will have thickened their original descriptions and/or perhaps will have taken the participants to places that they had not anticipated journeying towards. To quote Pinkola Estes again (1993: 1), 'one story leads to another, each re-telling offering a broader and deeper insight than a single story alone'.

OUTSIDER WITNESS PRACTICES

During outsider witness re-tellings people are not asked to evaluate the stories they have heard or people they have heard from (in terms of either applause and praise or any other judgement calls), but rather to identify the expressions that had most resonated with them; perhaps to describe the images that these expressions evoked, to recall stories from their own lives that these images brought to mind and possibly to articulate the ways in which the experience had somehow extended their ideas. This sense of the ceremony touching the lives of the witnesses (as well as the person at the centre) is described by White (1999: 73) as evoking:

> Turner's (1969) 'communitas' – that unique sense of being present to each other in entering liminal circumstances, betwixt and between known worlds.

The re-telling of stories without judgement by the witnesses can seem quite counter-cultural to contemporary tendencies, certainly in western societies, which are to critique or praise the teller, rather than re-tell the stories evoked. Careful preparation and support of the witnesses is required. Well-managed ceremonies (see White, 2005a, for useful guidelines) are nonetheless frequently experienced as creative and defining moments in people's lives, evoking comments such as: 'I had no idea my life could mean so much to other people,' 'I had no idea what I had to say could be so useful to others' (Russell and Carey, 2004b: 85) and 'I realised it was not to do with whether my story was true or not, or even to do with whether other people believed me: having it witnessed and knowing it made a difference to other people was what counted' (Midwinter et al., 2005).

Positioning Therapy Outcomes Research Differently

In the UK and the North Americas, at least, there is a rich and increasing variety of creatively written 'psychotherapy process research' studies and psychotherapy history and context studies. These multi-storied texts describe the experiences both of therapists and the people who consult them, and of the cultural contexts of therapy. Psychotherapy outcomes research, however (that is to say, the kind of research that governments, health authorities and medical insurance companies tend to refer to when deciding which kinds of 'treatment' to sanction and which kinds to remain sceptical about), has been dominated by 'quantitative' (statistically-based) research studies, occasionally supplemented by traditional thematically arranged qualitative (language-based) studies (see Roth and Fonagy, 1996; Rowlands and Goss, 2000, for overviews, and McLeod, 2001a: 161–80, for a critique). As McLeod points out, Bergin and Garfield's (1994) definitive and influential guide to work in this arena contains:

> 39 references to the word power. Most of these entries refer to the topic of statistical power . . . there are also some references to the interpersonal power of therapists . . . Nowhere in the book does there appear to be any consideration of the question of political power. (McLeod, 2001a: 162)

A number of the research studies that are becoming available within the narrative and related therapies, seem to have been conducted by practitioner and/or university researchers within a traditional, often large-scale model, using q-sorts, client questionnaires, and presenting themed 'smoothed' texts (see, for instance, Wallis, 2003; Tsun On-Kee, 2003). Indeed, some researchers have put forward the argument that these ways of researching are more appropriate if we want to influence social policy, since: 'People like stories, but governments want statistics' (Waldegrave, 2001).

I would not want to start 'othering' particular research stories or technologies, nor to argue against the political value of 'situated' statistics, such as, for example, those that shed light on the 'growing numbers of Pacific island clients being treated within the mental health area' (Tamasase, 2003: 195). I would want to question an assumption that policy makers are not also influenced by 'stories'. Policy makers are often credited with being solely interested in 'quantities': in whether it works, for whom and for how long, although, in the European Union, at least, the people who make policy also seem interested in funding research that 'sees things that would not otherwise have been seen and thinks about problems in ways that provide nuances and challenges to what is taken for granted' (Popkewitz, 2004: 74). There is certainly a history of powerful documentary films and fictionalised accounts influencing both public and political opinion in the UK. The impact of Dickens's novels, such as *David Copperfield* (1837–8), *Nicholas Nickelby* (1838–9) and *Oliver Twist* (1849–50), on child welfare, criminal justice and educational legislation is well documented, and a century later a series of televised docu-dramas in the 1960s, including *Cathy Come Home* (Loach, 1966) and *Edna: The Inebriate Woman* (Sandford, 1971), had a similar policy-shifting impact on British attitudes towards homelessness.

Having talked right up to the dizzy heights of Dickens's novels, I need to quickly back down to make more diffident claims for this chapter, which represents an incomplete account of the telling and re-telling of one woman's story of some of the outcomes of her experiences in narrative therapy. One of the hopes that Gina (see below) and I had for publishing an example of definitional ceremony as collaborative research in this chapter was to contribute to a different, more collaborative version of psychotherapy outcomes research. We hoped to demonstrate how one account of the outcomes of narrative therapy might be presented, and to encourage others to use the co-research practices of narrative therapy to produce their own accounts and to contribute to what might become a multi-storied, internationally available, archive.

David Epston's oft-quoted informal research (cited in White, 1995: 199–214), which suggested that the production of a therapeutic document was the equivalent of four therapy sessions, has had quite an impact on the working practices of certain therapy agencies. The accumulated stories of narrative therapy outcomes on people's lives might have a similar impact on service provision.

Many narrative therapists (see Drewery and Winslade, 1997) have also located their work within the traditions of poststructuralist inquiry and its attention to discourse and power relations. Unsurprisingly, considering it is emerging within the same moment in history, much new co-research practice outside the therapeutic domain has also been enriched by these ideas. The work of feminist researchers like Lather and Smithies (1997), excavating unheard and unhearable voices and conducting nomadic (St Pierre, 1997) and 'rhizomatic' research, seems very closely allied to some of the double listening practices and opening of conversational spaces advocated by narrative therapists and utilised in definitional ceremonies. Lather (1991) and subsequently other feminist researchers, after Deleuze and Guattari (1987), have put forward the rhizome as a research metaphor and encouraged studies that disappear under the surface and then burst up in unexpected, yet connected, ways to 'frame narratives that work against the terrain of controllable knowledge' (Lather, 2000: 221).

So how might these multi-storied, explicitly multiply-authored accounts of people's lives emerging from 'definitional ceremony' contribute to the wider body of life story research and, more specifically, research about the uses of the narrative therapies themselves? The second half of this chapter, wherein one woman's experience of narrative therapy outcomes is described to outsider witnesses, represents a small contribution to this domain.

Co-researching with Gina, and Others

This project developed from a chance meeting between Gina and myself in the centre of Bristol (the city in the South-West of England in which we both live and work). Gina is an experienced 'client', herself a counsellor, well versed in a range of therapeutic practices. She had consulted me some time ago about various concerns in her life. When we met, she started talking about how different her experience of this work had been from previous therapeutic encounters and about how much she had been noticing and thinking about these differences. After some discussion we agreed that I would interview Gina about these different outcomes and aftermaths and that we would invite an outsider witness group to join us.

The 'definitional ceremony' that we propose to write about lasted quite some time, so the re-presentation here can only provide a small glimpse into these events. These included a conversation with Gina, reflections from outsider witnesses, further reflections from Gina, some subsequent de-briefing, and further research and writing exchanges. The ideas and practices of definitional ceremony have been reviewed extensively elsewhere in the literatures of narrative therapy, which I can only touch on here. In engaging with each other and myself in re-tellings of what they experienced and what struck a chord for them in Gina's stories, the outsider witnesses contributed to richer and perhaps unexpected descriptions. In many ways this 'unexpectedness' also speaks to the 'rhizomatic' research practices described earlier: alternative re-tellings as a means of alternative narratives, connected under the surface and re-appearing in unexpected ways elsewhere.

Further re-tellings, in the shape of this chapter, have been written, in the main, by Jane Speedy, but have gone backwards and forwards across the email between Jane and Gina many times during the last few months, and more recently backwards and forwards between Jane and Gina and the outsider witnesses (Barry, Gina's partner and Sue, Gina's friend and colleague). The original re-telling in written form was undertaken by Jane, transcribing sections of the conversation from video-taped recordings (already an editing and therefore re-telling process). This re-telling would have been different had it been undertaken collaboratively, but Gina and Jane had different amounts of time available to engage with this study. This made a difference to the nature of the collaboration. Subsequently, in the re-editing and re-telling that has gone backwards and forwards, there has been a process of 're-engaging with the history of the present' as the text has moved backwards and forwards across from Gina to Jane.

Jane and Gina have had some discussions about whether to place these conversations within the context of the concerns in Gina's life that had initially brought her to therapy. In the first draft of this chapter, Jane added quite a lot of information about issues that had been troubling Gina, off and on, for much of her life. Gina argued that this came from Jane's 'professional' archive, not Gina's outcomes stories. In the end we took all of this out. Gina did have quite a number of things troubling her in the past and these same issues might well crop up again in her life, but we are not concerned with that here. We are more concerned with what happened next (and with whom) in Gina's life.

Email editing exchanges with the two outsider witnesses did not make such a difference to this text, although, since we have decided to opt for pseudonyms rather than given names, much careful thought and a considerable amount of humour has gone into the naming of all the participants. This took some time and was an interesting subplot in itself.

Here is the short story that we have come up with. You will notice flaws and particularities in the description (above) of the way this writing was constructed; indeed, if we were to construct this text again from the same 'raw data' it would almost certainly be different.

* * *

Jane: *So where would be a good place to start?*

Gina: Well, we started in Park Street really. In a way I hadn't thought of it, but bumping into you made me realise how different that experience had been, and not just for me, for everyone really.

Jane: *Would you be interested in talking about those differences?*

Gina: Yes, very. I mean I'm not saying better or worse, but very different. I suppose one thing's a bit odd, which is that it doesn't seem much like 'therapy' really, or at least, you're not exactly . . . like a 'proper' therapist. Is that all right to say? You won't get struck off or anything?

Jane: *Mmm . . . 'the gods of therapy' might try striking me down I suppose, but this building's got a lightning conductor, so I think we're safe. I'm not too comfortable with the claim of 'therapist' anyway these days. I think 'practitioner' might be my preferred description. So this time we spent together, quite a while on and off, that was 'not at all like therapy': do you have any kind of sense of what it was like? Is there another way of describing what we were engaged in that might fit better for you?*

Gina: I'm not sure what you mean.

Jane: *Well I was just interested, if it wasn't like therapy and I wasn't like a proper therapist, was there anything else that it was a bit like, or anything else that our conversations reminded you of then, or any other kind of image that perhaps springs to mind now, looking back . . .?*

Gina: Detectives!! It was more like I had hired myself a private detective. No that's not quite right. It was more like we were detectives together in the CID, on the trail, looking for clues, partners on the trail. I don't mean Sherlock Holmes and Doctor Watson, nothing quaint, more like 'The Bill' [a BBC police series]. So that's the image, quite fast moving, not messing about, both researching issues in my life. I had the 'local archive' as you put it, but you had more questions, no, more practice at asking interesting questions, and the archives of other people's experience to draw on, even other people to email or bring along. I guess that's another thing, it wasn't very hush hush. I mean, not only did I tell quite a lot of people about our conversations, there were a hell of a lot more people in them and that made a difference, no locked doors. Actually I had fewer conversations with you than I expected, but many more with other people like Barry and Sue and my mum of ALL PEOPLE. And that was a very different way around from sorting it all out with your therapist and then trying it out in real life later.

Jane: And do you have some ideas about what those conversations with Barry and Sue and your mum and others contributed to their lives, what difference it made to them and to their lives to be in those conversations?

Gina: I was thinking more of what they had to offer me actually

Jane: Well yes, I'd be really interested in exploring that too, in a moment, but I was also just wondering what this 'way round' of having many more conversations with people like Barry and Sue, do you think that might have contributed towards a different account of those relationships at all? It might not have; of course, I might be way off beam here . . .

Gina: I think more people, particularly my mum who'd always felt I was cross with her about stuff (which I was), to have her in that time as a witness. I think it blew her socks off really. We communicate differently now. Not all the time, we can still go for weeks and months talking about the weather, but I think this all contributed to having conversations with each other that we never expected to have. Conversations about my father, about me and Barry and I think that that is a contribution to her life. For Barry and Sue though, I think I was a bit 'full on' and it was more 'what did they contribute to my well being' . . .

*   *   *

This conversation continued with explorations of the ways in which Gina's life was more 'peopled', or at least the ways in which the connections with and commitments towards some of the key people on her team (particularly Barry and her mother) had shifted. We had had a conversation, some months previously, about my 'critical and hopeful' outlook on the world and the ways in which narrative therapy practices fitted with this position. Gina had always understood a critical outlook to be rather negative and nihilistic. My version placed a critique of the way things often were in the world alongside hopes for future possibilities within all sorts of life's domains. This conversation had stayed with Gina in relation to her mother in particular and had supported her in re-aligning her relationship with guilt in respect of her critical thoughts about her mother. This had all taken place some time after Gina's therapy had ended, in what she described as the slow 'drip drip drip' way that ideas that lingered in your mind gradually informed actions you took in your life.

It began to occur to me that this idea of 'criticalness' linking with 'hopefulness' had been at the heart of all our conversations (yours and mine, I mean) and it could really help out with mum and me. . . .

If we both got to a place where we were more critical of past muddles then we might both be hopeful about what happens now. We'll see. I'm not sure if this was entirely the result of our conversations, but then, I'm not sure if anything is.

But it was certainly somewhat connected with those ideas we talked about and it is 'in the spirit' of our time together, I think.

KNOWLEDGE OF THE PRACTICE

We also talked about the ways in which I would 'show my workings out' during the course of our exchanges by routinely discussing what I might ask and why, and also, on occasions, by emailing my online narrative practice group for suggestions when Gina and I were not sure where to go with things. All this had given Gina access to some of the ideas and many of the practices of working in narrative ways. She was pretty interested in all this and also in reading some of the books and journals exploring narrative practice. Gina was not at all comfortable with the expression 'externalising' but she did like the idea of interrogating issues about the ways that they were 'dogging her life'. She was especially struck by 'remembering' conversations as she had continued to have these with herself, by herself at home, and to write letters and journals keeping accounts of these exchanges. She appreciated my transparency about some of the practices of narrative therapy, although she found my love of 'postmodern hyphens' quite irritating and did not hesitate to remind me of a question that I had asked (and had had trouble letting go of) to do with 'dis-ease and dis-comfort' that had ended in absolute 'dis-aster'.

THE WITNESSES

Barry and Sue were subsequently interviewed as 'outsider witnesses' to Gina's stories and invited to recall expressions from Gina's life that struck a chord with them in some way and/or took them to unexpected places. Sue was most struck by the ways in which this kind of conversation had probably influenced Gina at work. She was interested in the kinds of questions Gina often seemed to ask people who had 'got themselves in a pickle' at work. Sue recalled a time when she had been stuck with a report and Gina had sat down and talked to her about other times when she had been in a jam with something and the kinds of resources and supporters that she had called on. Sue had ended up phoning old friends and behaving in quite unexpected ways in relation to her 'pickle'. Sue never knew what to expect from Gina.

Brian recalled that Gina had considerable expertise with regard to her own struggles and that this hadn't always served her well. 'Something of a stroppy cow' in the eyes of the mental health system, was Brian's expression. He was struck by Gina's image of the two detectives and the images of the 'maps and clues' that the detectives had pieced together. This particularly appealed to him as an ex-policeman, whose previous work experience had taught him that police work was most effectively undertaken by interdisciplinary teams. These images reminded him that Gina's considerable wisdom about her own life was legitimate and that this included an encyclopaedic knowledge of anti-depressant medications, tranquillisers, and their side effects, which he had not yet mentioned.

He was particularly touched by the way that she described her world as a 'more peopled place to live'. He now considered himself to be 'on the cast list' of those who also had some know-how about Gina and had a part to play in sustaining her at times of trouble in her life. This was different from previous times because he had had the distinct impression that he had been discouraged from even asking her about her therapy sessions before, let alone being invited along to take part in some of them. He said:

> I knew it had to be private and confidential and so on, but it also seemed quite exclusive, not only that I was shut out, but also that

I couldn't be part of it, that Gina had to do it all by herself all the time, in secret, with an 'expert'. We've been through quite a lot of experts in our time and I've had my doubts about a fair few of them, including you. I suppose I began to be heartened by the emails you sent. Some of them had her roaring with laughter . . . and I remember thinking . . . well, at least this one's got a sense of humour . . .

But the main difference for me has been that I wasn't shut out. In a way, I've always preferred the 'pill pushers' before, because they've often included me and other people in the family in discussions, maybe too much sometimes, but the 'talking cure types' on the other hand, that was all 'private, no entry, she's on her own with this'. I've never felt comfortable with that . . . its not that I'M NOSY . . . WELL I am actually (laughter) . . . its that I want to be part of the cure not just the problem.

This conversation left Barry pondering on the difference it made to him, being 'on the cast list'.

THE RE-TELLING OF THE RE-TELLING

Gina and I had a further conversation, reflecting on the contributions from Sue and Barry. Several of their expressions had made quite an impact on Gina. She had a sense that nowadays she had shifted the way she told herself and others about the issues that had concerned her throughout her adult life. This included talking at work in much more open ways. It was also a shift away from a search for the 'cure' and 'getting better'. It was a move towards living within a different 'spectrum of mental states' from those of most people and having a team of people to sustain that. It had only just come to her attention, in this conversation, that Barry had felt excluded from some of the other kinds of therapy that she had engaged with. This was important news as she had previously seen all her concerns as burdensome to others. She was also reminded of my lack of interest in making a fuss about her medication. Gina (who continues to take a range of medications) had developed a very clear idea of the ways that certain balances of medication worked for her and had been all set to 'do battle' with me over medication.

* * *

Gina: That's been my experience over the years, of the wars between the 'pill pushers' as Barry called them and the 'talking therapists'. The pill pushers are very matter of fact: 'take this dear, you'll feel better', sort of thing, which is true, I usually do . . . but then as soon as I get the dose right and feel better, I'm curious about why I felt like shit in the first place . . . it's that detective streak again . . . and I kind of want to know why.

. . . And so I'm on to the next talking cure . . . and they are generally dead set against medication, the talking ones . . . as if somehow, taking medication is for the 'duds' who don't have enough brains to figure it all out . . . that if I did enough proper 'IN DEPTH' talking and got to the bottom of things, then I'd be off medication for good. So I was a bit taken aback . . .

Jane: So you were expecting a different response, is that right, and then you were taken aback . . . where were you taken back to do you know?

Gina: Well yes, I just laid my cards on the table and made my position clear and all you did was check you'd got the right end of the stick and then ask me if I was interested in talking more about that or about something else, well 'SOMETHING ELSE' was the answer to that, and we've never even discussed it since, just in passing. So, well, I haven't thought about it for a while, but it was discombobulating, as if you just left all that to me because I was in charge of it, which is true. I bet I could train medical students about all this. What did you ask, where was I taken back to? Well just managing all that for myself, thank you very much and then you and I could explore what I was interested in, stuff I wasn't already a world expert in!

Jane: Anything else that caught your attention?

Gina: Well to continue the co-detectives theme. One difference is that I do have quite a lot of know-how about what we've been up to and despite being fairly widely-read across the 'inner state psychologies' as you would call them, I feel that some of this is more in my grasp as the client and that makes it more available to my colleagues and my family and so on. I mean, that story of Sue getting stuck, I remember sitting in her office and we had a conversation about the history of it all and investigated things . . . it was what you and I had been doing and it was within my grasp to explain that, talk about it with reference to 'my therapy' in just a very ordinary way.

Jane: *Anything else?*

Gina: Interestingly I've had all sorts of wobbles and things happening in life, how they do, in the subsequent months, well, well over a year. I'm still taking the tablets . . . different combination, but that's still part of life, but I haven't been back to a counsellor or to a therapist or anything. There's one at the Doctor's surgery now, but I haven't been, couldn't see the point.

I'm not saying I won't want to, won't get curious again. I'm sure I might find it helpful again. I'm absolutely not suggesting I've found the holy grail here or anything, but for the moment, I'm feeling connected with the people in my life and we're all much more part of this together than we used to be. Quite a cast list, to quote Barry, and with quite a lot of know-how.

*   *   *

RE-SEARCHING THIS CONVERSATION

Our time for reflecting on this conversation was very brief at the time as we had run over schedule, but Barry, Gina and I did meet a week or so later at their house to look at the videotape again and reflect a little more on this conversation, positioning ourselves very much as researchers and/or 'outcomes detectives'. I wrote this chapter on our behalf after this 're-research conversation' and consequently, although the descriptions above give the illusion of a linear appearance, they are, in fact, not particularly 'chronological'. Much of the description has been thickened by our subsequent reflections. That which is quoted is 'verbatim' and is in temporal sequence, but the nuances and selection processes that took place in re-tellings in our reflections and also in the re-tellings in our subsequent writings and re-writings have shaped much of the final outcome. This is not to suggest that we diverged from our commitments to verisimilitude, but rather to give voice to some of the complexities or 'storytelling technologies' of re-presentation, in which, 'there are always more things going on than you thought' (see Harraway, 2004: 232).

Much of what caught our attention this time around was to do with the kinds of questions that I asked and the frequency with which I asked them. My most frequent response was to ask 'What else?' or 'Anything else?' It was also apparent that I had asked the witnesses quite a lot of questions in relation to the guidelines that I had given them (see White,

2005a, 'outsider witness responses'). Barry felt that this kept things 'on track' and that it certainly maintained the ceremony as a 'storytelling technology' and a re-telling, rather than an opportunity to 'go off on one'.

It seemed that we had given Gina's experiences of narrative practice 'quite an airing' and that she was left feeling that she had more ways of sustaining herself, as someone living 'with a wider spectrum of mental states than most people', that were part of her 'real life', than she had had before. She had found this way of working and the sorts of questions that I had asked 'discombobulating', and quite transparent and 'easy to get a grasp of' at the same time. In terms of being a 'terrible expense to the British taxpayer' she was continuing to 'pop pills', but had had the 'longest time for many years' off the books of the 'talking therapists'. For the time being, at least, she was engaging in her own 'detective work', together with some of the other people on the 'cast list'.

None of these outcomes can be attributed directly and solely to narrative practice. Other interviewers might have asked different questions, or used less irritating hyphenated jargon, or found fewer things funny. At a different time in her life, Gina might not have been interested in 'engaging in her own detective work' in quite the same way, and Barry and Sue might have been less enthusiastic about their membership of the cast list. Similar 'outcomes' might equally have come about through other kinds of conversations. These are, nonetheless, the kinds of outcomes from our conversations that we attributed, to some extent at least, to the narrative practices of critical hopefulness, the storytelling ceremonies and technologies and the collaborative detective work that we have tried to describe here. This is not an exhaustive description of narrative therapy practice, or its 'outcomes'. This is an incomplete version of one experience of working in these ways in a particular context.

It is also an attempt to illustrate the ways that definitional ceremonies might be described and used as a form of collaborative research (not just with regard to researching narrative therapy practice, but across a range of human situations and contexts (see Russell and Carey, 2004a; Speedy, 2003a). In particular, this was a very different process from versions of research where therapeutic encounters are 'written up' by professionals. I was privileged as the professional and principal writer and as a researcher and therapist, yet the impetus for this chapter came from Gina, who remained at its heart. In our collaborative writing and putting together of this chapter as co-researchers (or detectives), Sue,

Barry, Gina and I were all members of a community of practice with different degrees of participation and different relationships with time, computer technology and different purposes.

So, What are our Outcomes?

This is one local story, put together by a therapist, one of the people consulting her and some of the witnesses from that person's 'cast list' of supporters. It is an exploration about the outcomes and aftermaths and ongoing reverberations she experienced. These research conversations took place well over a year after the initial therapeutic conversations. They blurred the edges between 'research' and 'therapy' practice partly through positioning narrative therapy practices (or do I mean co-research?) as research methods and partly because all the participants described this opportunity to re-connect with their experiences of narrative practice, reflect upon them and write about them, as therapeutic. To quote Gina:

> I have found it quite restorative of my hopes really, really quite a therapy of itself, 'doing research' and writing this paper. We found we all had quite a lot to say. I knew a lot more about all this than I thought. A lot of it has stayed in my heart.

This would be enough of an outcome for us in some ways, but we have still higher hopes and dreams for this project: if readers of this chapter who considered themselves co-researchers within a narrative therapy project, were to make one small, local and particular written contribution around this theme, we would produce an extensive (cumulative rather than conclusive) narrative-practice outcomes archive, which could be added to over time. This would not provide us with a definitive text about the outcomes of narrative therapy practice, for whom it works or for how long, but it might offer us some diverse and thick descriptions of the outcomes, aftermaths and reverberations of these experiences in the lives of different people at different times across different continents. This would be intriguing for us all, of course, but it might also provide policy makers with opportunities to (Popkewitz, 2004) 'see things that might otherwise not have been seen'.

Further reading

Definitional ceremony

Myerhoff, B. (1986) 'Life Not Death in Venice', in: V. Turner and E. Bruner (eds), *The Anthropology of Experience* (Champaign, Illinois: University of Illinois Press).
(A tautly written account by the originator of this expression.)

White, M. (2000) 'Reflecting Team Work as Definitional Ceremony Re-visited', in *Reflections on Narrative Practice: Essays and Interviews* (Adelaide: Dulwich Centre Publications).
(Michael White's radical take on the introduction of these ideas into therapeutic conversations.)

White, M. (2005b) workshop notes on: www.dulwichcentre.com.au
(Guidelines for outsider witness responses.)

Contemporary examples of outsider witness practices

Andrews, J. (2001) 'The Elder Project: Witnessing Lives', in *Working with the Stories of Women's Lives* (Adelaide: Dulwich Centre Publications).
(Re-engaging with isolated older women.)

Behan, C. (2002) 'Linking Lives around Shared Themes: Narrative Group Therapy with Gay Men', in Denborough, D. (ed.), *Queer Counselling and Narrative Practice* (Adelaide: Dulwich Centre Publications).
(People at the margins sustaining each other.)

7

Telling and Re-telling Life Stories: Collective Biography Practices

*Learning to write and to tell stories of self against the grain of hege-
monic discourses; making visible and therefore revisable the
discourses through which we make meanings and selves; deconstructing the individual as existing independent of various collectives, of discourse, of history, of time and place.*

(Davies et al., 2004: 369)

This chapter's version of the term 'collective' deserves some scrutiny
since it is co-authored by a middle-aged, female academic/narrative
therapist and a group of young men who at the time of writing were
aged between seventeen and twenty-three. The young men, who
described themselves collectively as the 'unassuming geeks', had all
spent some time in their lives seriously considering the possibility of,
and in some cases attempting, suicide.

One of the blurred meeting places between narrative research and
narrative therapy is that between the collective biography practices used
by feminist researchers and the outsider witness practices that have
emerged from the narrative therapies (described at some length in the
previous chapter). Feminist researchers, notably Crawford and
colleagues (1992) and Davies and colleagues (Davies, 1994, 2000a;
Davies et al., 1997, 2001, 2004; Gannon, 2001), have recently expanded
the 'collective memory' work developed by Haug and others (Haug,
1987) into a way of writing together that produces a form of collaborative research which challenges and disrupts the borders between culture
and agency, so that:

through the process of talking and listening, of writing and re-writing, the edges that mark off the texts of ourselves, one from the
other, are blurred.   (Davies et al., 2001: 169)

Outsider witness practices have been developed by narrative therapists (see above, plus White, 1995, 1997a, 1999, and also Andrews, 2001; Behan, 2002; Russell and Carey, 2004a) as a means of telling and re-telling the stories of people's lives to an 'audience' that privileges the process of telling and re-telling stories, rather than the expertise or person of the therapist (although both are present).

The 'unassuming geeks group', the co-authors of this chapter, started in the form of a group of outsider witnesses to one young man's concerns about his life, and gradually developed, slid, in fact, into becoming a collective biography group, but also moved backwards and forwards across these two ways of working. As the borders between narrative therapies and narrative research methods merged, a 'witnessed' collective biography method has emerged that has subsequently been used with other groups (Speedy, 2003a, 2003b).

Perhaps it would be useful, however, before describing the particularities of how this process took place with the unassuming geeks, to outline the characteristics of collective biography work and explore their 'fit' with outsider witness practices.

Collective Biography

A growing body of feminist research, spawned by the memory work of Haug (1987) and others, has described itself as 'collective biography': work that draws on the memories that people hold to in their lives through a process of telling, re-telling, writing and re-writing stories 'which reveal the ways in which we were (and are) collectively produced' (Davies et al., 2001: 169). Some of this work has been written by individuals through collective processes (see Davies, 2000a), some creatively layered and written in a collective voice by individual authors (see Gannon, 2001), and some, as in the case of this text, has been produced through collective processes and has at times been written in individual and at times in collective voices.

Like definitional ceremony, this process of talking, writing, reading aloud, reflecting and re-writing creates a kind of resonation chamber where the echoes of similar and different stories expand the spaces between culturally familiar or appropriate explanations and assumptions and the particularities of the stories people seek to tell and the language they might uncover in so doing. This process does not converge or disentangle culture, agency, object, subject, individual and collective. The threads that bind dominant discourses so tightly around us are, in the words of the 'geeks', dishevelled a little. In this dishevelment, threads of other stories, including some resistances, are teased out: different positions are taken up, no more or less real or true or core, just different 'discursive imperatives at play' (Davies et al., 2004).

Collective biography processes have varied (see Crawford, et al., 1992; Davies, 2000a; Davies et al., 1997, 2001, 2004; Gannon, 2001; Kamler, 1996) but have in common their origins in Haug's (1987: 47) memory work with women, wherein:

> it is possible to study the process whereby we have become the person we are as a sedimentation of different levels of working over of the social. If, for example, we write down and scrutinise any given memory from childhood, we find ourselves confronted with a diverse number of apparently fixed and given opinions, actions, attitudes, motives and desires, which in themselves demand explication. Once we have begun to disentangle the knots, the process becomes endless . . .

Most of these processes have included strategies for moving from conversations, to reveries, to writing, to reading aloud, to critically scrutinising each other's writing, to re-writing, and so on in a cycle. Gannon (in Davies, 2000a: 47/8) describes the conversational process, in ways that echo the experiences of 'witnesses' in definitional ceremonies:

> Once we start talking
> Stories spill out
> Lap over each other
> Wash us into other stories
> We give our gifts,
> Memories,
> to each other.

The moving back and forth from oral histories and live readings to moments of reverie and of producing written texts steps towards more 'embodied' writing. The critical scrutiny (following Haug, 1987) includes an interrogation of 'normative', rehearsed and familiar ways of making sense of things and suggests erasing explanations, justifications and clichés to make space for concrete, embodied memories. This process of discussion, questioning and re-writing the text in order to strip out the 'rationalisations, justifications, explanations, judgements'

(Davies et al., 1994: 84) can go on almost indefinitely and certainly the writings presented by the geeks, below, are considered 'work in progress' that has changed and may continue to change many times.

The work described in this chapter has, quite deliberately, not stripped away all the clichés, but rather has included, amplified and exaggerated some of them, some as themes and section titles, in order to place other ways of writing up against them. Thus familiar, everyday phrases, particularly those that had come from fathers, family doctors and other older men, such as: 'on the rampage', 'just the ticket', 'you need to get out more', 'just a phase' and 'think of others' are juxtaposed with the unexpected, embodied expressions that emerged, such as: 'collective curvature of the spine', 'an unassuming rampage itches gently' and 'we have considered suicide and erred in favour of breathing'.

There was much discussion about which writings should be included when they were deemed finished. This led to further discussions about authorship, ownership and subjectivities, eliciting comments such as:

> we passed the 'who wrote what' threshold some time ago. Now the fighting is just as fierce on the 'what goes where' front, but we are still finding the words and they are still eluding us.

This kind of work sits within feminist traditions of research and seems to have been used initially by women's groups to work almost therapeutically in developing strategies of resistance to dominant discourses of (see Haug, 1987), for example, female sexuality. More recent moves to describe this work as collective biography rather than memory work have brought with them a greater focus on re-searching and deconstructing meaning-making processes (Davies et al., 2004). I would suggest here, as in the rest of the book, that this is a matter of emphasis and that much that has been considered therapy can develop into published research, and much that has been constructed as research, as indicated by Gannon's poem, above, can achieve therapeutic as well as scholarly outcomes. This seems particularly the case where issues of identity, marginalisation, resistance and transgression are at play.

Should I have had concerns about using ways of working that had been devised by and for groups of women with a group of young men? I think not. Equations of 'feminist' with 'about women' have long since been disrupted. Pease (2000a, 2000b) has already used this work with men's groups, and Davies et al., (2004: 369) 'insist on remaining free to develop and change what we do in response to the particular questions we are asking' with regard to the emergence of 'collective biography' out of memory work.

It seems equally valuable and viable to learn from and use ways of working that have usefully explored the subjectivities, sexualities and gendered embodiments of one group from the margins with those from another such group. Conversations with young men who have considered suicide lend themselves to explorations of embodiment, gendered stances, sexualities, masculinities, transgressions and resistances. Collective biography seems a particularly fruitful vehicle for such a group seeking to research itself. Indeed, I hope to have already suggested that explorations of identities formed in the margins, trailing with them opportunities to transgress and even shift dominant discourses, are the 'bread and butter' of much counselling and psychotherapy research. Poststructuralist feminist researchers who are developing ways of researching such as collective biography have much to offer this whole field.

Should I have concerns about blurring the edges between that which has been constructed as 'research' and that which has been constructed as 'therapy'? In many ways this was our collective purpose. The 'unassuming geeks' wanted to be published in a book read by professional therapists. One of the geeks described 'therapists' in general as:

> Scared shitless of suicide. As soon as you say it, they panic and get you to agree to some contract that covers their agency or their arses. We need to tell them . . . I want to tell them. I think they must have crap training about all this.

And this is their chance. My own strong sense, also, is that as long as 'research' continues to identify itself as something esoteric and unavailable to practitioners and those consulting them, the published works emerging from the counselling and psychotherapy fields will continue to be dominated by academics and practitioners located in university settings (such as myself) rather than the voices of practitioners out in the field, and the clients they are working with.

Ethical Issues and Accountability

For the middle-aged, female facilitator of a group of young men between the ages of seventeen and twenty-three, issues of inappropriate intrusion into the 'collective' process of biography immediately arise, as do safeguards within and dilemmas about working with and publishing the work of people in relation to contemplations of their suicides.

The young men in this group were not, in fact, considering suicide, or anywhere near that point in their lives at the time of taking part in this project. The one person who came along as witness who was not yet ready to take up a position of drawing on memories rather than daily experience, was not included in this project. This does not detract in any way from his rich contributions as a witness to Gregory's life (the young man initially at the centre of the definitional ceremony, see Chapter 5), but it was simply not a good point for him to join this kind of writing group.

We had many discussions about moving from working together as a community of witnesses to each others lives towards writing together about those experiences ('therapeutic', 'experimental', 'writerly' and 'poetic' not being mutually exclusive terms, but rather words that contain large trace elements of each other).

It was Gregory's idea, influenced by the co-writing and exchanges of writing that he and I had undertaken, to 'translate ourselves' into a collaborative writing group, and my suggestion, influenced by the work of feminist researchers in New Zealand and Australia in particular, to work as collective biographers. The description 'feminist research' did not strike a chord with this group, but constructs of transgressive writing practices developed by groups at the margins with an interest in telling stories against the grain resonated immediately.

My work as a therapist was supervised by other professional therapists and this support continued, but the main ethical sustenance for undertaking this work together was our accountability structure as a community, borrowed heavily from the work of the 'just therapy centre' (see Waldegrave et al., 2004). In this way I was apprenticed to the group and accountable to them and to the friends and family members they had nominated to act as our team of consultants. My expertise as an interviewer, writing teacher and group facilitator was called upon and I was influential, although ultimately peripheral, to the group in relation to decisions about what constituted 'finished' pieces of writing, for example. With regard to the sections published here: I wrote the sections you are now reading, to which the unassuming geeks made very few changes. They selected the writing to be included from the group. I did not bump up against the concerns expressed by Gannon (2001: 787) about presenting or re-presenting texts produced by participants since the unassuming geeks have organised their own representations. As the facilitator of the process, however, I did have considerable influence over what was available and what was possible. I hoped to hold to a de-centred but influential position, which was not neutral, and involved negotiating and navigating the landscape of power relations and relationship transitions as well as issues of gender, age and educational status. Much of the later talking and writing took place without me, but the group was influenced and limited by my facilitation in ways that were made transparent by one member, who said:

> This is a bit the same, but different from being all men. We are all men and sometimes forget you are even in this project, but in some way we know you are in here somewhere and let's face it . . . you are my mum's age and that makes a difference to what I might write sometimes.

The practices of remaining accountable to the participants in this group went some way towards redressing and negotiating the complex territories between a middle-aged woman therapist and a group of young male mental health system users. Redressing and negotiating, however, is not the same as negating. These texts, collectively owned and constructed by the geeks, remain differently constructed than they might otherwise have been. In this sense the term 'collective' remains more contested and overtly problematic than in feminist accounts of women's workshops, although the purposes: to sustain the geeks in their quest to 'occupy the language, to make it live' (Davies, 2000a: 43) remain the same.

The tensions between confidentiality, particularly for family members (hence the collective pseudonym), and pride and ownership of the writings have been, and still are, a constant theme in our discussions (see Speedy, 2005c). Gregory (a pseudonym, already used in published works, see Speedy, 2000a and 2005d) and the collective term 'unassuming geeks' have been used in this text but this decision may become open to later revisions.

Selecting and Constructing this Text

This introduction to the processes of collective biography and background to the unassuming geek's contribution has been substantively written by Jane Speedy. The extracts from the collective biography work were chosen by the geeks. They selected and layered together the pieces presented below out of a much larger body of writing. These pieces included some writings inspired by the works of others and some that spoke, in embodied ways, to familiar expressions within the regimes of truth surrounding suicide, youth and maleness. The unassuming geeks originally met as a group of 'outsider witnesses' to the expressions of Gregory's life outlined in Chapter 5 and in response to his request for a team of quiet young men or 'unassuming geeks' to listen to and sustain the stories he was telling himself. This group consisted of four other young men (two of whom were known to me and two of whom were known to Gregory), plus Gregory, Gregory's mother and older brother and his older brother's friend. Gregory and some of the group of witnesses decided to form themselves into a support group, initially facilitated by me, somewhat in the manner described by Behan (2002) and Andrews (2001), but eventually becoming self-supporting. This group (now five men) later began writing together as a result of my own practice of sending them occasional poetic documents after meetings (see Chapter 5) and because they had begun to write to each other online between sessions.

Our writing sessions usually began with a conversation around a particular shared theme, such as 'suicide and selfishness', or with one of the group bringing a poem or some writing by someone they admired. I, for instance, brought Ntozake Shange's (1977) play: *For Colored Girls Who Have Considered Suicide When the Rainbow Is Enuf: A Choreopoem* in response to questions about plays and musicals with 'suicide' in the title, and this sparked a whole new genre of scenes written as 'men in coloured shirts'. Similarly the poems of R. S. Thomas were brought in by one of the group, as were newspaper articles and United Kingdom Department of Health (2003, 2005) reports. All these texts generated conversations that led into some of this writing.

The process of working together that has evolved consists of a conversation in which a particular story or theme or piece of writing is introduced by one person, whose contribution is witnessed by others in the form of re-tellings that resonate with their own lives (often in juxtaposition to dominant stories, or more frequently dominant silences, in relation to suicide), followed by re-re-tellings by the original narrator. The telling has been followed by writing, by reading aloud and then placing that writing under rigorous scrutiny within pairs or within the group. This process has then moved back and forward between critical scrutiny and re-writings. We looked for 'taken for granted' and familiar expressions, either to capture with ironic juxtapositions ('thinking of others' leading to the holding of breath to keep others at bay, for instance), or to burrow underneath 'explanations' such as 'we were looking towards the future' towards expressions like:

> A gaze that scours the landscape not only for the lives of current others, but for the children we might yet father . . .

The 'finished' works in progress have sometimes become collectively authored works and sometimes, individually authored in collective ways. My tasks and responsibilities have been to facilitate this process and provide safe online spaces and archives. None of the writings are 'mine', apart from co-authorship of the initial poetic account (shown in Chapter 5) of some of Gregory's life.

Extracts from the Collected Writings of the Unassuming Geeks

> The unassuming geeks are on the rampage.
> Such rampages start in the belly.
> They are gut twisters.
> An unassuming rampage itches gently
> against the skin and
> a modest amount of facial disquiet
> and bodily dishevelment may be experienced

We just have a few questions about relentless forward motion. We may not be the future and our spines may curve unexpectedly. Is this manly?

Dishevelment may follow . . .

> 'Don't say anything at school, you'll only frighten people.
> You have the right to burble on like madmen, but we prefer you to remain silent. Anything you do say will be taken down.'

It came to us later, on the breeze, that it was the silence at school that was eerie and we now reserve the right to remain dishevelled.

YOUR WHOLE LIFE AHEAD OF YOU, IT'S JUST A PHASE . . .

We have our whole lives ahead of us. How do they know?
What if less is more? What, then, makes a 'whole' life?

When I see ring-billed gulls picking on the flesh of decaying
carp, I am less afraid of death.
We are no more and no less than the life that surrounds us.
My fears surface in my isolation.
My serenity surfaces in my solitude.

> (Terry Tempest Williams, 2004)

Phases are like waves, waves are also particles,
it all depends on your gaze.
Are you looking for connections or at each of us in isolation?
Collective curvature of the spine produces
generations of hunched up men
although this could be just a phase.

THINK OF OTHERS FOR A MOMENT

There are many other lives to consider: soft amphibians with razor
sharp memories trying to cross the busy roads; cormorants seeking
oil-free wings; lovers of the future with soft downy skin and implor-
ing olive eyes. Follow our gaze: A gaze that scours the landscape not
only for the lives of current others, but for the children we might yet
father . . .

Thinking of others for a moment,
as a very small boy,
he could keep himself alive and
hopeful by thinking
that he still had the power of breath.
How did he know so much?

Thinking of others for a moment
He and no one else
had control of his breathing.
It was his body, his diaphragm,
and he could make it breathe, or not.

Thinking of others for a moment
He could hold his breath for the longest time
and keep all the others
at bay.

Heroes night: you should get out more . . .

Out for a drink with R. S. Thomas over many pints. Speaking of Wales and of furies and changing midway to Welsh. What was said? Well, it echoed very fierce.

The furies are at home
In the mirror, it is their address.
Even the clearest water,
If deep enough can drown
Never think to surprise them.
Your face approaching ever
So friendly is the white flag
They ignore. There is no truce

With the furies.
(R. S. Thomas, 1995)

THE COLLECTIVE MEDICAL PROFESSION PRESCRIBES FRESH AIR AND FREQUENT SEXUAL ACTIVITY

'You need to get out more, mate, sow a few oats, get laid'
'You need to get out more, mate, you need a good shag'
What prescriptions lurk beneath the skin for suicidal women?

ALL OF OUR STUFF

A performance, each one taking on a different colour: brown, yellow, green, blue, and orange.

Things not being what they had seemed or how they might have ever been imagined: somebody walking off with every single possible expectation of how our lives might unfurl into the wind. Ntozake Shange (1977) has all this written on her body. She had, in her eighteenth year, put her head in an oven, slashed her wrists, taken an overdose of Valium and driven her car into the Pacific. . . . By the time we got to read her words, she was elsewhere, not assuming too much.

PERFORMANCE

(A one-act play for five men in different coloured shirts):

Man in green: It says here that the average man thinks about sex every two minutes, what sort of sex, where does he feel it? How often does he think about death and where does he feel death?

Man in yellow: Less. He fills his head with sex so that death gets less space. The geographies of sex are unlimited, but surely death curdles the contents of the stomach?

Man in green: So, in an average life, an unassuming life, how often does a man think about death?

Man in brown: An unassuming life is not average. It would be extraordinary to live a whole life without assumptions and perhaps it would be very exhausting. Perhaps an unassuming life would be very short.

Man in orange: You can get a lot of sex into a short life but only one death.

Man in blue: You can only die once but you can think about dying as often as you like.

Man in green: death by hanging

Man in yellow: death by misadventure

Man in brown: death by drowning

Man in green: death by suffocation

Man in blue: You are very quiet.

Man in orange: I am thinking about sex.

SUICIDE PREVENTION

The UK government has a strategy
So we are running our lives beneath their radar
They speak of young white men and a lack of educational
    achievement
so some of us are sliding in beneath their lasers with
darker skins and good degrees

A space like this
A year or so ago
Would have been
Just the ticket
When it was
Hard to breath
In and out each day

Fewer thoughts flooding in, less stumbling,
Some quiet place
Like this
To get back to the future
Could have been
Just the ticket

STATISTICAL HOPEFULNESS

We are vital statistics. A 'worrying' trend.

'suicidal thinking in young people . . . dramatic increases in the
suicide rates for young black British men . . . young white men . . . In
western Australia, young men fifteen to twenty-four . . . male suicide
rates in Finland, Canada and the USA . . .'

There is much less private panic in all this. As part of a worrying
trend, we at last have something to grip on. Suicide rates go up and
down with unemployment figures. This all feels more sociable.
Everything has stopped smelling of disinfectant and bedpans and
isolation. There is a whole city running around here beneath the
radar. It is really quite cosy, back-to-back, cup of sugar? Aspirin?
Paracetemol? Codeine? Panadol?

This is girl's stuff, boys don't swallow their pride. We have other
means of suicide: our ropes and fumes and watery ends all sediments
of Saturday mornings huddled together in the dark in front of
cowboys, truckdrivers and tall, tall ships in battle.

Why do more young men top themselves than young women?

- Perhaps because young women breathe out more?
- Perhaps because young women watch different movies?
- Perhaps because of all that 'action learning', all that 'look what
  he made out of Lego': perhaps it;s better to talk it over with
  'Barbie' first?

We might be a source of sustenance and hope for each other.
We are not keeping this inside
We are not keeping this
We are not
We are not

We'll put it on all future application forms
inside the box called 'other'
White British/White European/
Black British/Black European/

other.

THE MEN IN THE BOX MARKED 'OTHER' HAVE CONSIDERED SUICIDE

Collecting statistics on those who commit suicide is a bit of a dead end job. We have considered suicide and erred in favour of breathing in and out.

COULD WE HAVE YOUR ATTENTION?

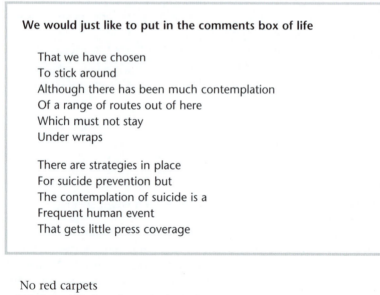

We would just like to put in the comments box of life

That we have chosen
To stick around
Although there has been much contemplation
Of a range of routes out of here
Which must not stay
Under wraps

There are strategies in place
For suicide prevention but
The contemplation of suicide is a
Frequent human event
That gets little press coverage

No red carpets
We just sidled in through the side entrance

We are stationed, breathing in and out, at the sign of hope.

We have not yet settled, but remain on our haunches
We are crouching in the shadows of statistics
We have not yet settled

There are dogs barking
At our heels
And loneliness threatens still
to eat away our hearts

And yet, our sweat gives off an unassuming
whiff of triumph

We are stationed, breathing in and out, at the sign of hope.

Future Possibilities and Pitfalls

The process of doing collective biography (see Davies and Gannon, 2006, for a contemporary overview) has much to offer psychotherapy researchers and service-user groups. The merging of outsider witness practices and collective biography outlined above offers even wider possibilities and perhaps a less intensive approach than the writing workshops described by Davies and Gannon (2006). Collective biographies offer groups at the margins a compelling and extremely social means of unpacking and exploring identities and histories in ways that constantly traverse the shifting landscapes between agency and culture. In my experience, collective biographies are complex undertakings that require constant and careful facilitation, but at the same time are always surprising and unlikely to generate any predictable outcomes. Principal researchers with a clear idea of where they are heading in their work and/or very specific time boundaries would be ill advised to enter this arena. Although face-to-face collective work together might be time-boundaried, collective decision-making about writing, even online, is a time-consuming and intense process. Davies and Gannon conducted many projects on intensive weeks away but the projects I have been involved with have all sprawled along. The geeks, for example, met sporadically over several years. The outcomes do not routinely make for easy reading, but they do uncover the histories of aspects of peoples lives, often those hidden or taken for granted, in uniquely discursive ways.

Further reading

Collective outsider witnessing

White, M. (2003) 'Narrative Practice and Community Assignments'. In: *International Journal of Narrative Therapy and Community Work*, 2003 (3): 17–56.

(Using outsider witness practices with whole communities.)

Collective biography

Davies, B. and Gannon, S. (2006) *Doing Collective Biography* (Buckingham: Open University Press).

(A collection of collective biographies that also explores their construction.)

Haug, F. (1987) *Female Sexualization* (New York: Verso).

(The original feminist text that describes 'memory work'.)

8

Writing as 'Inquiry': Failing to Come to Terms with Things[*]

> So this is part of my work. It is situated in the musical and silent environment of the text that produces effects in my writing. It is because I hear writing write.
>
> (Cixous and Calle-Gruber, 1997: 67)

> This is how I write: As if the secret that is in me were before me.

This chapter continues themes already alluded to in Chapters 1, 2, 3 and 5 of this book, concerning the blurring of genres between narrative inquiry within the social sciences and experiments with narratives within the arts. It borrows from discussions of the representational possibilities available to us as writers and practitioner-researchers and (see Richardson, 1997b, 2000a, Richardson and St Pierre, 2005; St Pierre, 1997) illustrates the reciprocity present in conversations, by juxtaposing three stories that are interrelated re-tellings from different writing genres.

In positioning poetic, auto-ethnographic, storied and more academic/interpretative texts alongside each other, we hope (the 'Jones' family and I) to trouble the edges between academic and creative writing as well as between practice and research. Similarly, if the inquiry takes place 'in the writing', conventional distinctions between data collection and data analysis become fuzzy, as 'thought happened in the writing' (St Pierre, 2005: 972). In placing these short stories next to each other we also seek to disrupt carefully contained 'client' and 'therapist' positions and hope to question some current bereavement orthodoxies.

---

[*] This chapter was written in conjunction with Margie, Fay, Jack, Pauline and Janice Jones (all pseudonyms).

Writing as Inquiry

All research studies require some kind of representation to their audiences, such as films, written texts, posters or other forms of visual portrayal or oral presentation (live or taped). All texts, such as those in this book, are edited, selected, pruned and spruced in order to draw the eyes of the reader towards certain spaces. Writing as a form of inquiry (as opposed to the 'writing up', a kind of mopping up process at the end of an otherwise apparently already completed study) makes these representational practices as explicit and transparent as possible. It is a form of research that uses writing both as a research tool or craft in its own right and/or as a method of re-presenting the words of participants. This is not new, either in the world of counselling or in that of research, wherein there is a history of experimental journal keeping (see Cixous, in Sellers, 2004; Johns, 1996) for both personal and professional purposes. Arts- and humanities-based research has always sustained a tradition of 'messy' texts, ranging from artists' sketchbooks to experimental performance, writing and film (see Bagley and Cancienne, 2002; Kahlo, 1995; Trinh, 1989). Writing as a performative methodology and 'performance as a way of knowing' (Pelias, 1999: ix) articulate choices about genre, about the uses of poetics, of stanza, of space on the page (and the stage), of liminality and of descriptive, interpretive and critical prose. The three stories offered below present a range of written performances, from left to right: a descriptive re-telling, a poetic account, and a more scholarly/interpretive account, all of which remain as stories rather than treatises. As Bochner (1997: 431) posited:

> Stories long to be used rather than analysed, to be told and retold rather than theorized and settled. And they promise the companionship of intimate details as a substitute for the loneliness of abstracted facts, touching readers where they live and offering details that linger in the mind.

Postmodernity has eaten away at the edges of authoritative traditions and has given many of us a space in which to speak with less authority about smaller parcels of knowledge-in-context and to tell more local stories. Writing as inquiry is an attempt to capture the readers' attention and engage them in conversation. It assumes and articulates a reflexive, situated researcher stance, but does not necessarily dwell there. It assumes and expresses a curiosity or even a thirst for knowledge about the contents of the study, but has no illusions that this might speak for itself. It leaves much unsaid, uncertain, and incomplete. It is, at best, a balancing act between form and content. It is often playful, often poetic, often experimental and often fictionalised. It tends towards distillation and description rather than explanation or analysis. It is best performed by those with a love of language and with the patience and resilience to spend time, a lot of time, writing and re-writing and re-writing their work. Above all, it attempts to provide sufficient substance to contribute towards scholarship in the field as well as sufficient space to engage the reader's imagination. As I have already described in outlining my various notebooks in Chapter 2, it is a process of creative thinking as well as writing, whereby:

> Thought happened in the writing. As I wrote I watched word after word appear on the computer screen – ideas, theories, I had not thought before I wrote them.   (St Pierre, 2005: 970)

In an earlier work, St Pierre (1997), writing from the Americas, describes this practice as nomadic, and I am grateful to Wojecki (2004) who, in an Australian context, has developed 'walkabout strategies'. On this small island off northern Europe (the UK), where space is at a premium, hedges are tightly clipped and 'indigenous methodologies' have an altogether different meaning within a postcolonial world, it is difficult to give expression to the geographies of such a practice. My pages are filled with nouns: fugitive, drifter, itinerant, wanderer, immigrant, deserter, traveller, imposter, asylum-seeker, and although there is some lineage and anchorage between these words and accompanying verbs, a shift to the sense of movement available in the continuous present tense (see Chapter 4, and Bird, 2004a, 2004b), of 'drifting' in and out of states of reverie and action, this was hard to hold to in such a tight space. Writing as inquiry, then, seems not only a risky, but also a slippery practice and I am struck once again by the constitutive power and interrelationship between language and place. I am frustrated by my own 'clipped hedge' limits, somewhat ashamed at the overt effort and grisly scrunching of gears as I 'shift' into drifting, only to slip unexpectedly out again. How hard the shift and easy the slip and what a thin skin lies on the language.

Various Practices of Writing as Research

Poetic and experimental representation of research participants is by no means the only style of 'writing as research' available to us (see

Richardson, 2000a, and Richardson and St Pierre, 2005, for a comprehensive overview): experimentation with font, layout, spacing and voices may occur in a variety of different texts. Narrative researchers may tell the same story from a range of different positions (see Etherington, 2003b). Performative ethnographers may produce plays giving voices to a range of characters both real and imagined (see Denzin, 2005; Gergen, 2001). Layered accounts may differentiate between different kinds of writing within the same text (see Ronai, 1995, 1998). In the text that follows, by myself and the Jones family, this is done by dividing different writing genres into parallel columns and inviting people to experiment with their reading. In Ronai's work (1998) chunks of text are differentiated with spaces or lines across the page. These include layers of personal narrative, vivid description, and theoretical discussion.

Similarly, Cixous's account (in Cixous and Calle-Gruber, 1997) of her family history and the impact of the Holocaust, includes extracts from interviews with her co-author, interspersed with key phrases written in different fonts and placed in boxes throughout the text, as well as photographic images, poetry, time lines, short stories and more traditional academic prose. Curiously, although exponents refer to this work as a 'blurring of genres' between social science and arts-based research methods, there seems to be reluctance surrounding any acknowledgement of antecedence within the creative arts. It seems as if 'proper' researchers cite each other rather than poets, novelists and other creative writers, perhaps because a blurring between different research genres does not trouble the edges of what constitutes 'academic' activity as much as a blurring of the borders between research and other forms of writing? Discussions of poetic representation such as those by Mair (1989) and Brady (1991, 2005) routinely recognise that: 'good ethnography always uses language poetically, and good poetry always brings a situation alive in the mind of the reader' (Denzin, 1997: 26), but rarely cite poets.

Positioned re-tellings of the same narrative through different lenses, such as those produced by Etherington (2003b) and Shostak (2000), invite similar 'multiple readings' to those offered by novelists like Walker (1992) or Shields (1993), whose novel *Happenstance* reads from the wife's point of view if held one way up and the husband's if held from another. Lather and Smithies' (1997) boxed and layered text and Ronai's (1995, 1998) layered accounts read in similar ways to Esquivel's novel (1993) *Like Water for Chocolate*, which intersperses boxed recipes and ingredients between layers of story from different time zones, and layers of cookery writing, and Lessing's (1972) *The Golden Notebook*, which intersects the main story with writings from a series of layered notebooks that 'separate things off from each other, out of a fear of chaos, of formlessness' (Lessing, 1972: 7).

I am not trying to suggest that any of these works of fiction are foundational to specific developments in research, but perhaps the creative arts genres that have informed experiments in research writing deserve something of a mention.

The 'creative and analytic processes' of writing as inquiry, and concomitant challenge to traditional distinctions between data collection and analysis (see Richardson, 2000a; St Pierre, 2005: 967–72), sound similar to those described by Atwood (2001) on writing novels, and Paz (1986) on writing poetry.

My own contribution, below, based on a very different counselling research text in three columns (Fetherston, 2002), comes after familiarity with all these and many similar works as well as with much contemporary poetry. Poets seem more capable of writing (and perhaps less professionally threatened by the 'crossovers'?) into the 'spaces in-between' and between such genres as autobiography (O'Reilly, 2002), biography (Duffy, 1985) and journalism (Donavan, 1999).

Opportunities and Constraints for Counselling Researchers

All these ideas have influenced contemporary forms of counselling and psychotherapy *practice*, such as narrative and discursive approaches and Lacanian analysis. Thus far, counselling research is still playing catch-up with educational, sociological, anthropological, feminist and queer studies in respect of producing creative, experimental 'research texts in progress'. This kind of work disrupts assumptions about written forms and about linearity. It takes us by surprise as readers and writers and shapes our experience in different ways from what we might have expected. At best, this work forms a written equivalent to contemporary arts installations that surprise, that stay in our mind's eye and make a difference to how we see the world, and maybe even to our future actions within it. These pieces are attempting to trouble and/or to delight, to tell incomplete and/or non-commensurate stories, to provoke more questions than answers and to have the audience reaching 'across our thresholds, towards a destination which is unknown, not foreseeable, not pre-existent' (Deleuze and Parnet, 1987: 25).

There are parallels between these research modalities and the conversational territories inhabited by counsellors, psychotherapists and the people consulting them. Tentative explorations into uncharted waters often characterise both these domains. This kind of arts-based research is best suited to small intimate studies and provides descriptive, evocative evidence of the particularities of conversational practice. It illustrates and suggests but it does not explain or evaluate. In an era when previously strongly held disciplinary boundaries are becoming blurred and challenged, 'writing as inquiry' *extends and questions* the repertoire of available research genres. These approaches are likely to appeal more to, and perhaps be conducted more by, practitioners and clients than by policy makers, agencies and health care trusts. Nonetheless, as attention to the art and craft of writing becomes a more legitimate consideration within some sectors of counselling and psychotherapy research, the whole field may become more concerned with writing in engaging and interesting ways.

Writing this Inquiry

We were not sure how to write this text, the Jones family and I. We had thought of starting at the end, or at least where our thinking ended in the moment. We had thought of writing a 'straight' text that disrupts and divides itself as it progresses, playing with font, font size and the use of space on the page. Eventually, this chapter was created, for the most part, as a multi-storied text in 'landscape', rather than in 'portrait'. In this way, you, the reader, are invited to turn either your head, or the text, around a little and in so doing, perhaps to engage with us, the writer(s), in a different way. We hope that the texts presented below will invite both playfulness and poignancy into your conversations. Turning the text to landscape had particular connotations for us, as we have had several conversations about Bruner's (1986a) landscapes of meaning and action (see Chapter 4, above) and about the ways in which narrative therapy practices attempt to position people as social agents, co-researching across the landscape of their lives, rather than as individuals in conversation with a therapist.

The stories, below, have been positioned together across the landscape in order to speak visually of some of the kaleidoscopic possibilities that exist alongside each other in conversations, to take note of the privileging of the stories of those who consult us in therapeutic work, but also to assert the value to all parties of the 'taking back' of therapists' own re-authored stories at some point (see Speedy, 2000a; White, 2000). This 'taking back' speaks to a *practice* of narrative ethics: an ethics that acknowledges the way in which conversations re-author and re-shape the lives of all participants, whether central or peripheral and whatever the principal purposes of the exchange. If conversations concerning loss and bereavement become re-membering conversations for the people consulting us, for example (conversations that both bring forth memories and increase the membership of the supporting team alongside people in their lives, see: Carey and Russell, 2002b; White, 1997a: 22–52), they are also quite likely to re-member the lives of therapists.

The juxtaposition of these stories was also an attempt to shed light on Michael White's (2002) work on responding to people's accounts of personal failure as possible points of entry to stories of 'resistance' in their lives (these ideas are reinforced by poststructuralist descriptions of discourses of resistance, see Thomas, 2002; Belsey, 2002; and Danaher et al., 2000: 46–82), and the work of White (1997a) and Hedtke and Winslade (2004) on remembering the dead and the dying. 'Never before', claims White (2004a: 151), 'has the sense of being a failure to be an adequate person been so freely available to people, and never before has it been so freely and willingly dispensed.'

The examples that we have given below emerge as stories of resistance to the prevailing discourses of bereavement in western societies and within the therapeutic domain. These discourses advocate 'coming to terms with' and 'moving on from' grief, and produce models of counselling that 'help the survivor complete any unfinished business with the deceased to be able to say the final goodbye' (Worden, 1991: 38).

There is a growing mainstream literature that questions these assumptions about stages of grief and 'doing grief work'. There is, for example, little evidence to support the existence of emotional stages of grief, or of discernible moments of 'recovery', or endpoints to bereavement, or of the universal application of grief theories across cultural contexts (see: Klass et al., 1996; Neimeyer, 2000). In this context, however, the Jones family and I found that it was not so much our standing in opposition or resistance to these ideas (in an either/or manner) that had opened up other possibilities for us, but rather, our taking up a postmodern stance of 'incredulity' towards commonly held beliefs about how to go about the business of mourning. This curious or incredulous stance became a way of positioning ourselves as anthropologists within our own cultures and families. In constructing our personal failures as possible resistances to the 'taken for granted' in our cultures, we found ourselves positioned more socially, more relationally and within an altogether different landscape.

As principal author I also had at least two overt intentions over and above those made explicit within the stories that we had decided to place alongside each other. First, I wanted to write about some of my work in uncertain, inconclusive, unfinished and questioning ways. As part of my own doctoral research (Speedy, 2001a) I had conducted surveys and extended interviews of counsellor educators in Britain and had discovered that in the main, they differentiated between research ('irrelevant, dry, academic and statistically inclined') and writing ('stories about our work that capture attention'). The majority of my correspondents saw 'research' as the high ground, conducted in universities, and 'writing about our work' as of lesser status, with a less certain outcome, and greater accessibility, and as about re-searching (re-telling the stories about therapeutic exchanges again, for a different audience, see Moodley, 2001). Many of my own research participants did not read the 'research journals' and several acknowledged leaving them 'lying in neat piles, still in their plastic wrappers' (Speedy, 2001a: 182–216). I wanted to create a piece of writing, to an extent collaboratively produced, that 'captured attention' as a piece of co-re-search and that somehow avoided staying in a neat pile in a plastic wrapper. I also wanted to write in a way that avoided all danger of reaching conclusions and that presented an invitation to others to write about the everyday particularities of their own work as therapists, or clients, or as human beings. Secondly, as an advocate of what has been described as one of the 'post-psychological therapies' (McLeod, 2004b, 2006), my last, but by no means least, purpose was to produce a text that was not wedded to the traditions of psychological/applied science research. I wanted to acknowledge the interdisciplinary nature of therapeutic work in Britain (see McLeod, 2003b: 13–15; Speedy, 2001a: 348–60) and to stand on the shoulders of those who went before me within (for example) experimental anthropological, sociological and arts-based research (see Brady, 1991, 2005; Finley, 2005; Goodall, 2000, and Mullen and Finley, 2003).

Having just given what seemed like an indispensable list of introductory citations, I should also add that I wanted to try and avoid the use of what Czarniawska (1998) describes as the 'shopping list referencing' that characterises mainstream psychological research (whereby authors preface each section of their argument with 'shopping lists' of references in order to establish disciplinary justification and credibility, often at the expense of aesthetic considerations and the flow of the text). To this end, albeit mindful of hooks's (1994) contention that the reading of endnotes is culturally specific and that many readers ignore them, I have provided few further citations, but have included endnotes containing sufficient referencing and background information for those that wish to develop these ideas. Above all, I wanted to take issue with the low- and high-ground positions in relation to 'writing' and 'research' outlined above and to promote and encourage ideas of scholarship (alongside research) within the therapeutic domain as a collaborative, writerly endeavour that produces troubling and incomplete texts: texts that explicitly invite ongoing conversation.

A short story about co-researching Margie's resistance to 'moving on' with her life	A quietly spoken poem about a complete failure in relation to coming to terms with my brother's death . . .	Some extracts from various conversations with dead, living and imaginary people
		I talk with dead people all the time. I have conversations with their books and scribble notes on their margins in my thin pink roller-pen. Ever since my older brother died and I continued to regularly chat to him and even have an annual day out together (see left), the construction of contemporary British discourses[7] of 'dialoguing with the dead' has become glaringly transparent to me. 'Scholarly' engagement with dead people is not only permitted, not only deemed a common-sense practice, but is sometimes even considered to be quite erudite. Published writings, preserved verbatim, are privileged legacies compared with oral histories, family memories and traces of conversation.
	There was silence and some subversion around our annual pact.	I can quite legitimately have daily conversations with the dead French 'historian of systems of thought', Michel Foucault, for instance, whose work and life I admire, am critical of, and feel connected with. I can trouble the edges of his ideas and their implications for my therapy and re-search practices. I can even conduct imaginary conversations with and between Foucault, my brother Chris and myself. They both died 'before their time' the former of AIDS, the latter from suicide. In my mind's eye they are somehow connected. They are partly linked in my mind's genealogies through their untimely deaths, partly
	It had captured us this lifelong commitment	
Margie had experienced difficulties in 'coming to terms' with her mother's death and had resolved, with the support of her family, to come and see me and enlist my support as a co-researcher[1] in her endeavours to 'sort this all out' and return to 'normal life'.	to spending our birthdays together	
Further excavations concerning these ideas about 'normal life' on our part painted a future picture in which the daily 'gnawing sense of missing Fay' might have faded from Margie's life and in which Margie did not expect Fay to re-appear. In this scenario, their ongoing conversations together ('or at least the out loud ones') would have come to an end. This, we discovered, would be what 'normal life' looked like, but it was not an attractive proposition at all. In fact, normal life 'sounded horrific' to Margie. It turned out that once she had described it clearly, out loud, she had	and was quite a transgression for siblings there was already something deliciously odd about that. It started at school, do you remember?	

through their non-traditional maleness and partly through having both influenced my ways of knowing/not knowing the world and my increasingly subversive ways of practising my craft.

I can imagine that Foucault's (1977b, 1980b, 1981, 1988) excavations into the history of power relations and 'madness' might have been of interest to Chris and might have sustained him in finding different places to stand in relation to 'manic depression' (now re-named 'bi-polar' disorder).

I imagine that Chris would have found Foucault's explicit out-there homosexuality discomforting and that Foucault would have found Chris's 'British civil servant goes hill walking' manners and dress sense a bit confusing. I also imagine that they would have enjoyed each other's company and found each other's unexpected take on life very funny. I imagine the three of us in a café somewhere on the Rive Gauche, roaring with laughter. This is all well within the bounds of the 'normalising gaze' of contemporary society. Scholarly conversations reinforcing therapeutic work and imaginary conversations sustaining and expanding fond memories are both within the acceptable parameters of the discursive field (the personal, cultural, social and spatial sites mapped out, permitted, shaped and constituted by the contemporary 'discourses'[8] of 'dialoguing with the dead'. It was the 'out-loudness' and continuingness of Margie's daily chunterings to her mother that stood outside what passes for common sense

---

no desire to return to 'normal life'. Margie would not be 'chuntering away' all the time as she went about her daily tasks and Fay's voice would not be 'trundling along' inside Margie's head. Margie would be 'left on her own at home in silence' and this is what was 'upsetting [her] the most'.

Many people, including Margie's daughters Janice and Pauline, were concerned that although Fay had died 'some time ago' (about three years), Margie could not seem to 'move on' in her life. They were very worried that she seemed to be 'stuck in the past'. Margie did not want to worry her daughters, who had 'enough on their plates'. She was also visited by some considerable anxiety about what life might be like with her mum (Fay) 'sorted out' of her life. For herself, she was 'quite comfortable with the conversations' that they continued to have. She maintained that:

'I would be really sad if I ever stopped missing her really. I would

---

I even missed a crucial
Latin test once

the whole of which
I later failed

quite extravagantly
'no such thing as crucial
Latin', you said.

and just before you died
we went to
the roller-disco in Camden
Town, do
you remember?

It was sometime later
that you

mentioned

your vital meeting with
the 'then prime-minister'

'no such thing as a vital
Tory' I said

in current British dealings with the dead ('normal life'), as do my annual outings with my brother.[9]

Margie and I had both, in our ways, failed to shape up to normalising judgements about bereavement processes and pathological versions of mourning. Indeed, I have no doubt that some of the readers of this paper are already 'policing' our lives in a well-intentioned way and pronouncing our bereavement behaviours further towards abnormality than normality on whatever scales, curves, continua, schemes or models of transition and bereavement that they have available to them. As it happens, we do not need further help with this process, for, like most people in contemporary society, we are already experts in the art of disciplining ourselves along these lines. We have, however, found in our life histories and in each other, and in Pauline and Janice and others, ways of sustaining our resistance to the appropriate technologies, scales and ratings of bereavement. We have found some other places to stand and make sense of things and have also found some other people to link our lives with and to join us in these endeavours. It has been the re-authoring[10] of our personal 'failures to come to terms with things' as acts of resistance to the discourses of bereavement that has most sustained us in finding these different places to stand. Indeed, these acts of resistance have turned out not only to be congruent with our histories and cherished values but also to be worthy of some celebration in our lives.

hope that I would always miss her.'[2]

Further quarries into Margie's life stories uncovered quite a history of 'failing to move on' in life. This history initially took some digging out, not because it was not remembered or valued by Margie, but because she anticipated that if she revealed these stories she would risk being judged as 'not quite up together' by others, including myself.

It transpired that she had failed to move on after she had finished college and had returned to her home town ('unlike the rest of [her] siblings and most educated twentieth-century adults'). She had lived her 'entire adult life' down the road from her parents, next door to her old primary school.

Pondering on what this failure to move on might say about her, Margie came up with a number of possibilities but the one that engaged her the most was her realisation that she:

> afterwards I tried
> to push on through
>
> February
>
> my pockets filled
> with pebbles
> and my eyes
>
> ablaze
>
> somehow my own
> birthday
> did not leave
>
> such a hollow stain on
> the calendar.
>
> Februaries came
> and went and
> *'time's healing powers'*
> and the
>
> *'terms'* I was supposed
> to come to
> and
>
> *'the natural course of
> things'*

These ways of describing our *relationship to* (as opposed to our *subjugation by*[11]) the discourses of 'bereavement' owe much to the work of Michael White, one of the founders of what have become known as the 'narrative therapies'. He has drawn extensively on the ideas of Foucault and other poststructuralists in his explorations of therapeutic practice. He has a keen interest in the 'personal failure' epidemic of 'advanced' western societies and has spent some time documenting the myriad ways in which we are recruited in 'modern' societies into experiencing failures in respect of personal identity. In these descriptions, not of negligence towards others, or errors of judgement, but rather of failures in relation to constructs of personal identity, he has observed that:

Never before has the sense of being a failure to be an adequate person been so freely available to people, and never before has it been so willingly and routinely dispensed.   (White, 2002: 35)

In tandem with these observations, White has described inquiries or co-research projects into people's responses to failure that have uncovered, amidst assorted attempts to fit with established 'regimes of truth', all sorts of expressions of life containing explicit or implicit traces of subjugated knowledges, divergent practices and alternative local stories including, as in Margie's story, the 'wilful abandonment of the pursuit of adequacy' (White, 2002: 45).

'Did not want to throw away good connections with people and places, but [she] wanted to appreciate history and family and being part of things and knowing lots of people around and about'.[3]

After several conversations together, we invited Margie's daughters, Janice and Pauline, to come and witness a re-telling of Margie's story.[4] We did so with some trepidation as this was not the story that they had anticipated hearing after their mum had 'been and sorted herself out'. Margie spoke about many aspects of her life, including her love for her daughters and her stand against contemporary 'throw away attitudes' towards families and places. She renewed her commitments to 'continue to miss [her] mother every day' and to continue to have both 'out loud' and 'in her head' conversations with Fay. She also reminded us that this was something of a 'family tradition' in that Fay had 'continued to chat to Jack', her husband, for at least forty years after his death.

just passed me by

and then, one February morning

I was out
collecting pebbles
for
my pockets

when you whispered:

'hang on. I've turned up
every year

It is you
that's broken
our agreement.'

and so we remain

bound together on our birthdays
which is quite

a transgression

Extended excavations have more richly described these territories as places of resistance to 'common-sense' regimes of truth and have elaborated their histories, connections and links to matters of ethical substance in people's lives and communities. In Margie's case, her resolve to 'chat out loud' every day not only spoke of commitments to her mother but also spoke implicitly to the values she placed on 'knowing lots of people around and about', only some of whom were living. The act of talking out loud to Fay turned out not to be a radical departure from 'normal life'. These were actions with a history, embedded in family tradition that could be traced across the landscapes of her life and woven into landscapes of identity, meaning and ethical substance.[12] These commitments, and her growing appreciation of a 'not quite up together' ethics of living, connected her life differently with the lives of her daughters. In turn, their lives also became linked with the lives of their grandparents and others, in a different way.

As to my own resistances to the current regimes of bereavement, my conversations with Margie reinforced certain of my cherished commitments. What seemed absent from the traditional literatures and conventions of bereavement was any kind of invitation to continue or develop our relationships with the dead, or to 'keep a plate set for Grandma'.[13] It was not until my conversations with Margie about some of these expressions of life and death within her own life that I began to talk openly to friends and colleagues about my 'secret annual assignations' with

for a dead person
and his sister

this year you would
have been fifty

we went
to the 'Tate Modern'
where there was an

exploding grand piano
suspended from the ceiling

next to an excruciating
treatise on post-
modernism
which had us

doubled-up

and we walked back
across
the millennium bridge

clutching our sides

our pockets filled with
memories.

Janice was still somewhat concerned about her mum's health in this atmosphere of 'not letting go' of things. She was nervous about Margie spending too much time alone with dead people and not enough time connected to 'the living world'. She also wondered 'what people would think'. She, nonetheless, acknowledged how moved she had been by her mum's words, which had reminded her of her grandmother who she was beginning to forget, and also that 'not moving on had often worked well' for Margie. Pauline, catching something of the 'under-cover flavour' of her mother's relationship with failures and lapses seemed delighted and amused to be able to add to the list of 'Margie's slip-ups' on this front, with a very lively account of the ways that Margie continued to 'not move on' from her ex-husband (Pauline's father), with whom she still 'went out to supper most Friday evenings', fifteen years after their divorce.

my brother. I wrote the poem on the left; for example, during the time that Margie and I were working together. It was also through my connections with the Jones family, that I remembered the beginnings of my own challenges to current bereavement orthodoxies. I recounted, in conversation with them, the ways in which the reclamation of my annual outings with my brother had been the direct result of a particularly significant conversation. I recalled a forgotten conversation with my own mother that had taken place a few years after my brother's death. She had been bemoaning the fact that she could not hear Chris's voice in her head, as I sometimes could. She wondered if this had anything to do with a facility for 'imaginary conversations' and reminded me that, as young children, Chris and I had had an imaginary friend called Mr Gingey. Mr Gingey had once persuaded me to take a day off primary school. There had been further incidents.

We had spent some time recollecting Mr Gingey (who we both acknowledged as Chris's invention or contribution) and re-telling each other several of his adventures and misdemeanours. This conversation had lifted my mother's spirits and she had resolved to talk more with people about her memories of Chris.

Later that night I drove home from my parents' house. My mind was brimming with half-remembered conversations with Chris and adventures with Mr Gingey. It occurred to me that if I had managed to take a day off

Following on from this conversation, all three of these women have stepped further into the spaces they have created and have continued to list and classify myriad 'lapses across the generations' in relation to moving on, letting go and coming to terms with things. Janice, in particular, has begun to take a more appreciative position with regard to what she affectionately describes as her mum's 'barking mad eccentricities'.

Margie has continued her conversations with Fay and continues to miss her every day. She has also begun to 'worry less about what other people might make of all this', although that's another story altogether . . .

At some point, somewhat further along this track, I told Margie about the ways in which some of the stories of her life had 'resonated with events in my own'.[5] I also gave her a copy of the poem that forms part of this text.

At yet another point, still further down the track again, we talked, and then talked again with Janice and Pauline, about 'co-writing this short story'.[6]

primary school with an imaginary friend when I was only six, I could easily 'bunk off' and go on an annual birthday outing with a dead brother now that I was in my forties. And so I do. Every year.

1   The process of narrative therapy, sometimes described as a 'post-psychological' therapy (McLeod, 2000), has been called an ethnographic or co-research process alongside people in their lives (see Epston, 1999, 2001).

2   Narrative practitioners, amongst others, have brought traditional models of grief and bereavement into question (see Hedtke 2001; Speedy, 2000a). White (1998) quotes the work of anthropologist Barbara Myerhoff (1982), who observed in her studies of elderly people that 'full recollection and retention may be as vital to well being as forfeiting memories' (p. 111).

3   Failing to measure up to common sense, received wisdom and/or the taken-for-granted psychological and social discourses of the day can sometimes be usefully regarded as an 'act of resistance' to the 'normalising gazes' of society (see White, 2002). These ideas in relation to 'pathological mourning' really captured Margie's attention and gave her, and her family, a completely different take on their positions.

4   Narrative therapy practices, which were at one time described as 'linking lives' therapy practices, are not so much concerned with restorative relationships within therapy settings as with the sustenance and acknowledgement of the therapeutic possibilities in people's daily lives and day-to-day relationships. In this regard, outsider witness practices (wherein witnesses are engaged in witnessing and re-telling people's stories), which make connections with communities and families, are readily and frequently engaged with. Space does not permit a more extensive description of the preparation of witnesses or the care-full conduct of such 'definitional ceremonies' here. (See White, 2000; Andrews, 2001; Behan, 2002; Speedy, 2004c, for more extensive explorations).

5   The possibility that the stories told in therapeutic (and other) conversations are constitutive of the lives of all participants has implications for therapists' lives and for their relationships with therapeutic exchanges as well as with the people consulting them. 'Taking it back' practices describe the conversational (and written) practices of acknowledging this two-way track with regard to the people currently consulting us, and the 'archives' they contribute to, in our future lives and work (see White, 1997, for further excavations of these issues).

6   All four of the co-writers contributed differently and equally to the writing of this short story. Jane Speedy sat down at her computer and wrote and re-wrote and re-wrote this piece. Most of the words and phrases used in the text are from Margie, Pauline and Janice. Those in inverted commas are verbatim. The text has been back and forth between the four co-writers several times. Margie, Janice and Pauline have also commented critically on the purposes and comprehensibility of the two columns of text to the right of their section, and on these footnotes.

7   'Discourse' is used by poststructuralist writers to describe the 'language in action' – the ideas and practices through which we shape and are shaped by our world and that allow us to both see and make sense of things. See Danaher et al. (2000), ch. 3: 'Discourses and Institutions', for a good introduction.

8   See McNay (2000), Danaher et al. (2000) and possibly Foucault (1972; not the easiest of his writings to read), for a more extensive exploration of these ideas.

9   Maori peoples routinely greet their ancestors 'out loud' on entering their Marae and the Mexican 'day of the dead' is a very raucous, nationally celebrated version of my outings with my brother.

10 The narrative practice of re-authoring conversations (see White, 1995, ch. 1: 'The Narrative Perspective in Therapy') is very different from notions of reframing (replacing one version with another). Re-authoring draws our attention to multiple possibilities and helps us to conceive of our lives as multi-storied rather than single or thinly storied. This provides a range of places to situate ourselves within the landscapes of our lives.

11 In his writings on the archaeology of knowledge (1972), Foucault developed the construct of subjugated knowledge: ways of knowing (in this case about relationships with the dead) that had been subjugated or submerged beneath the dominant discourses. In modern societies, surveillance of each other and ourselves could keep such knowledges subjugated, but implicit traces might remain. Michael White (2002) positions the narrative practitioner as an inquirer on the look out for people with these traces and glimmers of alternative knowledges and meanings and stories, and their relationship with the 'ethical substance' of people's lives.

12 Bruner (1986a) described storytelling as a series of events and happenings taking place over time within a 'landscape of action' that are made sense of and linked to meaning and identity within an adjacent 'landscape of consciousness'. Michael White (well illustrated by Payne, 2000, ch. 5) has described the position of the narrative practitioner as that of a curious questioner zigzagging back and forth across these landscapes, co-researching the links that people make between experience, sense-making, identity and performance.

13 Michael White's classic challenge to conventions of 'saying goodbye' to dead people is illustrated in his writings on 'saying hello again' (1998). These ideas have been most extensively taken up by Lorraine Hedtke and John Winslade. Lorraine's (Hedtke and Winslade, 2004: 85–94) description of keeping connections with her mother alive for her daughter (keeping a plate set for Grandma) resonated with my own daughter's commitments to keeping her relationship with her grandmother alive.

Further reading

Experiments in writing
Cixous, H. and Calle-Gruber, M. (1997) *Rootprints: Memory and Life Writing* (London: Routledge).
(A co-authored memoir, experimenting with different texts.)

Mair, M. (1989) *Between Psychology and Psychotherapy: The Poetics of Experience* (London: Routledge).
(A classic and beautifully written text within psychotherapy research.)

Shields, C. (1993) *Happenstance* (New York: Random House).
(A novel written, literally, from both sides of the text.)

Writing as methodology
Pelias, R. (1999) *Writing Performance: Poeticizing the Researcher's Body* (Carbondale and Edwardsville, IL: Southern Illinois University Press).
(A 'messy' text, exploring an array of performance ethnographies.)

Richardson, L. and St Pierre, E. (2005) 'Writing: a Method of Inquiry', in Denzin, N. and Lincoln, Y. (eds), *The Sage Handbook of Qualitative Research* (Thousand Oaks, CA: Sage).
(The third in a series of overviews of writing as inquiry within the social sciences.)

9

Creating and Performing Auto-ethnographies: Some Unfortunate Lapses – a Very Short Story

---

One of the main characteristics of an auto-ethnographic perspective is that the auto-ethnographer is a boundary crosser.

(Reed-Danahay, 1997: 3)

A self-narrative that critiques the situatedness of self with others in social contexts.

(Spry, 2001: 710)

Research, writing, story, and method that connect the autobiographical and personal to the cultural, social and political.

(Ellis, 2004: xix)

Auto-ethnography writes a world in a state of flux and movement – between story and context, writer and reader, crisis and denouement. It creates charged moments of clarity, connection and change.

(Holman-Jones, 2005: 764)

Auto-ethnography seems something of a slippery customer. As a research method it positions itself somewhere between ethnography (the study of cultures) and autobiography (people writing about their own lives). It also slides about in rather similar ways to the discussion of embodied and embedded reflexivities in Chapter 2, with some proponents veering more towards the 'auto' and the production of evocative texts, some more towards the 'ethno' and the scrutiny of culture and discourse (Reed-Danahay, 1997: 1–21; Ellis, 1995: 305–37; and Ellis and Bochner, 2000, chart some of the history and scope of the genre). These texts form part of a general resurgence in 'biographical research' (see Chamberlayne et al., 2000; Roberts, 2000), a further blurring of genres with literary and sociological memoirs, such as Conley's (2000) *Honky* and Sage's (2000) *Bad Blood*, both written in evocative styles that 'speak to culture' in similar ways to Ellis's (1995) influential auto-ethnography *Final Negotiations*.

Distinctions from other forms of biographical research are compounded by some of its practitioners (see Hayano, 1982; Reed-Danahay, 1997) using the term to describe all ethnographies in which researchers study 'their own people', and further compounded by the use of the related word 'auto/biography', a feminist/sociological term for writing about the lives of others that speaks as much to the life of the writer as to that of the 'researched' (see Stanley, 1992).

I would offer, that whatever else they include (and slipperiness might well be part of the package), auto-ethnographies invite an ethnographic approach to the study of aspects of self, wherein the principal researcher's life becomes the 'field of study' (see Bochner and Ellis, 2002; Ellis, 1995, 1997; Ellis and Bochner, 1996; Reed-Danahay, 1997; Sparkes, 2002b). Thus auto-ethnographies position themselves as very different genres from the kinds of personally embodied and/or culturally embedded reflexive researcher positions described in Chapter 2 and inhabit more ethnographic than biographical traditions and customs. Aspects of the researcher's life become the principal focus of the study in order to create 'intimate provocation' (Holman-Jones, 2005: 776) within the writer as reader/readers as audience. Interestingly, this is a field in which researchers do seem to cite creative artists as sustaining influences within their work (Holman-Jones, 2005, includes Raymond Carver, Sylvia Plath, Billy Holiday and Milan Kundera – a writer, poet, a jazz/blues singer and a novelist – amongst her muses, for instance). Ellis's book (1995) *Final Negotiations*, charting her relationship with her dying partner, and Ronai's (1996) work exploring aspects of a childhood living with 'mentally retarded' parents, are both evocatively written texts that 'claim the conventions of literary writing' (Ellis, 2004: xix).

Auto-ethnography, Self-indulgence and Purpose

Just as the ethics of the 'taking back practices' outlined in Chapter 8 with regard to failing to come to terms with things, would come in for some criticism from therapy practitioners who do not hold to a construct of identity as a social achievement (and therefore adhere to different 'boundaries'), auto-ethnography risks the criticism of 'self-absorption' and 'self-indulgence', as discussed by Mykhalovskiy (1997), Sparkes (2002b) and Coffey (1999: 132), who asks the critical question:

'Are we in danger of gross self-indulgence if we practise autobiographical ethnography?'

Pfister (1997) and Morrison (1998) both offer critiques of the cult of self-revelation and confession, the latter commenting (1998: 11) that 'it takes art. Without art, confessionalism is masturbation.' These kinds of writing do not always translate across oceans, and even practised North American exponents of the art of writing poignant evocative texts that 'work with the consciousness of death at [their] shoulders' (Lorde, 1980, in Ellis, 1995: 299) may find their more 'conversational' performances lost and out of context amongst European audiences (Clough et al., 2005, discussing Bochner and Ellis, 2002).

Sparkes (2002a: 73–106) and Ellis (2004: 284–327) give thoughtful consideration to these criticisms, particularly in critiquing the 'sensationalism' that ensues from:

> having the intention of producing a startling effect without proper consideration for participants, the audience or the narrative truth of what is being produced.   (Ellis, 2004: 320)

Sparkes (2002), borrowing from Church (1995) and Eakin (1999), counters charges of self-indulgence with challenges to misplaced assumptions about binary distinctions between individual and social experience. He draws our attention to the bearing of witness by audiences and to the place of evocation and resonance in the construction our own life stories and identities. At the end of her very powerful text on the death of her partner, Ellis (1995: 319), for instance, makes considerable demands of her readers: 'What text did you, the reader, create of my story?' She asks,

> Did this narrative make you think about or shed light on events in your own life? Would you have acted differently than we did? Would you have told the story the way I told it? Did the words I wrote elicit from you an emotional response to examine? What did you learn about yourself and your relationships through your responses to my text?

Auto-ethnographic Purposes and Power Relations within Counselling and Psychotherapy Research

Holman-Jones describes the 'intimate provocation' of this writing genre as a form of radical, democratic research (2005: 763) 'about the personal text as critical intervention in social, political and cultural life'. In this instance Holman-Jones is referring to both the writing from and witnessing of voices that criticise 'prevailing structures and relationships of power and inequity in a relational context' (Mutua and Swadener, 2004: 16). This description fits stories from clients within a therapeutic context (i.e., stories from the emotional/professional margins within the relationship, see Sands, 2000) as well as it does those from the indigenous Australian women who captured the politics of this genre in the title of their work *Telling our Stories in Ways that Make us Stronger* (Wingard and Lester, 2001).

Borrowing from White and Hales's (1997) challenges to the professional/personal and political divides within therapists' lives and Ellis's (2004: 130–44) invitations towards therapeutic, vulnerable and evocative texts, I would like to venture that auto-ethnographic research within the counselling and psychotherapy field also has a radical impact on power relations when **conducted by counselling and psychotherapy professionals**. 'Professional' research about therapy and the issues and concerns that people bring to therapy, albeit often reflexively and tentatively written from an 'I' position, has tended to focus on the stories of the clients (the 'others'), rather than regarding the lives of therapists themselves as 'fields of study'. There is a significant and radical distinction to be made here between 'vulnerable observers' of others and those whose vulnerabilities are placed under scrutiny. Currently an overview of published counselling and psychotherapy research with its focus on the stories of *clients*, might give an implicit impression of a field involving both practice and research by the distant, emotionally sorted, mentally stable, sexually 'normal', culturally dominant and, above all, undamaged population, upon the addicted, abused, abnormal, inadequate, Ethnic and cultural minority and damaged 'others' within society.

Auto-ethnographic writing that explicitly draws on the 'unsmoothed' and 'unsorted' life experiences of professional therapists and therapy researchers goes some way towards troubling these constructions of clients as 'other' (whilst at the same time not disrupting the purposeful and ethical 'way round' of therapeutic exchanges in focusing on the person who, *in that moment*, is in some distress or under some stress). This genre has informed practitioners writing (unpublished) dissertations (see Jackson, 2002; Cooper, 2003), but has remained underrepresented within the published counselling and psychotherapy research fields, although there are some notable exceptions in the form of contributions by therapy practitioners from a range of traditions to edited books (see Bochner and Ellis, 2002; Etherington, 2003a; White and Hales, 1997; Speedy, forthcoming).

Since including auto-ethnography within the remit of research methods training for therapists (see Speedy et al., 2003) I have also begun to notice an unexpected consequence that perhaps warrants further exploration than I have time for here. In unpacking in some detail the explicit and variously positioned differences between auto-ethnographies (which, although mostly written from the 'I' position, move continually backwards and forwards across and disrupt the 'space' between agency and culture in a way that most therapists have not come across) and the writing of traditional personal narratives (which most therapists have vast experience of), course participants begin to ask more cultural and *political* questions about the taken-for-granted assumptions of the 'personal problems industry' and to scrutinise their own professional identity stories more vigorously.

These are just my own tentative observations, but thus far the story seems to be more one of extending critical thinking than of self-absorption. I would hope that in the future more university-funded therapy researchers would consider positioning themselves as facilitators of consumer/client auto-ethnographies and will become increasingly interested and ethically committed to contemplating their own lives as fields of study rather than simply as opportunities to reflect on, or resonate with, the lives of others.

Performing 'Lapses in My Life'

According to Ellis, auto-ethnographies tend to focus on tragic and/or negative events. She claims that it is hard to write evocatively about happiness and joy (2004: 41–5). Indeed, much of the auto-ethnographic work emerging from the counselling and psychotherapy field, or currently drawn upon in the training of counselling practitioners, focuses on loss, trauma, abuse, illness and death (see Ellis, 1995; Etherington, 2003a; Keisinger, 1998; Speedy et al., 2003). This is not a light-hearted list. The short piece below, however, owes as much to the political pastiche, 'agitprop', performance traditions (see, for example, Cohen-Cruz, 1998) and to the critical community theatre practices advocated by Boal (1985) as it does to the literatures of auto-ethnography. Perhaps this piece contains too much playfulness and may express a humour that is peculiarly British, which does not translate across the Atlantic. It may also seem a strange choice as my exemplar of auto-ethnography in this book, rather than, for example, the more poignantly written poem in the previous chapter, or some of my other writings about my brother's death and/or about my family of choice (see Speedy, 2000a, 2001b).

I have included this piece partly as a contribution to the genre of auto-ethnographic performance, which has been described as the performative or 'cultural turn' in social research (see Alexander, 2005; Denzin, 1997; Rosaldo, 1998; Turner, 1982): a research genre that has, thus far, been underrepresented within the counselling and psychotherapy fields, apart from amongst communities of service users and others wanting to promote community engagements and actions. A genre that:

> seeks to implicate researchers and audiences by creating an experience that brings together theory and praxis in complicated, contradictory and meaningful ways.   (Holman-Jones, 2005: 770)

I have also included it because it is a piece that speaks to the ambiguity and fluidity of some of the border crossings that I have experienced in my own life that seem to strike a chord with the lives of others, and to engage audience members with events in both my life and their own (versions of this performance took place in Bristol, London and Liverpool during 2003).

If I were to place this short, flawed piece at the feet of any prominent literary figures from my own culture, I would apprentice myself to the playwright and commentator Alan Bennett and his *Talking Heads* (1988), a series of humorous and poignant monologues performed by leading British actors and first televised by the BBC in 1988.

I remain uncertain as to how this short performance piece will translate into the more constraining dimensions of a written document. As such, it has to stand its ground (or not) against at least some of the aesthetic criteria outlined in Chapter 3 – Does this text succeed aesthetically? Does it use creative practices that open up the text and invite interpretive responses? Is the text artistically shaped, satisfying and (above all) *not boring*?) Does the writing make my heart sing? – all of which seems alarming.

As 'intimate provocation' within a workshop context, however, the performing of this short story has routinely evoked discussions about the spaces between stereotyping and being stereotyped by others, and between humour, self-denigration and power relations; about the subtle and shifting nuances and constructions of age, gender, sexual and other social categories; about resonances between moments of belonging and not belonging; of slipping, falling and/or rocketing from one category to another; about differences between moments in my life of 'passing'/hybridity/migration and/or of accidentally slipping from one category to another and the barriers to this kind of movement, more frequently experienced in relation to issues of race and/or disability.

My performance of this text had an explicit purpose. Some of the ideas in this book are hard for people steeped in advanced capitalist cultures to grasp. Most students of counselling and research have a 'common-sense' knowledge that there are social and cultural forces at large in the world that will have some 'impact' on individuals. Equally, people are often intrigued by archaeological digs into the social histories of modern-day phenomena: Hepworth's (1999) *The Social Construction of Anorexia Nervosa*, for example. Similarly, the social construction of what is routinely described as 'drug abuse and addiction' in contemporary society often catches the attention of counsellors. Many people are fascinated with the tacit social acceptance of opium, laudanum and gin in seventeenth- and eighteenth-century Britain, alongside a condemnation of coffee houses (see Berridge, 1999; Davenport-Hines, 2001).

It seems much more difficult, however, for most of us (constructed to experience ourselves as autonomous individuals) to contemplate the current, lived discursivity of our own subject positions. Somehow my live performance of aspects of a life lived (not always intentionally) at various border crossings has seemed to evoke in people a sense of discourse as a constantly constitutive phenomenon.

When performed, this text has routinely (much to my surprise) provoked heated discussions between those audience members who are either excited or unexpectedly challenged by my experiences of happenstantially slipping between social/sexual categories, and others who are irritated, disbelieving and/or uncomprehending when faced with notions of 'failing to remember' which category we are supposed to stay in. Performances have always provoked laughter, sometimes tears, and a climate of intimacy. Workshop members have written a variety of moving responses to this work over the last few years, that I do not have the space or permission to publish here, concerning some of their own lapses in life. These have included a range of 'coming out' stories: 'lapses' in and out of acute mental distress, in and out of African/British/Black British/mixed race identities, in and out of a range of sexual relationships, categories and experiences, and in and out of love with themselves, their life partners and/or with their children. I would be interested to hear the responses to this 'performance', from what feels, as I write, to be the more distant and, as yet, unknown audience of readers of this book.

'Some Unfortunate Lapses in My Life' – a short one-act play for one woman

Props: One table, centre stage, containing three framed photographs: one of the narrator as a younger, slimmer woman in a 'Laura Ashley' frock, with her hair up, another of her in her 'brownie' uniform at the age of ten and another family portrait of four similar looking women, all with curly hair, of different ages: almost certainly the narrator's grandmother, mother, the narrator and her daughter. As the curtain goes up on an empty stage, Alma Cogan's 1950s UK hit 'Sugar, sugar' is playing in the background. There is one chair, back to the audience, downstage right.

Enter, stage left: A small, plump, middle-aged, curly haired white woman (the narrator), dressed as if in her 'mother-of-the-bride'/'Prunella Scales (a British actor who played the part of the Queen, see Alan Bennett, 1991) as Her-Majesty-the-Queen' outfit: Smart suit, cream 'Princess Diana' shoes and matching accessories, including hat and gloves. She moves to the centre of the stage, puts down her handbag on the table, carefully takes off her gloves, places them on the table alongside her handbag. She slowly picks up the photos one at a time, smiles at each one and puts them back down. The music fades. The woman turns towards the audience, smiles, slightly conspiratorially, begins to speak in a 'stage whisper', with a slightly 'Daphne Oxenford' English accent (Daphne Oxenford, presenter of 'Listen with Mother' on BBC radio throughout the 1950s, was considered quintessentially 'English').

It was such a small misdemeanour, such a minor transgression outside an otherwise exemplary girl-next-doorhood and quite acceptably 'English' kind of womanhood (if you like that sort of thing). I'm not sure, to this day, if I can explain to you how all this came about on my part. I know that for some people this sort of experience feels like an inevitability, more of a coming home than a coming out. Other people describe it as a choice, a deliberate seeking out of another place to stand. For myself, I just inadvertently stepped across a borderline that was really very hard to determine.

The woman moves downstage, leans forward slightly, placing her hands on the back of the chair, resting one knee on the seat, and 'chats' to the nearby audience, as if over the garden fence.

I had only initially intended the most temporary of toe-dips into nearby territories, but then, you see I apparently went too far. It is so hard to judge these things sometimes, don't you agree? It all began as a desultory meander down a nearby, inconsequential sort of a B-road, a brief sojourn off the main drag, so to speak. It was a bit off the usual route, I have to admit. The road was a little bit winding and perhaps it took a teeny bit longer to get where you wanted to go, initially at least. There again, I do think I should point out that this all started in the 1980s. Some of the main roads were becoming incredibly congested at that time and were not necessarily as well sign-posted as you might expect. And in the end, I lingered a bit too long, how you do, and then again, the extent and the ferocity of the love that I encountered was quite beyond my wildest expectations.

The woman pulls the chair towards her and sits down gracefully, neatly crossing her legs at the ankle, facing the audience. Clasping her hands together in her lap, she says:

In any case, one thing led to another and then, another. It's not as if some other more mainstream avenues aren't perfectly pleasant. Indeed, I've been up and down some of them in my day. It just seemed to me that I might possibly be having a whole lot more fun carrying on in the direction I was going. And another thing . . . after all that business with being spat at and so forth, I had had to take quite a stand. I mean I couldn't just meander along as if everything was hunky dory, could I?

Perhaps I should explain a little bit more about the spitting incident, since this was really quite a turning point. It all took place during the gay pride festival in London. It was the year that Charles was about to marry Diana, so central London was looking pretty smart and we were all wearing 'Don't do it Di' badges. (With hindsight, you must admit, we had a point.)

Anyway, this was the first of many times that gay pride was a celebration rather than a demonstration and we all got dressed up 'carnival style' for the occasion.

In front of us were the 'Brixton fairies', a bunch of very hairy men, with very hairless heads, dressed in tutus with wings, waving wands and, despite the baldness, managing somehow to sport an amazing assortment of tiaras. Behind us were the 'S and M Dykes', dressed in an intriguing array of interconnected leather gear, rubber gear and chains, which all looked very complicated and quite hard to extract yourself from. I remember hoping that they had all remembered to have a pee before they set out.

We were wearing our Laura Ashley frocks and handbags with matching accessories. My frock had puffed sleeves, a bow at the back, and was covered in small purple pansies. Anyway, you've probably guessed already that we were all marching under a banner saying 'Ooh! She can't be!'

But what you might be surprised to learn, or we certainly were, was that all along the route we were spat at by the crowds of onlookers. At first we all thought that they had been aiming for one of the groups in front of, or behind us and missed, but after a while, it became clear that there was something about our 'girl-next-door-at-her-cousin's-wedding' image that unsettled people. Men in frocks and outrageous women were expected, but in our 'Lady Di' shoes, 'nice-girl' pearly pink lipstick and pretty frocks, we were somehow not playing the game.

By the time we got to the Jubilee Gardens for the party at the end of the march we were covered in slime and confusion. It was at this point that we sat down on the grass with the 'S and M Dykes' and the 'Brixton fairies', with whom we became firm friends, and had the first of the many discussions I have had in my life about 'queerness'. In the UK at least, it seemed that at that point in this country's history we liked our 'queers' to be queer-looking and our 'straights' to be straight-looking, and then perhaps we would all know exactly where we were in the order of things and there could be no accidental crossings of borders.

Why on earth am I telling you about all this, when I imagine that this is way outside your experiences of life?

I suppose I just want you to get some of the flavour of my life. It's not as if I had intended to draw attention to myself. It was never my suggestion that I was revolting in the first place. As it happens (and it may surprise you to know this) I have routinely considered myself a bit of a stunner. You see, it has been said that I keep banging on about this, but it got to the point where something had to be done, and after that . . . well there was no looking back.

In any case, I had kind of forgotten which direction to look back in, and actually, now we come to be having this conversation, I'm not altogether sure what I was looking for. Let's face it, by that stage, the pitch had been well and truly queered.

The woman gets up off her chair, strolls gracefully over to the table, picks up her gloves and handbag and turns back to the audience.

So I'd just like to finish, by way of explanation, and point out in my defence, that it was all a complete accident really. It was a mixture of not really being bothered about 'moderation' in this instance and at the same time getting rather over-excited in the moment and then getting quite seriously waylaid, which, all-in-all, led to my totally forgetting to remember to remain heterosexual. A bit of a lapse really. It's surprisingly easily done. If you're interested, I know where the back roads start . . . but I don't quite remember which order I forgot what in. I didn't even know I hadn't remembered where to go next until I was a completely lost cause. Perhaps you should ask someone else?

Fade in music. Woman exits, stage left.

Further reading

Auto-ethnography
Ellis, C. (1995) *Final Negotiation: A Story of Love, Loss and Chronic Illness* (Philadelphia: Temple University Press).
(An extraordinary text, challenging accepted discourses of illness and death.)

Holman-Jones, S. (2005) 'Auto-ethnography: Making the Personal Political', in Denzin, N. and Lincoln, Y. (eds), *The Sage Handbook of Qualitative Research* (Thousand Oaks, CA: Sage).
(A short chapter that darts and folds between autobiography, performance and social activism.)

Reed-Danahay, D. (ed.) (1997) *Auto/ethnography: Re-writing the Self and the Social* (New York: Berg).
(An edited book containing a wide range of European takes on the genre.)

Writing about my life
Speedy, J. (2000) 'White Water Rafting in Cocktail Dresses: Taking it Back Practices and Re-membered Conversations in the Narrative Therapies'. In: *Counselling,* 11(10): 628–33.
(An introduction to narrative therapy that enfolds the author's life and relationship with her brother.)

Speedy, J. (2001) 'Making Ourselves Up as we Go Along', in *Working with the Stories of Women's Lives,* ed. Dulwich Centre Publications (Adelaide: Dulwich Centre Publications).
(One of a collection of stories of lives lived in non-traditional families.)

10

Crossing the Borders between Fiction and Research

Consulting and Consorting with Gargoyles

I used to work in the Wills Memorial Building, up in the tower, but now my office is on the other side of the square and I look out across the trees, towards the mullioned windows of my erstwhile fifth-floor eyrie. I used to call it my 'Rapunzel' room (see Lucas, 1909), perched up there beneath the bell tower, arched casements on both sides, each complete with its own stone window seat. Nobody ever ventured up there. There was an ancient professor in the room opposite, who appeared about once a year, and a rarely open, poorly lit library at the far end of the corridor. In summer it became warm enough to open the windows and hear the hubbub and noise of the traffic on Park Street below, but for the rest of the year there was only the occasional crematorium-swoosh of the lift to interrupt the stillness. It was very out of the way and forgotten, very quiet, and at night very spooky. And I had my very own gargoyle.

The Wills family, local tobacco magnates, had donated vast sums of money to the University over the years and the Wills building, 'the largest mock-gothic structure in Europe', was their show piece. My gargoyle was at the top of the back spiral staircase leading up to the fifth floor and she watched over me and any visitors that might come my way.

It was not until our department moved over to the other side of Berkeley Square that I came to reflect on the impact of space and place on the climate and tenor of our teaching and research within the University. I started to consider the different constraints, permissions, and lurking sediments that sustain that which might be imagined within dark, wood-panelled rooms and reached via wide stone steps, shared with elusive astronomers, compared with what might occur in purpose-built teaching spaces and permanently designated 'small group/video practice' rooms. Perhaps, suggests Massey (2005: 9), 'we could imagine space as a simultaneity of stories-so-far'.

The Wills Memorial Building was built long before, and indeed, totally flies in the face of competency-based learning. It is grandiose, ridiculous and impractical and a large population of gargoyles inhabit its corridors and precincts. Once we had moved across to a 'sensible' place to conduct the business of educating therapists, I began to more closely interrogate constructs of space, place and reverie within the development of our work.

A substantial body of counselling research has emerged from the University of Bristol over the last decade, almost entirely without reference to the built environment it has taken place in. Meanwhile, unbeknownst to the counsellors, the geography department, tucked just behind the bell tower, was conducting intense conversations about the various productions and practices of social space, and the power geometries operating across them (see Hubbard et al., 2002; Massey, 1994, 2005). What would we have learned about ourselves and the way we constructed the therapeutic spaces we inhabited, I wonder, if we had attended more to the colleagues with whom we shared our geographical space? Perhaps if we had considered McDowell's (1999: 4) contention that: 'Places are made through power relations which construct the rules which define boundaries,' we might have found ourselves looking about the place to discern these power relations and their ways of operating. McDowell (1994) went on to state:

> these boundaries are both social and spatial – they define who belongs to a place and who may be excluded, as well as the location or site of the experience. (1994: 4)

I had once previously, in a paper on narrative therapy supervision, referred to the way in which the gargoyles in our building had infiltrated the work that we did. I had done so by quoting the 'facts' from a note slipped under my office door by a student who had been left waiting for me to turn up for a supervision session that I had, unforgivably, forgotten all about. Her note said:

> I waited for 30 minutes, and have now gone to the library. My time was not wasted. I consulted at some length with the gargoyle at the top of your staircase. I found him in many ways a most satisfactory supervisor. He has a pleasing and quizzical countenance and regards me with the mixture of soul and oomph that I find most useful when reflecting on my practice. He also arrived on time. (Speedy, 2000c: 10)

What I had not mentioned (had excluded?) were the 'fictions' that were equally significantly held to within this, and other, learning relationships and how the quirks, mouldings and corridors of the building had come to form part of our curriculum. I had not realised this at the time of writing. It is only in retrospect that I notice the staircase gargoyle has been constructed as a coda at the end of a 'realist tale'. I had not muddied the waters with stories of gargoyles floating down from the rafters and joining in (sometimes even rudely interrupting) our conversations in the 'Rapunzel' room. I had wanted to be thought of as scholarly and not as some dodgy character who could not tell 'fact' from 'fiction'. I had also wanted to get my work published, and notice that both Sparkes (2005) within the UK and Richardson (1997a) from the US comment on the pressure for academics to conform. Richardson's (1997: 198) 'Professor Z', for instance, 'writes well . . . but is it sociology?' Sparkes (2005) and Clough (2002) both mention the pressures of the research assessment exercise within the UK, which favours tried and tested research methods rather than experimentation, in order that academics get sufficient scholarly publications out in the world in the 'right' journals.

There are, of course, established traditions of fictionalised research within the social sciences. From psychotherapy, Yalom (1991, 2000) has contributed a series of novels that portray 'symbolic equivalents' of his clients, a method of portraying people and events it would not otherwise be ethical or possible to portray. Clough (2002) has drawn extensively on Yalom's work in order to generate short stories that depict tales of schooling that might otherwise remain untold. Like Yalom, Clough (2002: 9) substantiates his claims towards research by his presence in the field as witness to such events:

> they are stories which could be true, they derive from real events and feelings and conversations but they are ultimately fictions: versions of the truth which are woven from an amalgam of raw data, real details and where necessary symbolic equivalents.

Sparkes (2002a) differentiates between fictionalised accounts, whose validation rests on 'being there', and creative fictions that rely on the production of evocative texts and on verisimilitude rather than presence at events that have taken place. He draws upon Bochner and Ellis's (1996b) distinction between 'making something' (of aesthetic merit) and 'making something up' (off the top of your head). Creative fictions have been used to good effect by writers within the counselling arena to tell stories that are too painful to be told in other ways. Etherington (2000) and Etherington et al. (2003a) use fictionalised/poetic accounts to give voice to stories of abuse and trauma. Mienczacowski et al. (2002) dramatise experiences of mental illness, and Keisinger (1998) uses a poetic account of a starving dove to portray a life lived with anorexia.

With few exceptions (see Bolton, 2003, and Keisinger, above), all these writers make explicit, transparent distinctions between fictionalised and other accounts of their research. Clough (2002) offers a critique of the tradition of apology that seems to accompany fictionalised social research. He nonetheless divides his own text between vivid fictionalised short stories in some chapters and academic prose in others. Banks (1998: 11) introduces herself as a researcher with the words: 'I've been reading fiction for a long time,' and quotes from Isabel Allende (1997: 11), maintaining:

> through this fiction I am revealing myself . . . I can't say who I am because the boundaries between reality and fantasy are totally blurred.

But she restricts herself to an academic discussion of the possibilities, rather than providing a demonstration of movement between reality and fantasy within a research text.

Magical Realist Accounts

> *'Magical realism' the 'transgressive and subversive' fictional genre, whereby the magical, the mythical and the 'impossible' blend seamlessly and unapologetically with the actual and the real*
>
> (Bowers, 2004: 67)

My experience of working as a therapist, and indeed, as a human being, consistently undermines neat distinctions between imagined and real experiences. Bruner (1986a) explored narrative ideas in order to move actual minds and possible worlds into closer proximity, but what of impossible, magical and mythical worlds. Bowers (2004, above; see also Faris, 2004) describes the genre of magical realism as transgressive in several senses. Importantly, magical realism flies in the face of fiction/faction dualities. It emanates from writers at the margins of dominant cultures and it is these writers, who wear both realist and magical guises lightly, that seem to capture most accurately the day-to-day experience of my working life. Rushdie (1981) moves gracefully between historical accounts of the partitioning of India and 'magical' versions of the lives of midnight's children, those born at the exact hour of Indian Independence, who possess telepathic powers. Allende (1986) moves effortlessly between military coups in Chile and the life stories of characters living, dead and mythical, and Marquez (1970) includes conversations with the living (one of whom is pregnant by an iguana), the dead and the not yet born. None of these fractures in time, space or place require justification or explanation. Things happen, just as, in my experience at least, they do in therapeutic exchanges with no demarcation lines between the layers of reality.

In counselling conversations people are also often at marginal moments in their lives (indeed, a disproportionate number of those seeking counselling live their lives fairly permanently at society's margins); they also seem to shift effortlessly from conversing with the dead to the living to the hoped-for and not yet born and back again.

At times of stress, turmoil and grief they invoke the support of the people and places that are available to them 'in reality', as well as angels, fairies and other magical creatures, times and landscapes. This is not remotely disturbed or disturbing. People may well afford different cultural and symbolic meanings to expressions like 'god', 'angel', 'demon' and 'ghost', but only a very, very few have any difficulty distinguishing between their own versions and/or taken-for-granted and socially accepted versions of fantasy and reality (and even then, mostly only for a very short time). In effect, almost all of these conversations about making sense and meaning out of difficult life experiences, however tentative and bewildering they might be, seem to slip easily between different time zones and different realities (see, for example, Etherington, 2000; Lock et al., 2004; McLeod and Lynch, 2000).

Many close readings of counselling conversations, then, might emanate from a 'magical realist' stance that has not yet been recognised or taken up by researchers and writers in the field. Could it be, perhaps, that we are too preoccupied with the professional trajectories and status that we imagine 'realist tales' will steer us towards? Perhaps, as workers staking a claim in the precarious 'sanity' business, we are reluctant, for the most part, to admit to inhabiting territories along the borders of fantasy and reality. Perhaps the medical discourses of madness (see Foucault, 1965, 1975) militate against explicitly leaning towards the magical rather than the realist? For whatever reasons, for the most part even the creative, fictionalised psychotherapy research texts that exist have not, thus far, espoused a seamless, subversive movement between realist and imaginary tales. Such seditious border crossings have been smoothed out of the literatures of our field.

Exotic Tales of the Everyday

I am on very risky ground here. Earlier in this book, having talked myself up to the heights of Charles Dickens's legacies, I had to talk back down towards a more modest and local effort, and now I seem to be comparing my small contribution to counselling research with acclaimed magical realist texts, many of them Booker Prize winners, including (Rushdie, 1981) 'the Booker of Bookers'. This would be a tall order indeed, if I were making this claim for myself and my writing. The best of magical realism, sitting at the edge and picking up the slippage between traditional and modern cultures as it does, is a seamless ride for the reader. Words and phrases slip under the surface of skin 'like water for chocolate' and linger in the mind's eye. But I am not making those claims, or expecting those glittering literary prizes for myself. I am making such claims for the extraordinary and exotic expressions of life that I have recorded and have available to me in notebooks and on videotapes. It speaks to much about human ingenuity and resilience that when actual minds find possible worlds constraining or oppressive many of them can find a way through life's thornier thickets by recourse to impossible and magical worlds: not as a retreat from reality, but as a way of tunnelling through to life's different possibilities.

Hyatt, for example, featured in Chapter 5, above, had a very particular relationship and affection for the bones she shared with her ancestors and much-loved brothers. She had had minimal contact with her one living brother in adult life, but had a strong sense that her bones connected them to each other. Once off the danger list and out of the hospital system, she had the energy and space to reflect on the stories that had sustained her relationship with anorexia, acknowledging that some of them were destructive, but also that some addressed her sense of family and connection. Hyatt, now very differently positioned, recently caught me up on some of the history of those times and on her current relationship with her bones, as somebody from a Caribbean island, surviving a northern European winter:

> When I was stick-bone thin most
> people, specially people my age,
> were afraid of me,
> but they were also fascinated.

Like the circus I suppose, like at a freak show.
In the changing rooms at school
people would look away,
look down,
go silent.
There would be this deathly hush and
then I would catch them peeking,

their mouths horror-movie wide, you know,
like they'd walked in on
  'last night of the zombies'
or something.
It's not comfortable, the freak position, but
it also feels quite powerful.
Witchy-powerful really.

the rest of them didn't have that control
and power over their bodies
Not like I had.
They had no access to their bones

I could slide my hands inside my skin at night
and take out the bones.
I could clutch the bones of my ancestors tight
I could hold them up to the window,
translucent and white in the moonlight and
then slip them back into my limbs in the morning
  and no one would know.

my bones are still there, but
I have different powers now
no longer a witch, but a woman
My bones are no longer extractable
But we can still communicate with each other

My bones are part of my look out system
You know, in quiet moments when I'm just
Chilling – I'll be going to work, say,
and my bones might say:

  'Hey girl, you skipped lunch yesterday,
You need to watch out for that'

And I'll say:
'It's okay, I'm looking out and
I'll look after you, I'll make sure you're well
covered for the British winter'

And they'll say:
'We're looking out for you too, girl, but if you really loved us, you'd take
us home before the winter'

The next extract is taken from a very different conversation with Josh, who was talking to me about wanting his family to take him a little bit less for granted. Unlike Hyatt, he came to see me very few times and we did not build up a particulary strong relationship or commitment to the work we were engaged in together. This did not seem to limit his magical as well as realist expressions of life. By way of explanation of how this 'taking for granted' had come about on the part of his family, he slipped seamlessly into the story of how he got swallowed up and spat out into a life as a 'nest of tables':

You can hear me more clearly now
because I am not speaking to you
through a thick wall of flesh.

My mother-in-law swallowed me whole
    fairly early on in the marriage I think.
It wasn't what I expected really,
to be gobbled up suddenly and with such gusto.
I spent twenty years down inside that churning stomach,
voice muffled, nobody even
noticing I was there really.

And then, at the hour of her death,
she kind of rose up and spat me out.
Her last act.

So, here I am,
back from beneath the folds of flesh,
but even so, everyone is used to my absence.
I have become invisible within my own family,
like a wall or a window

or maybe a nest of tables
in the corner of the room.

It is hard to know which fragments to pick, there are many to choose from and I feel certain that counsellors reading this will feel familiar with the many moments in which people consulting them have slipped through the semi-permeable membranes from the 'real' to either the 'imagined' or the 'magical'.

I'll finish with a conversation with Pauline (not a client, but a counselling student), who is talking here, looking back across her life some twenty years on, about what helped her sustain a strong sense that despite 'a crap start in life' she was going to really seriously amount to something. At the time of this conversation, Pauline had just been awarded a Master's degree in counselling.

* * *

JS (Jane Speedy): So, looking back, was there anybody around, anybody at all in your life at that time? Anyone who was supporting you in nurturing this secret, other idea of yourself, this idea that you might amount to something one day?

Pauline: No.

JS: No one at all?

Pauline: No one. They were all bastards, actually.

JS: They were all bastards in the home. Were they all bastards at school, as well? I'm not suggesting that they weren't. It sounds like 'bastard city'. I'm just trying to piece together this picture of you as a young girl, surrounded by bastards, and I'm interested in this idea that you held onto in secret that you were going to amount to something.

Pauline: Well, like I said, it came from my Nan. Even when she was ill, right up until she died, I would go round to hers on the weekend. And she'd cook me a roast dinner, you know, with all the trimmings and she'd tell me I was all right. Know what I mean? She'd say that she knew I was going to amount to something one day and then they'd all see. I believed her you see. She was my Nan and I believed her. I mean, who would you put your money on? Your Nan, who loved you, or a bunch of losers?

JS: Mm, well I suppose I'd put my money on my Nan. What was it she saw in you as a young child, do you think, that made her so sure you'd amount to something?

Pauline: Dunno really.

JS: But somehow, whatever she saw in you sustained this secret idea you had of yourself, this sense of amounting to something that no-one else could see, even after she died.

Pauline: Yup.

[*Pause*]

Pauline: Yup. Well she still came and talked to me you know. After she died. She used to come and sit on the end of my bed in the home and have a chat. Right up until I was sixteen.

JS (slightly confused):   So . . . that was after she died, she'd visit you at the home then?

Pauline: Yes. I'd wake up in the night, you know, and there she'd be, mug of tea in one hand, fag in the other, chatting away: Chat, chat, chat. I never got a word in. Never wanted to really, I'd just lie there and listen and she'd chat away and she'd always tell me just to wait, and then they'd see. I'd amount to something one day and those poor bastards 'd still be stuck doing shit work at a kid's home, or most probably out of work.*
    She was right.*
    Funny thing is, she never ever came to see me at the home when she was alive. Not once. But as soon as she upped and died you couldn't keep her away. Then when I left that was it, never saw her again.*
    I sort of half expected her to turn up on degree day, you know, but she never did. But it stayed with me all that time, you know, it was like our little secret, us against the world.

JS: What do you think she'd have said on degree day?

Pauline: Well, something vulgar probably. Something vulgar and loud about all the posh buggers on the podium in their robes and gold braid and all the swank and pomp of it all, but she'd have had a lump in her throat just the same and tears in her eyes, and when I went up to get my degree, she'd have clapped and clapped and clapped until her hands were sore.

*   *   *

SO WHAT?

So what? I hear some of my colleagues saying. All I have done here is extract movements in and out of different realities and ways of telling life stories that many counsellors and the people consulting them will be familiar with. My argument is that this is the daily territory we inhabit in therapeutic work. Magical realist writers have emerged as a subversive strand of literature, poised between first and third worlds. Their work transcends powerlessness in the ways that people consulting therapists aspire to, but this is rarely represented within the literatures of therapy process. Successful therapy outcomes are routinely reported, and this is sometimes described as the outcome of an initially imagined or 'magical' or 'miracle' scenario. I have a strong sense that counselling and psychotherapy researchers might present their work differently, and perhaps more precisely, if magical realism gained more legitimacy as a 'research' genre. Knights (1995), for instance, advocated the study of literature and poetry for counsellors in training, and I would particularly recommend adding magical realist texts to this curriculum.

Performative Alchemies

For my part, I cannot claim this seamless ease. My dreams may be magical but slipping into them by day, without recourse to the cranking machinery of tried and tested literary devices, seems to elude me. I should probably never have drifted off to sleep in the great hall of the Wills Memorial Building with the proofs of this book in my hand, but it was hot that day and I was drawn to the coolness of the carved wooden benches at the back . . . [See Sparkes (2002a) for differentiated representations of fictionalised accounts, creative non-fiction and creative fiction as research genres, all of which, he points out, might be open to the charge: *'the bastards are making it up'* (2002a: 186).]

Richardson (2000a) described her book *Fields of Play* (1997a) as a 'pleated text' (1997b), wherein stories were pleated in between academic papers and could be unfurled or folded back at any time. Perhaps I had just such a purpose here: to pleat further material into the text, in such a way that it was both *connected*, but not *of* the original writing.

The Alchemist's Meta-phora

*S*ubtle wines, soft redlipped women,

the silent companionship of tall hunting dogs,
all this and more has conspired to keep me from grasping
at the edges of some strangeness in the skies

I am held just beyond the brink

I spend my days tinkering with slow mouldering alloys,
distillations that separate out by sunset
and dissolve into the night

distracted by laughter and the taunts of the wind
my fingers have slipped from the caul of the page,
precious manuscripts have fallen from the shelves
and been lost to the dust and mites of my workshop floor, where

*H*alf-deciphered fragments congregate in corners

The night, pressing against the window and plump with pollen
has diverted my gaze from the delicate traceries and
filigrees of ancient words,

precise negotiations betwixt mouse and rat
smelling maidenly in some tongues and of machismo in others,
have been lost forever in the cultural sloppiness
of translation to 'rodent'

*S*ome nights I have fallen asleep at my bench

dreaming fitfully of the movement of clouds over forests
and waking in ri. ulets of regret
at the passing of time

it seems that greater diligence was required, a harsher mind
was necessary, a sharper narrowing of the eyes and quickening of the
*   reflexes*
to grasp the flourish of light that comes before unending rains, hold
*   steady*
against the current and, one-handed, sculpt this pitcher before the sun
poured in to bake it firm, concrete and unyielding

Perhaps some private certainty eludes me

I waited for the sucked-in silences of pending storms
shaped each vessel according to the precise calculations of
the grand tradition, employed only the finest crimson terracotta
and still my metaphors remained unstable, damp and slippery

each container that I turned out (and there have been many over this
lifetime) seemed to slip away beneath the floorboards and, on occasion,
re-appear elsewhere in the house, fashioned in a different way

Nomadic tendencies persisted within each and every pot

produced

my metaphors, in manufacturing themselves, simply refused to stand
*   still*
and yet, even in the face of feigned disappointment at the hours consumed
loafing in cafés, performing bath time oratorios and watching apricots
ripen in the sun; I am not persuaded of my own culpability

whilst the codes and ciphers of alchemical practice include
copious warnings against the hazards of daydreaming and
other brands of negligence, I owe my own survival to such reveries

I am no closer to immortality than you are

but I can show you myriad ways of staying out of focus
long enough to spot some ruptures upon the skin of silence
besides which, I remain suspicious of perfectly formed antiquities
that shatter effortlessly on impact

My own flawed works remain porous, unglazed
and too unpredictable to transport elixirs
from this world to the next

the incessant flaring of meta-phora throughout my dwelling
remains outside the standard alchemical procedures
and makes for untidy, muddy living, but brings
a growing sense of modest pride

I am dog-tired now and fart involuntarily with every step

I doubt the authorities will trouble themselves to seize the
    (unpublished) ramblings
of an elderly scholar or requisition my foundry and
smelting equipment. Nonetheless I am engraving
the inside of my mortar with

This short memorandum for those who follow.

Further reading

Extending research genres
Banks, A. and Banks, S. (eds) (1998) *Fiction and Social Research, by Ice or Fire* (Walnut Creek, CA: Alta Mira).
(Exemplars of fictionalised research studies from across the social sciences.)

Sparkes, A. (2002) *Telling Tales in Sport and Physical Activity: A Qualitative Journey* (Champaign, IL: Human Kinetics).
(A thoughtful, critical text excavating the different qualitative genres available within the sports sciences.)

Magical realism
Allende, I. (1986) *The House of the Spirits* (London: Black Swan).
(A magical realist novel from South America.)

Bowers, M. (2004*) Magic(al) Realism: The New Critical Idiom* (London: Routledge).
(A literary critique of magical realism as subversion.)

Rushdie, S. (1981) *Midnight's Children* (London: Jonathan Cape).
(The Booker of Bookers: a much heralded magical realist novel.)

Afterwords: Electronic and Cinematic Tools and some Future 'Nomadic' Possibilities in Narrative Counselling and Psychotherapy Research

I mentioned at the beginning that this book would just fizzle out, and here's the fizzle into future possibilities. The previous chapters have presented various narrative practices that are already being used, albeit some of them in small ways, amongst counselling researchers. The blurring of genres between arts-based and social-science approaches to the study of human beings is constantly being extended as the parameters around disciplines unravel and are challenged, particularly by those within more established professions such as education and community work (see, for instance, the 'Artography' website).

Education researchers have begun to experiment with the representation of more traditionally collected data and have commissioned dance, community theatre and 'reader's theatre' performances from their work (see Bagley and Cancienne, 2002; Bagley, 2005; Davis and Sumara, 2005; Speedy and Worth, 2007). Perhaps counselling and psychotherapy researchers will catch on to the tail of this trend and, seeking to disseminate their work more widely, will consider different representational genres?

Video-papers and Documentaries: the Visual Narrative Turn

Many counsellors and psychotherapists already routinely use videotaping equipment within their day-to-day work, as a means of recording and supervising work and as a key factor in therapist training and development. Contemporary advances in computer technology allow for the integration of both written and filmed text (or, more precisely, the integration of clips of conversation alongside written reflection). This kind of text, or 'video-paper' as it has become known, is increasingly used within the training and development of teachers and might well be incorporated into therapist training in order for students to more fluidly and commensurately present their work (see Olivero et al., 2004).

Traditions of documentary filmmaking have long been established (and critiqued, see Trinh, 1999) within the work of anthropologists, and perhaps in these days of 'i-movie' and the digital revolution, a wide range of more visual and cinematic research methods may also spread to counselling and psychotherapy, genres that seem well suited to this form of documentation and exploration. Currently, much of the data that becomes narrative counselling research is captured on audio- or videotape and then 'translated' or negotiated across to written text in order to become part of a greater whole, and also in order to preserve confidentiality. The development of cheap, readily available digital recording and editing equipment will perhaps, in time, render some of these translations redundant and the 'messy' narrative texts emerging from future research will include short, experimental and documentary films as well as books and papers. Techniques for disguising identity, and/or video diaries and short vignettes that portray life stories and experiences without betraying confidentiality, are increasingly possible and have become well-known devices from popular TV programmes.

Issues of confidentiality and the protection of clients change constantly as we move increasingly in a world of reality television, in which people are prepared to expose the intimate details of their lives on primetime national television (see Greer, 2001). In this sense it is, I suspect (and hope), client groups that will contribute more and more towards broadening the scope and style of therapy research and its dissemination.

Again, the availability of inexpensive digital film and photographic equipment lends itself to an increasing democratisation of research and to the movement of research out of the academy and into the streets. People are increasingly recording their lives by digital camera, by digital phone/camera and by digital video, and by posting these images up on the Internet. The collection and web-archiving of visual narratives is becoming easier and easier to achieve, and many educational researchers have already exploited the appeal of such methods with young people by undertaking user-led or collaborative research projects with school children that use web logs, digital, visual (and other) narratives and life-story projects involving the use of disposable and other kinds of available camera equipment (see Luttrell, 2005; O'Donoghue, 2004; Photovoice, 2005).

Working in a school of education, as I do, I am privy to these developments, and cannot help but wonder at the possible benefits of their application in my own field, in which talking about events that take place in contexts and space over time is key not only to understanding what is happening in people's lives, but also to imagining what might happen. Photographs and films can record images of people's lives. They might, surely, also speak to the images that are not there: the absent but implicit stories, just outside the frame of the photograph, waiting to be told? As Arnheim (1969/1997: 89) points out:

> Visual knowledge is also responsible for the many examples in which the absence of something functions as an active component of a precept . . . to see emptiness means to place into a precept something that belongs there, but is absent, and to notice its absence as a property of the present. A setting in which a lively action took place or is expected to take place looks strangely motionless: the emptiness may appear pregnant with events to burst forth.

Nomadic and Digital Texts

There's an irony, not lost on this author, in plotting 'the end of the book' at the end of my book, and my own love of literature is far too passionate for me to be found advocating such a turn of the page. Nonetheless, I have been conscious of the limitations of written texts throughout the production of this one. Set down in a linear way, meanings often appear more fixed than I might have wished for. I have frequently longed to imply greater fluidity, movement and multiplicity than the setting down of one word followed by another and then another might imply. The tables and charts describing research criteria and mapping various conversational landscapes in Chapters 3 and 4, for example, appear very differently from how they would as web pages in hypertext, which would provide opportunities for readers to change them around, delete those criteria which were irrelevant, or add maps and charts of their own.

My dreams towards less fixed and more nomadic research practices might be supported by the inclusion of more visual technologies, particularly moving pictures within the currently fairly static archives of counselling research. The documentary and experimental filmmaker Trinh Minh-Ha (1992) speaks of filmmaking as a hybrid practice of constant re-assemblage with fiction at its heart. Thus visual and moving images, already in day-to-day use amongst therapy practitioners, seem an exciting and untapped resource that might be extended much further through the use of digital technologies.

The salient characteristic of hypertext lies in its representation of intertextuality through electronic links between parts of a work and between works (written, visual, film clips, etc.). From the outset, I had my heart set on this manuscript as a traditional paper book. Perhaps I am just an old-fashioned girl? During the course of its production, however, it has repeatedly occurred to me that many of my frustrations with seemingly fixed and apparently two-dimensional or linear representations of complex phenomena might be overcome by the use of hypertext. Hypertext is not only a non-linear, but also a multi-sequential space (see Landlow, 1994; Morgan, 2000) in which 'either/or' is abandoned in favour of 'and/and/and' (Douglas, 1996), and in which readers can re-order and, in some cases, re-create the text in any way they choose. Many critical moments of weakness within this book, such as not having the space to include audience reflections on my performance piece in Chapter 9 or only including short quotes or the titles of works cited, rather than extensive and pithy extracts from key texts, could have been avoided through the production of an electronic text. Had this been the case, readers could continue to add links from the expressions of my life that caught their attention, into stories from their own lives and cultures, at any time:

> It blurs the boundaries between authors and readers, giving the latter more power to construct the text in reading, choosing pathways through the material and thereby juxtaposing textual segments in a one-off assemblage.   (Morgan, 2000: 131)

The lip service paid to readers and audiences in poststructuralist texts, such as this one, would take on a new collaborative and democratic power if clients, practitioners and others reading psychotherapy research texts were visibly and permanently supported in contributing their co-constructions of the stories they read. Perhaps Derrida's (1976) infinite possibilities available in conversations and Geertz's (1983) 'multi-storied' worlds would begin to appear out of the abstract mists as more of a visible practice of collaborative narrative inquiry, if counselling research 'went digital'.

Complex Narratives: Moving from De-centred to De-human-centred Research and Practice in Therapy

This book has covered a lot of the shifting ground between individual-istic and social ways of theorising what it means to be human. It has also crossed and re-crossed several of the borders between arts-based and social-sciences research. It may not have achieved success as a substantive contribution, as suggested amongst the criteria for readers in Chapter 2, but it has found a fragmented, partial, local, nomadic place to stand and make a transgressive, transparent, reflexive contri-bution of aesthetic merit in parts. Much value has been placed, throughout, on practices of co-research in which collaborative projects have been described, and the local knowledge gained has been valued and recorded. Throughout the text, apart from rhizomatic metaphors for research processes and some reference to the geographical and cultural spaces we inhabit, the entire world is referenced as if human beings constructed it. I stand by the ideas I have outlined above about the significance and constitutive powers of the stories we tell ourselves about our lives. There is also, as Harraway (2004) would say, 'really a lot else going on besides' that which is storied, or not, by human beings.

Just as attention to the social and the cultural has provided a more complex, less individualistic practice of therapy and of co-research, an understanding of the complex non-human sites and systems that we inhabit and co-exist with, might lead to more questioning of anthropo-morphic notions about human beings as central actors in the shaping of their worlds. Ideas of a multi-storied world generating infinite local possibilities have generated a modest sense of therapist/researcher expertise in relation to the stories people might tell us about their lives. Consideration of the positions and contributions to those lives on the part of birds in flight, weather conditions, pollution in cities, global warming and a myriad complex and interconnected eco-systems, posi-tions human beings even more modestly upon the surface of the planet. Consideration of the contribution of human beings to such complex phenomena reduces their chosen place at the centre of things still further (see Byrne, 1998; Cilliers, 1998; and Hayles, 1990, for overviews of these ideas).

One quick re-read of this text before it goes to the publishers reminds me how much everything I have written about focuses on human beings and their communities as if they were somehow disconnected from other species on the planet or the geographical and ecological forces and discourses that surround them. The research and therapy practices I have described here have moved away from privileging god, or individuals, as autonomous beings. They have also steered clear of deterministic ideas of socio-cultural construction and have avoided generating models, frameworks and structures to explain the stories of people's lives. The forms of knowing and not knowing included in this book, however, have centred entirely on human undertakings as if these were at the top of some imagined hierarchy. Hayles (1990: 176), a writer more interested in physical and geographical than peopled worlds, claims: 'where scientists see chaos as the source of order, poststructuralists appropriate it to subvert order'.

Perhaps these do not have to remain binary positions. Perhaps there are infinite possibilities in the space between sources and subversions of order. And perhaps now that we have started to work with people, and research their lives in ways that link them with each other in a social world, we can begin to make further, less anthropomorphic connections with the spaces, landscapes, geographies and ecologies that people form part of. There is much said about such ideas, and has been for some time, within the related literatures of psychotherapy, spirituality and the interconnectedness of all things (the work of James Hillman, Satish Kumar, Vandanya Shiva, Fritjof Capra and others springs to mind here, representatives of a group of thinkers working across the boundaries of spirituality, psychotherapy and ecology, see www.schumachercollege.org.uk and www.resurgence.org for more about their work), but I am not discussing philosophical positions or debates about values here. I am talking about the development of a therapeutic or co-research *practice* that might release human beings from the centre of their own stage and take account of the linking of lives with (literal) landscapes.

As I write, I am at the edges of what I know, with little idea about how the practice of a more globally, ecologically interconnected therapeutic or co-research endeavour might look.

Turning once again to a magical realist to sustain me in my endeavours, I shall end with Salman Rushdie, who seems to understand such matters in ways that both I, and most of my chosen profession, seem to have grasped only dimly. This text is not fizzling out here with some kind of abstract and distant esoteric discussion. This book has come to a fizzle at a point where its author has understood that the 'hall of mirrors' people find themselves in as they try and make sense of the world, reflects and refracts far more than the great anonymous murmur of *human* discourses. She is not at all sure, for the moment, where to go with all this. She is left pondering Rushdie's commentary on the limits of human discourses and the fragile light that they alone might shed upon our lives. In his own words he argues that:

> *To understand one life you have to swallow the world.*
>
> (Rushdie, 1981: 126)

References

Abbott, H. (2002) *The Cambridge Introduction to Narrative* (Cambridge: Cambridge University Press).

Adair, M. (2003) 'Living in the Kingdom of Yuck', unpublished MSc. thesis, University of Bristol.

Alexander, B. (2005) 'Performance Ethnography: the Re-enacting and Inciting of Culture', in Denzin, N. and Lincoln, Y. (eds), *The Sage Handbook of Qualitative Research* (Thousand Oaks, CA: Sage).

Allende, I. (1986) *The House of the Spirits* (London: Black Swan).

Allende, I. (1997) 'An Interview with Isabel Allende', in Iftekharuddin, F., Rohrberger, M. and Jackson, M. (eds), *Speaking of the Short Story: Interviews with Contemporary Writers* (Jackson: University of Mississippi Press).

Alvermann, D. (2000) 'Researching Libraries, Literacies, and Lives: a Rhizoanalysis', in St Pierre, E. and Pillow, W. (eds), *Working the Ruins: Feminist Poststructural Theory and Methods in Education* (London: Routledge).

Alvesson, M. and Skoldberg, K. (2000) *Reflexive Methodology* (London: Sage).

Andersen, T. (1987) 'The Reflecting Team: Dialogue and Meta-dialogue in Clinical Work'. In: *Family Process*, 26: 415–28.

Anderson, H. and Goolishan, H. (1992) 'The Client as the Expert: a Not Knowing Approach to Therapy', in *Therapy as a Social Construction*, ed. S. McNee and K. Gergen (London: Sage).

Andrews, J. (2001) 'The Elder Project: Witnessing Lives', in: *Working with the Stories of Women's Lives* (Adelaide: Dulwich Centre Publications).

Andrews, M. (2004a) 'Memories of Mother: Counter-narratives of Early Maternal Influence', in Bamberg, M. and Andrews, M. (eds), *Considering Counter-narratives: Narrating, Resisting, Making Sense* (Amsterdam: John Benjamins).

Andrews, M. (2004b) 'Refusing to tell the expected tale as a form of counter-narrative', paper given at the 9th International Pragmatics Conference, http://webhost.ua.ac.be/tisp/index.php

Angus, L. and Hardtke, K. (1994) 'Narrative Processes in Psychotherapy'. In: *Canadian Psychology*, 35(2): 190–203.

Angus, L. and McLeod, J. (eds) (2004a) *The Handbook of Narrative and Psychotherapy Practice, Theory and Research* (London: Sage).

Angus, L. and McLeod, J. (2004b) 'Toward an Integrative Framework for Understanding the Role of Narrative in the Psychotherapy Process', in Angus, L. and McLeod, J. (eds), *The Handbook of Narrative and Psychotherapy Practice, Theory and Research* (London: Sage).

Aristotle (1932 edn) *The Poetics* (Cambridge, MA: Loch Classical Library).

Arnheim, R. (1969/1997) *Visual Thinking* (Berkeley, CA: University of California Press).

Artography: arts-informed research association, http://m1.cust.educ.ubc.ca:16080/Artography/ (accessed June 2005).

Atkinson, P. and Delamont, S. (2005) 'Analytic Perspectives', in Denzin, N. and Lincoln, Y. (eds), *The Sage Handbook of Qualitative Research* (Thousand Oaks, CA: Sage).

Atkinson, P. and Silverman, D. (1997) 'Kundera's Immortality: the Interview Society and the Invention of Self', *Qualitative Inquiry*, 3(3): 304–25.

Atwood, M. (1985) *The Handmaid's Tale* (London: Virago).

Atwood, M. (2001) *Negotiating with the Dead: A Writer on Writing* (Cambridge: Cambridge University Press).

Bachelard, G. (1971) *The Poetics of Reverie* (Boston, MA: Beacon Press).

Bachelard, G. (1986) *The Poetics of Space* (New York: Beacon Press).

Bagley, C. (2005) 'Keynote Performance', Arts-based Educational Research Conference, Drama Studio, Queen's University, Belfast.

Bagley, C. and Cancienne, M. (2002) *Dancing the Data* (New York: Peter Lang).

Bakan, D. (1996) 'Some Reflections about Narrative Research, Hurt and Harm', in Josselson, R. (ed.), *Ethics and Process in the Narrative Study of Lives* (Thousand Oaks, CA: Sage).

Bakhtin, M. (1981) *The Dialogic Imagination: Four Essays*, trans. C. Emerson and M. Holquist (Austin, TX: University of Austin Press).

Bakhtin, M. (1986) *Speech Genres and Other Late Essays* (Austin, TX: University of Austin Press).

Bamberg, M. and Andrews, M. (2004) *Considering Counter-narratives: Narrating, Resisting, Making Sense* (Amsterdam: John Benjamins).

Bamberg, M. and McCabe, A. (1998) Editorial. In: *Narrative Inquiry* 8(1): iii–v.

Banks, A. (1998) 'Some people would say I tell lies', in Banks, A. and Banks, S. (eds), *Fiction and Social Research, by Ice or Fire* (Walnut Creek, CA: Alta Mira).

Behan, C. (1999/2002) 'Linking Lives Around Shared Themes: Narrative Group Therapy with Gay Men'. In: *Gecko: A Journal of Deconstruction and Narrative Ideas in Therapeutic Practice*, 2: 18–35. Republished 2002 in Denborough, D. (ed.), *Queer Counselling and Narrative Practice* (Adelaide: Dulwich Centre Publications).

Behan, C. (2003) *Rescued Speech Poems: Co-authoring Poetry in Narrative Therapy*, http://narrativeapproaches.com

Behar, R. (1993) *Translated Woman: Crossing the Border with Esperanza's Story* (Boston, MA: Beacon Press).

Belsey, C. (2002) *Post-structuralism: A Very Short Introduction* (Oxford: Oxford University Press).

Bennett, A. (1988/2003) *Talking Heads* (New York: Picador).

Bennett. A. (1991) *A Question of Attribution*, BBC, UK.

Bennett, A. and Royle, N. (1999) *Introduction to Literature, Criticism and Theory*, 2nd edn (Harlow: Prentice Hall).

Bergin, A. and Garfield, S. (eds) (1994) *Handbook of Psychotherapy and Behavioural Change*, 4th edn (Chichester: Wiley).

Berridge, V. (1999) *The Opium of the People: Opiate Use and Drug Control in Nineteenth and Early Twentieth Century England* (London: Free Association Books).

Besley, T. (2001) 'Foucauldian Influences in Narrative Therapy: an Approach for Schools'. In: *Journal of Educational Enquiry*, 2(2): 72–92.

Betterton, E. and Epston, D. (1998) 'Imaginary Friends: Who are They? Who Needs Them?' In: *Catching Up with David Epston: A Collection of Narrative Practice-based Papers* (Adelaide: Dulwich Centre Publications).

Bird, C. (2005) 'How I Stopped Dreading and Learned to Love Transcription'. In: *Qualitative Inquiry*, 11: 226–48.

Bird, J. (2000) *The Heart's Narrative: Therapy and Navigating Life's Contradictions* (Auckland: Edge Press).

Bird, J. (2004a) *Talk that Sings* (Auckland: Edge Press).

Bird, J. (2004b) 'Narrating the Difference', in Strong, T. and Paré, D. (eds), *Furthering Talk: Advances in the Discursive Therapie* (New York: Kluwer Academic/Plenum Publishers).

Blake, William, 'Gnomic Verses', in Stevenson, W. (ed.) (1989), *Blake, the Complete Poems* (Harlow: Longman).

Bloom, L. (1998) *Under the Sign of Hope: Feminist Methodology and Narrative Interpretation* (Albany, NY: State University of New York Press).

Boal, A. (1985) *Theatre of the Oppressed* (New York: Theatre Communications Group).

Bochner, A. (1997) 'It's About Time: Narrative and the Divided Self'. In: *Qualitative Inquiry*, 3: 418–38.

Bochner, A. (2000) 'Criteria Against Ourselves'. In: *Qualitative Inquiry*, 6(2): 266–72.

Bochner, A. (2001) 'Narrative's Virtues'. In: *Qualitative Inquiry*, 7(2): 131–57.

Bochner, A. and Ellis, C. (1996a) 'Talking over Ethnography', in Ellis, C. and Bochner, A. (eds), *Composing Ethnography* (Walnut Creek, CA: Alta Mira Press).

Bochner, A. and Ellis, C. (1996b) 'Taking Ethnography into the Twenty-first Century'. In: *Journal of Contemporary Ethnography*, 25(1): 3–5.

Bochner, A. and Ellis, C. (2002) *Ethnographically Speaking: Autoethnography, Literature and Aesthetics* (Walnut Creek, CA: Alta Mira Press).

Bolton, G. (2003) 'Around the Slices of Herself', in Etherington, K. (ed.) (2003), *Trauma, the Body and Transformation* (London: Jessica Kingsley).

Bolton, G., Howlett, S., Lago, C. and Wright, J. (2004) *Writing Cures: An Introductory Handbook of Writing in Counselling and Psychotherapy* (London: Brunner-Routledge).

Bond, T. (2004a) *Ethical Guidelines for Researching Counselling and Psychotherapy* (Rugby: British Association of Counselling and Psychotherapy).

Bond, T. (2004b) 'An Introduction to the Ethical Guidelines for Researching Counselling and Psychotherapy'. In: *Counselling and Psychotherapy Research*, 4(2): 4–10.

Booker, D. (2004) *The Seven Basic Plots: Why We Tell Stories* (London: Continuum).

Bourdieu, P. (1988) *Homo Academicus* (Stanford, CA: Stanford University Press).

Bowers, M. (2004) *Magic(al) Realism: The New Critical Idiom* (London: Routledge).

Brady, I. (1991) *Anthropological Poetics* (Savage, MD: Rowman & Little).

Brady, I. (2005) 'Poetics for a Planet: Discourse on some Problems of Being-in-Place', in Denzin, N. and Lincoln, Y. (eds), *The Sage Handbook Of Qualitative Research*, 3rd edn (Thousand Oaks, CA: Sage).

Broadhurst, S. (1999) *Liminal Performance* (London: Cassell).

Bruner, J. (1986a) *Actual Minds: Possible Worlds* (Cambridge, MA: Harvard University Press).

Bruner, J. (1986b) 'The Inspiration of Vygotsky', in *Actual Minds: Possible Worlds* (Cambridge, MA: Harvard University Press).

Bruner, J. (1990) *Acts of Meaning* (Cambridge, MA: Harvard University Press).

Bruner, J. (1991) 'The Narrative Construction of Reality'. In: *Critical Inquiry*, 18: 1–21.

Bruner, J. (2002) *Making Stories: Law, Literature, Life* (New York: Farrar, Straus & Giroux).

Buckroyd, J. (2005) 'Compare and Contrast'. In: *Counselling and Psychotherapy Research*, 5(1): 51–2.

Burr, V. (2003) *Social Constructionism*, 2nd edn (London: Routledge).

Butler, J. (1993) *Bodies that Matter: On the Discursive Limits of Sex* (New York: Routledge).

Butler, J. (1997) *Excitable Speech: A Politics of the Performative* (New York: Routledge).

Buzan, T. and Buzan, B. (2003) *The Mind Map Book: Radiant Thinking – Major Evolution in Human Thought* (London: BBC Books).

Byrne, D. (1998) *Complexity Theory and the Social Sciences* (London: Routledge).

Calgut, C. (1999) 'A Fair Deal for Lesbians in Therapy – an Ethical Issue?' In: *Counselling*, 10(4): 285.

Calgut, C. (2005) 'Lesbians and Therapists: the Need for Explicitness'. In: *Counselling and Psychotherapy Journal*, 16(4): 8–11.

Capshew, J. (1999) *Psychologists on the March: Science, Practice and Professional Identity, 1929–1969* (Cambridge: Cambridge University Press).

Carey, M. (1999) 'Reflecting on our Reflections: the Use of Reflecting Processes in Community Gatherings'. In: *Gecko: A Journal of Deconstruction and Narrative Ideas in Therapeutic Practice*, 2: 83–91.

Carey, M. and Russell, S. (2002a) 'Externalising – Commonly Asked Questions'. In: *International Journal of Narrative Therapy and Community Work*, 2: 76–85.

Carey, M. and Russell, S. (2002b) 'Remembering: Responding to Frequently Asked Questions'. In: *International Journal of Narrative Therapy and Community Work*, 3: 23–33.

Carter, A. (1984) *Nights at the Circus* (London: Virago).

Carter, A. (1992) *Wise Children* (London: Virago).

Cavallaro, D. (2003) *French Feminist Theory* (New York: Continuum).

Chamberlayne, P., Bornat, J. and Wengraf, T. (2000) *The Turn to Biographical Methods in Social Science: The Comparative Issues and Examples* (London: Routledge).

Charmaz, K. and Mitchell, R. (1997) 'The Myth of Silent Authorship: Self, Substance and Style', in: Hertz, R. (ed.), *Reflexivity and Voice* (Thousand Oaks, CA: Sage).

Charon, R. (2004) *Program in Narrative Medicine, College of Physicians and Surgeons, Columbia University*, on: www.narrativemedicine.org

Chase, S. (2003) 'Learning to Listen: Narrative Principles in a Qualitative Research Methods Course', in Josselson, R., Lieblich, A. and McAdams, D. (eds), *Up Close and Personal: The Teaching and Learning of Narrative Research* (Washington, DC: American Psychological Association).

Chaudry, L. (1997) 'Researching "my" People, Researching Myself: Fragments of a Reflexive Tale'. In: *International Journal of Qualitative Studies in Education*, 8(3): 229–38.

Church, K. (1995) *Hidden Narratives* (London: Gordon & Breach).

Ciardi, J. (1979) *For Instance* (New York: W. W. Norton).

Cilliers, P. (1998) *Complexity and Postmodernism: Understanding Complex Systems* (London: Routledge).

Cixous, H. (1991) 'Readings', in Blyth, I. and Sellers, S. (eds) (2004), *Hélène Cixous: Live Theory* (New York: Continuum).

Cixous, H. (1993) *Three Steps on the Ladder of Writing* (New York: Columbia University Press).

Cixous, H. and Calle-Gruber, M. (1997) *Rootprints: Memory and Life Writing* (London: Routledge).

Cixous, H. and Clement, C. (1986) *The Newly Born Woman* (Manchester: Manchester University Press).

Clandinin, J. and Connelly, P. (2000) *Narrative Inquiry: Experience and Story in Qualitative Research* (San Francisco, CA: Jossey-Bass).

Clough, P. (2000) 'Comments on Setting Criteria for Experimental Writing'. In: *Qualitative Inquiry*, 6(2): 278–91.

Clough, P. (2002) *Narratives and Fictions in Educational Research* (Buckingham: Open University Press).

Clough, P., Henry, M., Riessman, C., Sparkes, C. and Speedy, J. (2005) Roundtable discussion on Auto-ethnography (Centre for Narratives and Transformative Learning, University of Bristol).

Coffey, A. (1999) *The Ethnographic Self* (London: Routledge).

Cohen-Cruz, J. (ed.) (1998) *Radical Street Performance: An International Anthology* (London: Routledge).

Collins, P. (1990) *Black Feminist Thought: Knowledge, Consciousness and the Politics of Empowerment* (New York: Routledge).

Conley, D. (2000) *Honky* (Berkeley, CA: University of California Press).

Cooper, L. (2001) 'Re-searching My Self: an Auto-ethnography of My Personal Experience of Work-related Stress, Drawing on Personal, Professional and Research Narratives', unpublished MSc thesis, University of Bristol.

Crawford, J., Kippax, S., Onyx, J., Gault, U. and Benton, P. (1992) *Emotion and Gender: Constructing Meaning from Memory* (London: Sage).

Crockett, K. (2004) 'From Narrative Practice in Counselling to Narrative Practice in Research: a Professional Identity Story'. In: *International Journal of Narrative Therapy and Community Work*, 2: 63–8.

Crockett, K., Drewery, W., McKenzie, W., Smith, L. and Winslade, J. (2004) 'Working for Ethical Research in Practice'. In: *International Journal of Narrative Therapy and Community Work*, 3: 61–7.

Currie, M. (1998) *Postmodern Narrative Theory* (Basingstoke: Macmillan).

Czarniawska, B. (1998) *A Narrative Approach to Organisation Studies* (Thousand Oaks, CA: Sage).

Dale, S. (2005) 'Where Angels Fear to Tread: an Exploration of the Experience of Having Conversations about Suicide within a Counselling Context', unpublished MSc thesis, University of Bristol.

Danaher, G., Schirato, T. and Webb, J. (2000) *Understanding Foucault* (London: Sage).

Danchev, D. (1998) Paper on Issues of Transcription and Representation, presented at: BAC Research Conference, University of Birmingham.

Davenport-Hines, R. (2001) *The Pursuit of Oblivion: A Global History of Narcotics, 1500–2000* (London: Weidenfeld & Nicolson).

Davies, B. (1991) 'The Concept of Agency: a Feminist Post Structural Analysis'. In: *Social Analysis*, 30: 42–53.

Davies, B. (1994) *Poststructuralist Theory and Classroom Practice* (Geelong: Deakin University).

Davies, B. (2000a) *(In)Scribing Body/Landscape Relations* (Walnut Creek, CA: Alta Mira).

Davies, B. (2000b) *A Body of Writing, 1990–1999* (Walnut Creek, CA: Alta Mira).

Davies, B., Browne, J., Honan, E., Laws, C., Mueller-Rockstroh, B. and Bendix Petersen, E. (2004) 'The Ambivalent Practices of Reflexivity'. In: *Qualitative Inquiry*, 10(3): 360–89.

Davies, B., Dormer, S., Gannon, S., Laws, C., Rocco, S., Taguchi, H. and McCann, H. (2001) 'Becoming Schoolgirls: the Ambivalent Process of Subjectification'. In: *Gender and Education*, 13(2): 167–82.

Davies, B., Dormer, S., Honan, E., MacAllister, N., O'Reilly, R., Rocco, S. and Walker, A. (1997) 'Ruptures in the Skin of Silence: a Collective Biography'. In: *Hecate: A Women's Interdisciplinary Journal*, 23(1): 62–79.

Davies, B. and Gannon, S. (2005) 'Feminism/Poststructuralism', in Somekh, B. and Lewin, C. (eds), *Research Methods in the Social Sciences* (London: Sage).

Davies, B. and Gannon, S. (2006) *Doing Collective Biography* (Maidenhead: Open University Press).

Davies, B. and Harré, R. (1990) 'Positioning: the Discursive Production of Selves'. In: *Journal for the Theory of Social Behaviour*, 19(4): 43–63.

Davis, B. and Sumara, D. (2005) Normalizing Fictions of Teacher Education: a Readers' Theatre Performance: CLIO Seminar, Graduate School of Education, University of Bristol.

Deleuze, G. and Guattari, F. (1987) 'Introduction: Rhizome', in *A Thousand Plateaus: Capitalism and Schizophrenia* (Minnesota: University of Minnesota Press; originally published 1980).

Deleuze, G. and Parnet, C. (1987) 'Many Politics', in *Dialogues* (New York: Columbia University Press).

Denborough, D. (2002) *Community Song-Writing and Narrative Practice*, www.dulwichcentre.com.au (website accessed July 2005).

Denzin, N. (1997) *Interpretive Ethnography* (Thousand Oaks, CA: Sage).

Denzin, N.(2000) 'Aesthetics and the Practices of Qualitative Inquiry'. In: *Qualitative Inquiry*, 6(2): 256–66.

Denzin, N. (2005) 'Emancipatory Discourses and the Ethics and Politics of Representation', in Denzin, N. and Lincoln, Y. (eds), *The Sage Handbook of Qualitative Research* (Thousand Oaks, CA: Sage).

Denzin, N. and Lincoln, Y. (2000) 'Introduction: the Discipline and Practice of Qualitative Research', in Denzin, N. and Lincoln, Y. (eds), *Handbook of Qualitative Research* (Thousand Oaks, CA: Sage).

Department of Health (2003) *National Suicide Prevention Strategy*, on: www.dh.gov.uk/publicationsandstatistics/publications

Department of Health (2005) *Lowest Suicide Rate for Young Men for Nearly 20 Years*, on: www.dh.gov.uk/publicationsandstatistics/publications

Derrida, J. (1976) *Of Grammatology* (Baltimore, MD: Johns Hopkins University Press).

Derrida, J. (1978) *Writing and Difference* (Chicago: University of Chicago Press).

Derrida, J. (1981) *Positions* (Chicago: University of Chicago Press).

Dickens, C. (1837–8) *David Copperfield* (London: Hazell, Watson & Viney).

Dickens, C. (1838–9) *Nicholas Nickleby* (London: Hazell, Watson & Viney).

Dickens, C. (1849–50) *Oliver Twist* (London: Hazell, Watson & Viney).

Donavan, K. (1999) 'The Report', in *Entering the Mare* (Newcastle-on-Tyne: Bloodaxe Books).

Douglas, J. (1996) 'Abandoning the either/or for the and/and/and: Hypertext and the Art of Argumentative Writing'. In: *Australian Journal of Language and Literacy*, 19(4): 305–16.

Drewery, W. (2005) 'Why We Should Watch What We Say: Position Calls, Everyday Speech and the Production of Relational Subjectivity'. In: *Theory and Psychology*, 15(3): 305–24.

Drewery, W. and Winslade, J. (1997) 'The Theoretical Story of Narrative', in Monk, G., Winslade, J., Crocket, K. and Epston, D. (eds), *Narrative Therapy in Practice: The Archaeology of Hope* (San Francisco, CA: Jossey-Bass).

Duffy, C. (1985) 'The Biographer', in *Selected Poems* (Harmondsworth: Penguin).

Duffy, C. (1993) *Mean Time* (London: Anvil Press).

Eakin, P. (1999) *How our Lives Become Stories* (New York: Cornell University Press).

Eco, U. (2003) *Mouse or Rat? Translation as Negotiation* (London: Weidenfeld & Nicolson).

Ellington, L. (1998) ' "Then You Know How I Feel": Empathy, Reflexivity and Identification in Field Work'. In: *Qualitative Inquiry*, 4(4): 492–514.

Ellis, C. (1995) *Final Negotiation: A Story of Love, Loss and Chronic Illness* (Philadelphia: Temple University Press).

Ellis, C. (1997) 'Evocative Ethnography, Writing Emotionally about our Lives', in Tierney, W. and Lincoln, Y. (eds), *Representation and the Text, Reframing the Narrative Voice* (Albany, NY: State University of New York Press).

Ellis, C. (2000) 'Creating Criteria: an Ethnographic Short Story'. In: *Qualitative Inquiry*, 6(2): 273–7.

Ellis, C. (2004) *The Auto-ethnographic 'I': A Methodological Novel about Teaching and Doing Ethnography* (Walnut Creek, CA: Alta Mira).

Ellis, C. and Berger, L. (2001) 'Their Story/My Story/Our Story: Including the Researcher's Experience in Interview Research', in Gubrium, J. and Holstein, J. (eds), *Handbook of Interview Research: Context and Method* (Thousand Oaks, CA: Sage).

Ellis, C. and Berger, L. (2003) 'Their Story/My Story/Our Story: Including the Researcher's Experience in Interview Research', in Gubrium, J. and Holstein, J. (eds), *Postmodern Interviewing* (Thousand Oaks, CA: Sage).

Ellis, C. and Bochner, A. (eds) (1996) *Composing Ethnography: Alternative Forms of Qualitative Writing* (Walnut Creek, CA: Alta Mira).

Ellis, C. and Bochner, A. (2000) 'Auto Ethnography, Personal Narrative, Reflexivity: Researcher as Subject', in Denzin, N. and Lincoln, Y. (eds), *Handbook of Qualitative Research*, 2nd edn (Thousand Oaks, CA: Sage).

Ellis, C. and Flaherty, M. (1992) *Investigating Subjectivity: Research on Lived Experience* (Newbury Park, CA: Sage).

Ellis, C., Kiesinger, C. and Tillman-Healy, L. (1997) 'Interactive Interviewing: Talking about Emotional Experience', in Hertz, R. (ed.), *Reflexivity and Voice* (Thousand Oaks, CA: Sage).

Ellos, W. (1994) *Narrative Ethics* (Aldershot: Avebury).

Epston, D. (1999) 'Co-research: the Making of an Alternative Knowledge', in *Narrative Therapy and Community Work: A Conference Collection* (Adelaide: Dulwich Centre Publications).

Epston, D. (2000) *The History of the Archives of Resistance – Anti-anorexia/Anti-bulimia*: www.narrativepapproaches.com (accessed, 2004)

Epston, D. (2001) 'Anthropology, Archives, Co-research and Narrative Therapy: an Interview with David Epston', in Denborough, D. (ed.), *Family Therapy: Exploring the Field's Past, Present and Possible Futures* (Adelaide: Dulwich Centre Publications).

Epston, D. (2004) 'From Empathy to Ethnography: the Origin of Therapeutic Co-research'. In: *International Journal of Narrative Therapy and Community Work*, 2: 31.

Epston, D. and White, M. (1992) 'Consulting your Consultants: the Documentation of Alternative Knowledges', in *Experience, Contradiction, Narrative and Imagination* (Adelaide: Dulwich Centre Publications).

Esquivel, L. (1993) *Like Water for Chocolate* (New York: Doubleday).

Etherington, K. (1996) 'The Counsellor as Researcher: Boundary Issues and Critical Dilemmas'. In: *British Journal of Guidance and Counselling*, 24(3): 339–46.

Etherington, K. (2000) *Narrative Approaches to Working with Adult Male Survivors of Child Sexual Abuse: The Client's, the Counsellor's and the Researcher's Story* (London: Jessica Kingsley).

Etherington, K. (2001) 'Research with Ex-Clients: an Extension and Celebration of the Therapeutic Process'. In: *British Journal of Guidance and Counselling*, 29(1): 5–19.

Etherington, K. (ed.) (2003a) *Trauma, the Body and Transformation: A Narrative Inquiry* (London: Jessica Kingsley).

Etherington, K. (2003b) 'The Weaver's Tale: Yarns and Threads', in: Etherington, K. (ed.) (2003a), *Trauma, the Body and Transformation* (London: Jessica Kingsley).

Etherington, K. (2004) *Becoming a Reflexive Researcher: Using Our Selves in Research* (London: Jessica Kingsley).

Evans, M. (1999) *Missing Persons: The Impossibility of Auto/Biography* (London: Routledge).

Faris, W. (2004) *Ordinary Enchantments: Magical Realism and the Remystification of Narrative* (Nashville, TN: Vanderbilt University Press).

Ferguson, M., Salter, M. and Stallworthy, J. (eds) (1996) *Norton Anthology of Poetry* (New York: W. W. Norton).

Fetherston, B. (2002) 'Double Bind: an Essay on Counselling Training'. In: *Counselling and Psychotherapy Research*, (2)2: 108–27.

Filax, G., Sumara, D., Davis, B. and Shogan, D. (2005) 'Queer Theory/Lesbian and Gay Approaches', in Somekh, B. and Lewin, C. (eds), *Research Methods in the Social Sciences* (Thousand Oaks, CA: Sage).

Fine, M., Weis, L., Weseen, S. and Wong, L. (2000) 'For whom? Qualitative Research, Representations and Social Responsibilities', in Denzin, N. and Lincoln, Y. (eds), *Handbook of Qualitative Research*, 2nd edn (Thousand Oaks, CA: Sage).

Finley, S. (2005) 'Arts-based Inquiry: Performing Revolutionary Pedagogy', in Denzin, N. and Lincoln, Y. (eds), *The Sage Handbook of Qualitative Research*, 3rd edn (Thousand Oaks, CA: Sage).

Fontana, A. and Frey, J. (2000) 'The Interview: from Structural Questions to Negotiated Text', in Denzin, N. and Lincoln, Y. (eds), *Handbook of Qualitative Research* (Thousand Oaks, CA: Sage).

Fontana, A. and Frey, J. (2001) 'Postmodern Trends in Interviewing', in Gubrium, J. and Holstein, J. (eds), *Handbook of Interview Research: Context and Method* (Thousand Oaks, CA: Sage).

Fontana, A. and Frey, J. (2005) 'The Interview: from Neutral Stance to Politcal Involvement', in Denzin, N. and Lincoln, Y. (eds), *The Sage Handbook of Qualitative Research* (Thousand Oaks, CA: Sage).

Foucault, M. (1965) *Madness and Civilisation: A History of Insanity in the Age of Reason* (London: Routledge).

Foucault, M. (1972) *The Archaeology of Knowledge* (London: Routledge).

Foucault, M. (1975) *The Birth of the Clinic: An Archaeology of Medical Perception* (New York: Random House).

Foucault, M. (1977a) 'What is an Author?', in Bouchard, D. (ed.), *Language, Counter-Memory Practice* (Ithaca, NY: Cornell University Press).

Foucault, M. (1977b) *Discipline and Punish* (London: Allen Lane).

Foucault, M (1980a) 'Truth and Power', in Gordon, C. (ed.), *Michel Foucault: Power/Knowledge: Selected Interviews and Other Writings, 1972–1977* (Brighton: Harvester).

Foucault, M. (1980b) *Power/Knowledge: Selected Interviews and Other Writings* (New York: Pantheon Press).

Foucault, M. (1981) *The History of Sexuality*, Vol. One: *An Introduction* (Harmondsworth: Penguin).

Foucault, M. (1982) 'The Subject and Power: an Afterword', in Dreyfus, H. and Rabinow, P. (eds), *Michel Foucault: Beyond Structuralism and Hermeneutics* (Chicago: University of Chicago Press).

Foucault, M. (1988a) 'The Ethic of Care for the Self as a Practice of Freedom', in Bernasser, J. and Rasmussen, D. (eds), *The Final Foucault* (Cambridge, MA: MIT Press).

Foucault, M. (1988b) 'Technologies of the Self' and 'The Political Technology of Individuals', in Gutman, M. and Hutton, P. (eds), *Technologies of the Self* (Amherst, MA: University of Massachusetts Press).

Foucault, M. (1989) *Foucault Live: Interviews, 1966–1984* (New York: Semiotext).

Foucault, M. (2000) *Essential works, 1954–84*, Vol. 1: *Ethics*, ed. P. Rabinow (Harmondsworth: Penguin).

Frank, A. (1995) *The Wounded Storyteller: Body, Illness, and Ethics* (London: University of Chicago Press).

Freedman, J. and Combs, G. (1996) *Narrative Therapy: The Social Construction of Preferred Realities* (New York: W. W. Norton).

Freeman, J. Epston, D., and Lobovits, D. (1997) *Playful Approaches to Serious Problems: Narrative Therapy with Children and their families* (New York: W. W. Norton).

Freeman, M. (1998) 'Mythical Time, Historical Time and the Narrative Fabric of the Self'. In: *Narrative Inquiry*, 8(1): 27–50.

Freire, P. (1982) 'Creating Alternative Research Methods: Learning to Do It by Doing It', in Hall, B., Gillette, A. and Tandon, R. (eds), *Creating Knowledge: A Monopoly?* (New Delhi: Society for Participatory Research in Asia).

Freire, P. (1998) 'Pedagogy of the Heart', in Freire, A. and Macedon, D. (eds), *The Paolo Freire Reader* (New York: Continuum).

Friedman, S. (1995) *The Reflecting Team in Action: Collaborative Practice in Family Therapy* (New York: Guilford).

Gannon, S. (2001) '(Re)presenting the Collective Girl: a Poetic Approach to a Methodological Dilemma'. In: *Qualitative Inquiry*, 7(6): 787–800.

Gatens, M. (1995) 'Between the Sexes: Care of Justice', in Almond, B. (ed.), *Introduction to Applied Ethics* (Oxford: Blackwell).

Gee, J. (1991) 'A Linguistic Approach to Narrative'. In: *Journal of Narrative and Life History*, I: 15–39.

Geertz, C. (1973a) *The Interpretation of Cultures* (New York: Basic Books).

Geertz, C. (1973b) 'Thick Description: Towards an Interpretative Theory of Culture', in Geertz, C., *The Interpretation of Cultures* (New York: Basic Books).

Geertz, C. (1980) 'Blurred Genres: the Refiguration of Social Thought'. In: *The American Scholar*, 49(2): 165–79.

Geertz, C. (1983) *Local Knowledge* (London: Fontana).

Gergen, K. (1992) *The Saturated Self: Dilemmas of Identity in Contemporary Life* (New York: Basic Books).

Gergen, K. (1997) 'On the Poly/Tics of Postmodern Psychology'. In: *Theory and Psychology*, 7(1): 31–6.

Gergen, K. (1999) *An Invitation to Social Construction* (London: Sage).

Gergen, M. (2001) *Feminist Reconstructions in Psychology, Narrative Gender and Performance* (Thousand Oaks, CA: Sage).

Gergen, M. (2003) *'Generating Research'. Videotape in Conversations on Social Construction*, www.masterswork.com/

Gergen, M. (2004) *Generating Research: A Conversation with Mary Gergen*, film distributed by masterswork.com

Gerrig, R. (1993) *Experiencing Narrative Worlds: On the Psychological Activities of Reading* (Boulder, CO: West View Press).

Gilligan, C. (1982) *In a Different Voice: Psychological Theory and Women's Development* (London: Harvard University Press).

Goodall, H. (2000) *Writing the New Ethnography* (Oxford: Alta Mira).

Greer, G. (2001) 'Watch With Brother', *Observer*, 24 June.

Gremillion, H. (2003) *Feeding Anorexia: Gender and Power at a Treatment Center (Body, Commodity, Text)* (Durham, CT: Duke University Press).

Grosz, E. (1994) 'A Thousand Tiny Sexes: Feminism and Rhizomatics', in Boundas, C. and Olkowski, D. (eds), *Gilles Deleuze and the Theater of Philosophy* (New York: Routledge).

Gubrium, J. and Holstein, J. (eds) (2001) *Handbook of Interview Research: Context and Method* (Thousand Oaks, CA: Sage).

Gunaratnam, Y. (2003) *Researching Race and Ethnicity* (London: Sage).

Harding, S. (1987) *Feminism and Methodology* (Buckingham: Open University Press).

Hare-Mustin, R. and Marecek, J. (1990) *Making a Difference: Psychology and the Construct of Gender* (New Haven, CT: Yale University Press).

Harraway, D. (1988) 'Situated Knowledges: the Science Question in Feminism and the Privilege of Partial Perspective'. In: *Feminist Studies*, 14(3) 575–99.

Harraway, D. (2004) *The Harraway Reader* (New York: Routledge).

Harris, L. (1985) *Holy Days* (New York: Macmillan).

Hart, N. and Crawford-Wright, A. (1999) 'Research as Therapy, Therapy as Research: Ethical Dilemmas in New Paradigm Research'. In: *British Journal of Counselling and Guidance*, 27(2) 205–15.

Haug, F. (1987) *Female Sexualization* (New York: Verso).

Hayano, D. (1982) *Poker Faces: The Life and Work of Professional Poker Players* (Berkeley, CA: University of California Press).

Hayles, N. (1990) *Chaos Bound* (Ithaca, NY: Cornell University Press).

Hedke, L. and Winslade, J. (2004) *Re-membering Lives: Conversations with the Dying and the Bereaved* (New York: Baywood).

Hedtke, L. (2001) 'Stories of Living and Dying'. In: *Gecko: A Journal of Deconstruction and Narrative Ideas in Therapeutic Practice*, (1): 4–27.

Hedtke, L. and Winslade, J. (2004) *Re-membering Lives: Conversations with the Dying and the Bereaved* (New York: Baywood Publications).

Henry, M. (2003) 'Where Are You Really From? Representation, Identity and Power in the Fieldwork Experiences of a South Asian Diasporic'. In: *Qualitative Research*, 3(2): 229–42.

Hepworth, B. (1985) *A Pictorial Autobiography* (London: Tate Gallery).

Hepworth, J. (1999) *The Social Construction of Anorexia Nervosa* (London: Sage).

Herman, L. (2005) 'Researching the Images of Evil Events: an Arts-based Methodology in Liminal Space'. In: *Qualitative Inquiry*, 11(3): 468–80.

Heron, J. and Reason, P. (1997) 'A Participatory Inquiry Paradigm'. In: *Qualitative Inquiry*, 3(3): 274–94.

Hertz, R. (1996) 'Introduction: Ethics, Reflexivity and Voice'. In: *Qualitative Inquiry* 19(1): 3–9.

Hertz, R . (ed.) (1997) *Reflexivity and Voice* (Thousand Oaks, CA: Sage).

Hoeg, P. (1983) *Miss Smilla's Feeling for Snow* (London: Harvill Press).

Hollway, W. and Jefferson, T. (1997) 'Eliciting Narrative through the In-Depth Interview'. In: *Qualitative Inquiry*, 3(1): 53–70.

Hollway, W. and Jefferson, T. (2000) *Doing Qualitative Research Differently: Free Association, Narrative and the Interview Method* (London: Sage).

Holman-Jones, S. (2005) 'Auto-ethnography: Making the Personal Political', in Denzin, N. and Lincoln, Y. (eds), *The Sage Handbook of Qualitative Research* (Thousand Oaks, CA: Sage).

hooks, b. (1994) *Teaching to Transgress* (London: Routledge).

hooks, b. (2000a) *Feminism is for Everybody: Passionate Politics* (Cambridge, MA: South End Press).

hooks, b. (2000b) *Feminist Theory: From Margin to Center*, 2nd edn (London: Pluto Press).

Hubbard, P., Kitchin, R., Bartley, B. and Fuller, D. (2002) *Thinking Geographically: Space, Theory and Contemporary Human Geography* (London: Continuum).

Humphries, B. (2000) 'From Critical Thought to Emancipatory Action: Contradictory Research Goals?', in: Truman, C., Mertens, D. and Humphries, B. (eds), *Research and Inequality* (London: University College London Press).

Humphries, B., Mertens, D. and Truman, C. (2000) 'Arguments for an Emancipatory Research Paradigm', in Truman, C., Mertens, D. and Humphries, B. (eds), *Research and Inequality* (London: University College London Press).

Hurston, Z. (1942) *Dust Tracks on a Road: An Autobiography* (Urbana and Chicago, IL: University of Illinois Press).

Ifegwunigwe, J. (1999) *Scattered Belongings: Cultural Paradoxes of Race, Nation and Gender* (London: Routledge).

Irigaray, L. (1985) *This Sex, Which is not One* (New York: Cornell University Press).

Irigaray, L. (1993) *Sex and Genealogies* (New York: Columbia University Press).

Irigaray, L. (2004) *Key Writings* (New York: Continuum).

Irigaray, L. and Whitford, M. (1991) *The Irigaray Reader* (Oxford: Blackwell).

Irwin, R. and Cosson, A. (eds) (2004) *a/r/tography: Rendering Self through Arts-based Living Inquiry* (Vancouver: Pacific Educational Press).

Jackson, D. (2002) 'An Auto-Ethno Biographical Exploration of War and Post Traumatic Stress Disorder (PTSD)', unpublished MA thesis, University of East Anglia.

Johns, H. (1996) *Personal Development in Counselling Training* (London: Cassell).

Johnson, J. and Weller, S. (2001) 'Elicitation Techniques for Interviewing', in Gubrium, J. and Holstein, J. (eds), *Handbook of Interview Research: Context and Method* (Thousand Oaks, CA: Sage).

Jones, R. (2004) ' "That's very rude, I shouldn't be telling you that": Older Women Talking about Sex', in Bamberg, M. and Andrews, M. (eds), *Considering Counter-narratives: Narrating, Resisting, Making Sense* (Amsterdam: John Benjamins).

Jordan, J. (1995) *June Jordan's Poetry for the People* (New York: Routledge).

Josselson, R. (ed.) (1996a) *Ethics and Process in the Narrative Study of Lives* (Thousand Oaks, CA: Sage).

Josselson, R. (1996b) 'On Writing Other People's Lives: Self-Analytic Reflections of a Narrative Researcher', in Josselson, R. (ed.), *Ethics and Process in the Narrative Study of Lives* (Thousand Oaks, CA: Sage).

Josselson, R. (1999) 'Introduction', in Josselson, R. and Lieblich, A. (eds), *Making Meaning of Narratives: The Narrative Study of Lives*, vol. 6 (Thousand Oaks, CA: Sage).

Josselson, R. and Lieblich, A. (eds) (1993) *The Narrative Study of Lives*, vol. 1 (Thousand Oaks, CA: Sage).

Josselson, R. and Lieblich, A. (eds) (1995) *Interpreting Experience: The Narrative Study of Lives*, vol. 3 (Thousand Oaks, CA: Sage).

Josselson, R. and Lieblich, A. (eds) (1999) *Making Meaning of Narratives: The Narrative Study of Lives*, vol: 6 (Thousand Oaks, CA: Sage).

Josselson, R., Lieblich, A. and McAdams, D. (eds) (2003) *Up Close and Personal: The Teaching and Learning of Narrative Research* (Washington, DC: American Psychological Association).

Josselson, R., Lieblich, A., Sharabany, R. and Wiseman, H. (1997) *Conversation as Method: Analysing the Relational World of People who were Raised Communally* (Thousand Oaks, CA: Sage).

Kahlo, F. (1995) *The Diary of Frida Kahlo* (London: Bloomsbury).

Kamler, B. (1996) 'From Autobiography to Collective Biography: Stories of Ageing and Loss'. In: *Women and Language*, 19(1): 21–6.

Katz, A. and Shotter, J. (1996) 'Hearing the Patient's Voice: Towards a Social Poetics in Diagnostic Interviews'. In: *Social Science Medicine*, 43(6): 919–31.

Keisinger, C. (1998) 'Portrait of an Anorexic Life', in Banks, A. and Banks, S. (eds), *Fiction and Social Research, by Ice or Fire* (Walnut Creek, CA: Alta Mira).

Kennedy, C. (2005) reported in: Branigan, T., 'Kennedy Prepares for the Next Step', *Guardian*, 20 May: 11.

Kincheloe, J. (2005) 'On to the Next Level: Continuing the Conceptualisation of the Bricolage'. In: *Qualitative Inquiry*, 11(3): 323–50.

Klass, D., Silverman, P. and Nickman, L. (eds) (1996) *Continuing Bonds: New Understandings of Grief* (London: Taylor and Francis).

Knights, B. (1995) *The Listening Reader: Fiction and Poetry for Counsellors and Psychotherapists* (London: Jessica Kingsley).

Kong, T., Mahoney, D. and Plummer, K. (2001) 'Queering the Interview', in Gubrium, J. and Holstein, J. (eds) (2001) *Handbook of Interview Research: Context and Method* (Thousand Oaks, CA: Sage).

Kristeva, J. (1974) 'Revolution in Poetic Language', in Oliver, K. (ed.), *The Portable Kristeva* (New York: Columbia University Press).

Kristeva, J. (1987) 'Tales of Love', in: Moi, T. (ed.), *French Feminist Thought* (Oxford: Blackwell).

Kvale, S. (1988) 'The 1,000-page Question'. In: *Phenomenology and Pedagogy*, 6(2): 90–106.

Kvale, S. (1996) *Inter Views: An Introduction to Qualitative Research Interviewing* (Thousand Oaks, CA: Sage).

Kvale, S. (1999) 'The Psychoanalytic Interview as Qualitative Research'. In: *Qualitative Inquiry*, 5(1): 87–113.

Labov, W. (1982) 'Speech Actions and Reactions in Personal Narrative', in Tannen, D. (ed.), *Analyzing Discourse: Text and Talk* (Washington, DC: Georgetown University Press).

Labov, W. and Waletzky, J. (1967) 'Narrative Analysis: Oral Versions of Personal Experience', in Helm, J. (ed.), *Essays on the Verbal and Visual Arts* (Seattle: University of Washington Press).

Laird, J. (2001) '"Women's stories", an interview', in Denborough, D. (ed.), *Family Therapy: Exploring the Field's Past, Present and Possible Futures* (Adelaide: Dulwich Centre Publications).

Landlow, G. (ed.) (1994) *Hyper/text/theory* (Baltimore, MD: Johns Hopkins University Press).

Langellier, K. (2001). '"You're marked": Breast Cancer, Tattoo, and the Narrative Performance of Identity', in Brockmeier, J. and Carbaugh, D. (eds), *Narrative and Identity: Studies in Autobiography, Self and Culture* (Amsterdam and Philadelphia: John Benjamins).

Langellier, K. and Peterson, E. (2004) *Storytelling in Everyday Life* (London: Routledge).

Lapadat, J. and Lindsay, A. (1999) 'Transcription in Research and Practice: from Standardisation of Technique to Interpretive Positionings'. In: *Qualitative Inquiry*, 5(1): 64–87.

Lather, P. (1991) *Getting Smart: Feminist Research and Pedagogy With/In the Postmodern* (New York: Routledge).

Lather, P. (1993) 'Fertile Obsession: Validity after Post-structuralism'. In: *The Sociological Quarterly*, 34(4): 673–94.

Lather, P. (1995) 'The Validity of Angels: Interpretive and Textual Strategies in Researching the Lives of Women with HIV/AIDS'. *Qualitative Inquiry*, 1(1): 41–68.

Lather, P. (2000) 'Post Book: Working the Ruins of Feminist Ethnography'. In: *Signs: Journal of Women in Culture and Society*, 27(1): 199–227.

Lather, P. and Smithies, C. (1997) *Troubling the Angels: Women Living with HIV/Aids* (Boulder, CO: West View Press).

Leftwich, A. (1998) ' "But I must also feel it as a man": the Experience of Male Bereavement', unpublished MSc thesis, University of Bristol.

Lessing, D. (1972) *The Golden Notebook* (London: Panther).

Lessing, D. (1974) *Memoirs of a Survivor* (London: Octagon Books).

Lewin, R. (1993) *Complexity: Life on the Edge of Chaos* (London: Phoenix).

Lieblich, A., Tuval-Mashiach, R. and Zibler, T. (1998) *Narrative Research: Reading, Analysis and Interpretation* (Thousand Oaks, CA: Sage).

Linnell, S. (2004) 'Towards a Poethics of Therapeutic Practice: Extending the Relationship of Ethics and Aesthetics in Narrative Therapies through a Consideration of the Late Work of Michel Foucault'. In: *International Journal of Narrative Therapy and Community Work*, 4: 42–55.

Loach, K. (1966) *Cathy Come Home*, BBC Films.

Lock, A., Epston, D. and Maisel, R. (2004) 'Countering that which is Called Anorexia'. In: *Narrative Inquiry*, 14(2): 275–301.

Lodge, D. (1995) *Therapy* (Harmondsworth: Penguin).

Lorde, A. (1980) *The Cancer Journals* (Midway, IL: Spinster's Ink).

Lucas, E. (trans.) (1909) 'Rapunzel', in *The Fairy Tales of the Brothers Grimm* (London: Constable).

Luttrell, W. (1997) *School-Smart and Mother-Wise: Working-Class Women's Identity and Schooling* (New York: Routledge).

Luttrell, W. (2003) *Pregnant Bodies, Fertile Minds: Gender, Race and the Schooling of Pregnant Teens* (New York: Routledge).

Luttrell, W. (2005) 'Framing Childhood: Visual Imagery and Image-Making's Role in Training Educators'. Interview in: *Harvard Graduate School of Education News*, www.gse.harvard.edu/news (accessed January 2005).

Lynch, M. (2000) 'Against Reflexivity as an Academic Virtue and Source of Privileged Knowledge'. In: *Theory, Culture and Society*, 17(3): 27–56.

Lyons, D. (1999) *Postmodernity*, 2nd edn (Buckingham: Open University Press).

Lyotard, J. (1984) *The Post-Modern Condition: A Report on Knowledge* (Manchester: Manchester University Press).

Macbeth, D. (2001) 'On "Reflexivity" in Qualitative Research, Two Readings, and a Third'. In: *Qualitative Inquiry*, 7(1): 35–69.

Malouf, D. (1998) *A Spirit of Play: The Making of Australian Consciousness* (Sydney: ABC Books).

Mair, M. (1989) *Between Psychology and Psychotherapy: The Poetics of Experience* (London: Routledge).

Marcus, G. (1994) 'What comes just after 'post'? The Case of Ethnography', in Denzin, N. K. and Lincoln, Y. S. (eds), *Handbook of Qualitative Research* (Thousand Oaks, CA: Sage).

Marquez, G. (1970) *One Hundred Years of Solitude* (London: Cape).

Marsalis, W. (2004) *Wynton Marsalis to Perform Jazz Narrative: 'Suite for Human Nature'*, www.wyntonmarsalis.net

Massey, D. (1994) *Space, Place and Gender* (London: Methuen).

Massey, D. (2005) *For Space* (London: Sage).

Mathiessen, P. (1962) *Under the Mountain Wall* (London: Penguin).

May, T. (1998) 'Reflexivity in the Age of Reconstructive Social Science'. In: *Social Research Methodology: Theory and Practice*, 1(1): 7–25.

McAdams, D. (1993) *The Stories We Live By: Personal Myths and the Making of the Self* (New York: Guilford Press).

McAdams, D., Josselson, R. and Lieblich, A. (eds) (2001) *Turns in the Road: Narrative Studies of Lives in Transition* (Washington, DC: American Psychological Association).

McAfee, N. (2003) *Julia Kristeva* (London: Routledge).

McDowell, L. (1999) *Gender, Identity and Place: Understanding Feminist Geographies* (Cambridge: Polity Press).

McLeod, J. (1997) *Narrative and Psychotherapy* (London: Sage).

McLeod, J. (1999) 'Counselling as a Social Process'. In: *Counselling*, 10: 217–26.

McLeod, J. (2000) 'Introduction', in Payne, M., *Narrative Therapy: An Introduction for Counsellors* (London: Sage).

McLeod, J. (2001a) *Qualitative Research in Counselling and Psychotherapy* (London: Sage).

McLeod, J. (2001b) 'Developing a Research Tradition Consistent with the Practices and Values of Counselling and Psychotherapy: Why Counselling and Psychotherapy Research is Necessary'. In: *Counselling and Psychotherapy Research*, 1(1): 3–12.

McLeod, J. (2001c) 'Counsellors, Psychotherapists and Research: a Response'. In: *Counselling and Psychotherapy Journal*, 12(2): 10–11.

McLeod, J. (2003a) *Doing Counselling Research*, 2nd edn (London: Sage).

McLeod, J. (2003b) *An Introduction to Counselling*, 3rd edn (Buckingham: Open University Press).

McLeod, J. (2004a) *Beginning Postcolonialism* (Manchester: Manchester University Press).

McLeod, J (2004b) 'The Significance of Narrative and Storytelling in Post-psychological Counselling and Therapy', in Lieblich, A., McAdams, D. and Josselson, R. (eds), *Healing Plots: The Narrative Basis of Psychotherapy* (Washington, DC: American Psychological Association).

McLeod, J. (2006) 'Narrative Thinking and the Emergence of Post-psychological Therapies'. In: *Narrative Inquiry*, 16(1): 201–10.

McLeod, J. and Balamoutsou, S. (1996) 'Representing Narrative Process in Therapy: Qualitative Analysis of a Single Case'. In: *Counselling Psychology Quarterly*, 9: 61–76.

McLeod, J. and Lynch, G. (2000) ' "This is our Life": Strong Evaluation in Psychotherapy Narrative'. In: *European Journal of Psychotherapy, Counselling and Health*, 3(3): 389–407.

McNay, L. (2000) *Gender and Agency: Reconfiguring the Subject in Feminist and Social Theory* (Cambridge: Polity Press).

Midwinter, R. (2004) 'Through someone else's eyes! An autoethnographic insight into the passing-on of trauma', unpublished MSc. thesis, University of Bristol.

Midwinter, R., Nott, J. and Speedy, J. (2005) 'Definitional Ceremony as a Form of Collaborative Research', BACP Research Conference presentation, Nottingham.

Mienczakowski, J. (2000) 'Ethnography in the Form of Theatre with Emancipatory Intentions', in Truman, C., Mertens, D. and Humphries, B. (eds), *Research and Inequality* (London: University College London Press).

Mienczakowski, J., Smith, L. and Morgan, S. (2002) 'Seeing Words – Hearing Feelings: Ethnodrame and the Performance of Data', in Bagley, C. and Cancienne, M. (eds), *Dancing the Data* (New York: Peter Lang).

Mishler, E. (1986) *Research Interviewing: Context and Narrative* (Cambridge, MA: Harvard University Press).

Mishler, E. (1991) 'Representing Discourse: the Rhetoric of Transcription'. In: *Journal of Narrative and Life History*, 1: 255–80.

Mishler, E. (2000) *Storylines: Craftartists' Narratives of Identity* (Cambridge, MA: Harvard University Press).

Moi, T. (1986) *Sexual/Textual Politics* (London: Routledge).

Moi, T. (1987) *French Feminist Thought* (Oxford: Blackwell).

Monk, G., Winslade, J., Crockett, K. and Epston, D. (eds) (1997) *Narrative Therapy in Practice: The Archaeology of Hope* (San Francisco: Jossey-Bass).

Moodley, R. (2001) '(Re)Searching for a Client in Two Different Worlds: Mind the Research-practice Gap'. In: *Counselling and Psychotherapy Research Journal* (1)1: 18–24.

Morgan, A. (2000) *What is Narrative Therapy?* (Adelaide: Dulwich Centre Publications).

Morgan, W. (2000) 'Electronic Tools for Dismantling the Master's House: Poststructuralist Feminist Research and Hypertext Poetics', in St Pierre, E. and Pillow, W. (eds), *Working the Ruins: Feminist Poststructural Theory and Methods in Education* (London: Routledge).

Morrison, B. (1998) *Too True* (London: Granta).

Mullen, C. and Finley, S. (eds) (2003) Special issue: 'Arts-based Approaches to Qualitative Inquiry'. In: *Qualitative Inquiry* (9)2: 165–297.

Mutua, K. and Swadener, B. (2004) *Decolonising Research in Cross Cultural Contexts: Critical Personal Narratives* (Albany, NY: University of New York Press).

Myerhoff, B. (1980) *Number Our Days* (New York: Simon & Schuster).

Myerhoff, B. (1982) 'Life History among the Elderly: Performance, Visibility and Re-Membering', in Ruby, J. (ed.), *A Crack in the Mirror: Reflective Perspectives in Anthropology* (Philadelphia: University of Pennsylvania Press).

Myerhoff, B. (1986) 'Life Not Death in Venice', in: Turner, V. and Bruner, E. (eds) *The Anthropology of Experience* (Champaign, IL: University of Illinois Press).

Mykhalovskiy, E. (1997) 'Reconsidering Table-Talk: Critical Thoughts on the Relationship between Sociology, Autobiography and Self-Indulgence', in Hertz, R. (ed.), *Reflexivity and Voice* (Thousand Oaks, CA: Sage).

Neimeyer, R. (2000) 'Narrative Disruptions in the Constructions of the Self', in R. Neimeyer and J. Raskin (eds), *Constructions of Disorder: Meaning-making*

Frameworks for Psychotherapy (Washington, DC: American Psychological Association).

O'Donoghue, D. (2004), 'Constructions of Men and Masculinity in Primary Teacher Education in Ireland': conference presentation, American Educational Research Association Conference.

O'Reilly, C. (2002) 'Autobiography', in *The Nowhere Birds* (Newcastle-on-Tyne: Bloodaxe Books).

Oakley, A. (1981) 'Interviewing Women: a Contradiction in Terms?', in Roberts, H. (ed.), *Doing Feminist Research* (London: Routledge & Kegan Paul).

Ochs, E. (1979) 'Transcription as Theory', in Ochs, E. and Scheifflin, B. B. (eds), *Developmental Pragmatics* (New York: Academic Books).

Ochs, E. and Capps, B. (2001) *Living Narrative: Creating Lives in Everyday Storytelling* (Cambridge, MA: Harvard University Press).

Oliver, K. (ed.) (1997) *The Portable Kristeva* (New York: Columbia University Press).

Oliver, M. (2002) 'Wild Geese', in Astley, N. (ed.), *Staying Alive* (Newcastle-on-Tyne: Bloodaxe Books).

Olivero, F., Sutherland, R. and John, P. (2004) 'Learning Lessons with ICT: Using Videopapers to Transform Teachers' Professional Knowledge'. In: *Cambridge Journal of Education*, 34(2): 179–91.

Ortiz, S. (2001) 'How Interviewing became Therapy for Wives of Professional Athletes: Learning from a Serendipitous Experience'. In: *Qualitative Inquiry*, 7(2): 192–221.

Parker, I. (ed.) (1999) *Deconstructing Psychotherapy* (London: Sage).

Payne, M. (2000) *Narrative Therapy: An Introduction for Counsellors* (London: Sage).

Payne, M. (2006) *Narrative Therapy: An Introduction for Counsellors*, 2nd edn (London: Sage).

Paz, O. (1986) *On Poets and Others* (New York: Seaver Books).

Pease, B. (2000a) 'Beyond the Father-wound: Memory Work and the Deconstruction of the Father–Son Relationship'. In: *Australian and New Zealand Journal of Family Therapy*, 21(1): 9–15.

Pease, B. (2000b) 'Reconstructing Heterosexual Subjectivities and Practices with White Middle Class Men'. In: *Race, Gender and Class*, 7(1): 133–45.

Pelias, R. (1999) *Writing Performance: Poeticizing the Researcher's Body* (Carbondale and Edwardsville: Southern Illinois University Press).

Pfister, J. (1997) 'Beyond the Talking Cure: Listening to Female Testimony on the Oprah Winfrey Show', in Pfister, J. and Schnog, N. (eds), *Inventing the Psychological: Towards a Cultural History of Emotional Life in America* (Cambridge, MA: Yale University Press).

Phoenix, A. (1994) 'Practicing Feminist Research: the Intersection of Gender and "Race" in the Research Process', in M. Maynard and J. Purvis (eds), *Researching Women's Lives* (London: Taylor & Francis).

Photovoice (2005) website, www.photvoice.com (accessed February 2006).

Piercy, M. (1985) *My Mother's Body, Poems by Marge Piercy* (London: Pandora Press).

Pinkola Estes, C. (1993) *The Gift of Story: A Wise Tale about What is Enough* (London: Rider).

Polkinghorne, D. (1988) *Narrative Knowing and the Human Sciences* (New York: State University of New York Press).

Polkinghorne, D. (2004) 'Narrative Therapy and Postmodernism', in Angus, L. and McLeod, J. (eds), *The Handbook of Narrative and Psychotherapy Practice, Theory and Research* (London: Sage).

Popkewitz, T. (2004) 'Is the National Research Council Committee's Report on Scientific Education Scientific? On Trusting the Manifesto'. In: *Qualitative Inquiry*, 10(1): 62–79.

Prowell, J. (1999) 'Reflecting on Issues of Culture'. In: *Gecko, A Journal of Deconstruction and Narrative Ideas in Therapeutic Practice*, (2): 43–51.

Pullman, P. (2003) *Lyra's Oxford* (Oxford: David Fickling Books).

Rawnsley, A. (2002) 'New Labour Grows Up', in *The Observer*, 21 April.

Reed-Danahay, D. (ed.) (1997) *Auto/ethnography: Re-writing the Self and the Social* (New York: Berg).

Reinharz, S. and Chase, S. (2001) 'Interviewing Women', in Gubrium, J. and Holstein, J. (eds) (2001), *Handbook of Interview Research: Context and Method* (Thousand Oaks, CA: Sage).

Richards, W. (2006) 'Race, identity and agency: a heuristic investigation into the experience of crossing the race boundary', unpublished PhD thesis, University of Manchester.

Richardson, L. (1991) *Writing Strategies: Reaching Diverse Audiences* (London: Sage).

Richardson, L. (1992) 'The Consequences of Poetic Representation: Writing the Other, Rewriting the Self', in Ellis, C. and Flaherty, M. (ed.), *Investigating Subjectivity: Research on Lived Experience* (Newbury Park, CA: Sage).

Richardson, L. (1993) 'Poetics, Dramatics and Transgressive Validity: the Case of the Skipped Line'. In: *Sociological Quarterly*, 34(4): 695–710.

Richardson, L. (1997a) *Fields of Play: Constructing an Academic Life* (New Brunswick: Rutgers University Press).

Richardson, L. (1997b) 'Skirting the Pleated Text: De-disciplining an Academic Life'. In: *Qualitative Inquiry*, 3(3): 295–303.

Richardson, L. (1999a) 'Dead Again in Berkeley: an Ethnographic Happening'. In: *Qualitative Inquiry*, 5(1): 141–44.

Richardson, L. (1999b) 'Feathers in our Cap'. In: *Journal of Contemporary Ethnography*, 28(6): 660–8.

Richardson, L. (2000a) 'Writing: a Method of Inquiry'. In: Denzin, N. K. and Lincoln, Y. S. (eds), *Handbook of Qualitative Research*, 2nd edn (Thousand Oaks, CA: Sage).

Richardson, L. (2000b) 'Introduction – Assessing Alternative Modes of Qualitative Ethnographic Research: How Do We Judge? Who Judges?' In: *Qualitative Inquiry*, 6(2): 251–3.

Richardson, L. (2000c) 'Evaluating Ethnography'. In *Qualitative Inquiry*, 6(2): 253–6.

Richardson, L. (2001) 'Poetic Representation of Interviews', in Gubrium, J. and Holstein, J. (eds), *Handbook of Interview Research* (Thousand Oaks, CA: Sage).

Richardson, L. and St Pierre, E. (2005) 'Writing: a Method of Inquiry', in Denzin, N. and Lincoln, Y. (eds), *The Sage Handbook of Qualitative Research*, 3rd edn (Thousand Oaks, CA: Sage).

Riessman, C. (1993) *Narrative Analysis* (Thousand Oaks, CA: Sage).

Riessman, C. (2000) 'Even if we don't have children, we can live', in Mattingly, C. and Garro, L. (eds), *Narratives and the Cultural Construction of Illness and Healing* (Berkeley, CA: University of California Press).

Riessman, C. (2004) 'New Readings of an Old Story', in Hurwitz, B., Greenhalgh, T. and Skultans, V. (eds), *Narrative Research in Health and Illness* (Oxford: Blackwell).

Riessman, C. (2005) personal website, on: www2.bc.edu/~riessman (accessed, July 2005).

Riessman, C. and Speedy, J. (2006) 'Narrative Inquiry in the Psychotherapy Professions: a Critical Review', in Clandinin, Jean (ed.), *The Handbook of Narrative Inquiry* (Thousand Oaks, CA: Sage).

Rimmon-Kennan, S. (1983) *Narrative Fiction: Contemporary Poetics* (London: Routledge).

Robbins, R. (2000) *Literary Feminisms* (Basingstoke: Macmillan).

Roberts, B. (2000) *Biographical Research* (Buckingham: Open University Press).

Rogers, A., Casey, M., Eckert, J., Holland, J., Nakkula, V. and Sheinberg, N. (1999) 'An Interpretive Poetics of Languages of the Unsayable', in Josselson, R. and Lieblich, A. (eds), *Making Meaning of Narratives: The Narrative Study of Lives*, vol. 6 (Thousand Oaks, CA: Sage).

Rogers. M. (1998) *Contemporary Feminist Theory: A Text/reader* (New York: McGraw-Hill).

Ronai, C. (1992) 'A Night in the Life of a Dancer/Researcher: a Layered Account', in: Ellis, C. and Flaherty, M., *Investigating Subjectivity: Research on Lived Experience* (Newbury Park, CA: Sage).

Ronai, C. (1995) 'Multiple Reflections of Child Sex Abuse: an Argument for a Layered Account'. In: *Journal of Contemporary Ethnography*, 23: 395–426.

Ronai, C. (1996) 'My Mother is Mentally Retarded', in: Ellis, C. and Bochner, A. (eds), *Composing Ethnography* (Walnut Creek, CA: Alta Mira).

Ronai, C. R. (1998) 'Sketching with Derrida: an Ethnography of a Researcher/Erotic Dancer'. In: *Qualitative Inquiry*, 4(3): 405–20.

Ronai, C. (1999) 'The Next Night Sous Rature: Wrestling with Derrida's Mimesis'. In: *Qualitative Inquiry*, 5(1): 114–30.

Rosaldo, R. (1989) *Culture and Truth: The Re-making of Social Analysis* (Boston, MA: Beacon Books).

Roth, A. and Fonagy, P. (1996) *What Works for Whom? A Critical Review of Psychotherapy Research* (New York: Guilford Press).

Rowlands, N. and Goss, S. (eds) (2000) *Evidence-based Counselling and Psychological Therapies* (London: Routledge).

Roy, A. (1998) *The God of Small Things* (London: Flamingo).

Ruby, J. (ed.) (1982) *A Crack in the Mirror: Reflexive Perspectives in Anthropology* (Philadelphia: University of Pennsylvania Press).

Ruby, J. (2000) *Picturing Culture: Explorations in Film and Anthropology* (Chicago: Chicago University Press).

Rushdie, S. (1981) *Midnight's Children* (London: Cape).

Russell, S. and Carey, M. (2004a) *Narrative Therapy: Responding to your Questions* (Adelaide: Dulwich Centre Publications).

Russell, S. and Carey, M. (2004b) 'Outsider Witness Practices: some Answers to Commonly Asked Questions', in *Narrative Therapy, Responding to your Questions* (Adelaide: Dulwich Centre Publications).

Sage, L. (2000) *Bad Blood* (London: Fourth Estate).

Salinger, J. (1951; reprinted 1987) *Catcher in the Rye* (Harmondsworth: Penguin).

Sandford, J. (1971) *Edna: The Inebriate Woman*, BBC Films.

Sands, A. (2000) 'Falling for Therapy'. In: *Counselling and Psychotherapy Journal*, 11(100): 614–16.

Sarbin, T. R. (1986) 'The Narrative as a Root Metaphor for Psychology', in Sarbin, T. R. (ed.), *Narrative Psychology: The Storied Nature of Human Conduct* (New York: Praeger).

Sarris, G. (1994) *Mabel Mckay: Weaving the Dream* (Berkeley, CA: University of California Press).

Sellers, S. (1994) *The Hélène Cixous Reader* (Oxford: Blackwell).

Sellers, S. (ed.) (2004) *Hélène Cixous: The Writing Notebooks* (New York: Contimuum).

Shange, N. (1977) *For Colored Girls who have Considered Suicide when the Rainbow is Enuf: A Choreopoem* (New York: Macmillan).

Shange, N. (1995) *Liliane* (London: Methuen).

Shields, C. (1993) *Happenstance* (New York: Random House).

Shostak, M. (2000) *Nisa – the Life and Works of a !kung Woman* (Cambridge, MA: Harvard University Press).

Sliep, Y. (2004) 'Narrative Theatre as an Interactive Community Approach to Mobilizing Collective Action'. In: *Families, Systems and Health*, 22(3): 306–20.

Smith, J. and Deemer, D. (2000) 'The Problem of Criteria in the Age of Relativism', in Denzin, N. K. and Lincoln, Y. S. (eds) (1994), *Handbook of Qualitative Research* (Thousand Oaks, CA: Sage).

Sparkes, A. (2002a) *Telling Tales in Sport and Physical Activity: A Qualitative Journey* (Champaign, IL: Human Kinetics).

Sparkes, A. (2002b) 'Auto-ethnography: Self-indulgence or Something More?', in Bochner, A. and Ellis, C. (2002) *Ethnographically Speaking: Autoethnography, Literature and Aesthetics* (Walnut Creek, CA: Alta Mira Press).

Sparkes, A. (2005) Introductory keynote address, Arts-based Educational Research Conference, Queen's University, Belfast.

Speedy, J. (2000a) 'White Water Rafting in Cocktail Dresses: Taking it Back Practices and Re-Membered Conversations in the Narrative Therapies'. In: *Counselling and Psychotherapy Journal*, 11(10): 628–33.

Speedy, J. (2000b) 'The Storied Helper: an Introduction to Narrative Ideas in Counselling and Psychotherapy'. In: *European Journal of Psychotherapy, Counselling and Health*, 3(3): 361–75.

Turner, V. (1969) *The Ritual Process* (New York: Cornell University Press).

Turner, V. (1982) 'Dramatic Ritual/Ritual Drama: Performative and Reflexive Anthropology', in Ruby, J. (ed.), *A Crack in the Mirror: Reflexive Perspectives in Anthropology* (Philadelphia: University Of Pennsylvania Press).

Turner, V. and Bruner, E. (eds) (1986) *The Anthropology of Experience* (Champaign, IL: University of Illinois Press).

Van Maanen, J. (ed.) (1983) *Qualitative Methods* (Thousand Oaks, CA: Sage).

Van Maanen, J. (1988) *Tales of the Field: On Writing Ethnography* (Chicago: University of Chicago Press).

Varela, F. (1999) *Ethical Know-how: Action, Wisdom and Cognition* (Stanford, CA: Stanford University Press).

Vygotsky, L. (1978) *Mind in Society: The Development of Higher Psychological Processes* (Cambridge, MA: Harvard University Press).

Waldegrave, C. (2001) Keynote address given at the International Narrative Therapy and Community Work Conference, Adelaide.

Waldegrave, C., Tamasase, K., Tuhaka, F. and Campbell, W. (2004) *Just Therapy – A Journey: A Collection of Papers from the Just Therapy Team* (Adelaide: Dulwich Centre Publications).

Walker, A. (1984) *In Search of Our Mother's Gardens: Womanist Prose* (London: Women's Press).

Walker, A. (1988) *Revolutionary Petunias* (London: Women's Press).

Walker, A. (1989) *The Temple of My Familiar* (Harmondsworth: Penguin).

Walker, A. (1992) *Possessing the Secret of Joy* (London: Vintage).

Walker, A. (2004) *Now is the Time to Open Your Heart* (London: Weidenfeld and Nicolson).

Wallis, J. (2003) 'Narrative Therapy: Definition and Practice in the UK', paper delivered at the International Narrative Therapy and Community Work Conference, Liverpool.

Webster's Third International Dictionary (1966) (Springfield, MA: Merriam Webster).

Weedon, C. (1997) *Feminist Practice and Poststructuralist Theory* (Oxford: Blackwell).

Welch, S. (1999) *Sweet Dreams in America: Making Ethics and Spirituality Work* (New York: Routledge).

Wengraf, T. (2001) *Qualitative Research Interviewing: Biographic Narrative and Semi-structured Methods* (London: Sage).

White, C. and Hales, J. (1997) *The Personal is the Professional: Therapists Reflect on their Families, Lives and Work* (Adelaide: Dulwich Centre Publications).

White, M. (1995) *Re-Authoring Lives: Interviews and Essays* (Adelaide: Dulwich Centre Publications).

White, M. (1997a) *Narratives of Therapists' Lives* (Adelaide: Dulwich Centre Publications).

White, M. (1997b) 'The Mouse Stories', in White, C. and Hales, J. (eds), *The Personal is the Professional: Therapists Reflect on their Families, Lives and Work* (Adelaide: Dulwich Centre Publications).

Index